Aspectual Prefixes in Early English

STUDIES IN ENGLISH MEDIEVAL LANGUAGE AND LITERATURE
Edited by Jacek Fisiak

Advisory Board:
John Anderson (Methoni, Greece), Ulrich Busse (Halle),
Olga Fischer (Amsterdam), Marcin Krygier (Poznań),
Roger Lass (Cape Town), Peter Lucas (Cambridge),
Donka Minkova (Los Angeles), Akio Oizumi (Kyoto),
Katherine O'Brien O'Keeffe (UC Berkeley, USA),
Matti Rissanen (Helsinki), Hans Sauer (Munich),
Liliana Sikorska (Poznań), Jeremy Smith (Glasgow),
Jerzy Wełna (Warsaw)

Vol. 43

Vlatko Broz

Aspectual Prefixes
in Early English

Bibliographic Information published by the Deutsche Nationalbibliothek
The Deutsche Nationalbibliothek lists this publication in the Deutsche Nationalbibliografie; detailed bibliographic data is available in the internet at http://dnb.d-nb.de.

Library of Congress Cataloging-in-Publication Data
Broz, Vlatko, 1975-
　Aspectual prefixes in early English / Vlatko Broz. – Peter Lang Edition.
　　p. cm. – (Studies in English medieval language and literature; Vol. 43)
　ISBN 978-3-631-64529-1 – ISBN 978-3-653-03645-9 (E-Book) 1. English language–Aspect. 2. English language--Suffixes and prefixes. 3. English language–Old English, ca. 450-1100–Suffixes and prefixes. 4. English language–Middle English, 1100-1500–Suffixes and prefixes. I. Title.
　PE1306.B77 2014
　425'.63–dc23
　　　　　　　　　　　　　　　　　　　　　　2014020484

ISSN 1436-7521
ISBN 978-3-631-64529-1 (Print)
E-ISBN 978-3-653-03645-9 (E-Book)
DOI 10.3726/978-3-653-03645-9

© Peter Lang GmbH
Internationaler Verlag der Wissenschaften
Frankfurt am Main 2014
All rights reserved.

Peter Lang Edition is an Imprint of Peter Lang GmbH.

Peter Lang – Frankfurt am Main · Bern · Bruxelles · New York ·
Oxford · Warszawa · Wien

All parts of this publication are protected by copyright. Any utilisation outside the strict limits of the copyright law, without the permission of the publisher, is forbidden and liable to prosecution. This applies in particular to reproductions, translations, microfilming, and storage and processing in electronic retrieval systems.

This publication has been peer reviewed.

www.peterlang.com

Acknowledgements

I owe the greatest debt of gratitude to my parents, Biserka Garac and the late Eduard Broz, who put me through school and have always given me their unconditional love and support in every possible way. I also thank my grandmother, Marija Budimir, who eagerly followed wherever my education led me.

I gratefully acknowledge the Open Society Institute for helping me with funding during my stay in Leuven during 2009 and 2010, as well as OSI/FCO Chevening for funding my research at the University of Oxford in 2007-2008. I am also thankful to the Croatian Science Foundation for their scholarship in 2010.

It is hard to overstate my gratitude to both my Croatian and Belgian supervisors for their invaluable advice, trust and patience. Special thanks are due to Prof. Dr. Dora Maček for always finding time to read and comment on my work. I will always be indebted to Prof. Dr. Hubert Cuyckens for introducing me to his research group, for inviting me to write a PhD thesis in Leuven and for all his thoughtful suggestions and critical comments which have greatly helped to improve this dissertation.

I would like to thank Prof. Dr. Milena Žic Fuchs for all her support, for believing in me and for telling me to believe in myself, as well as for all our inspiring regular chats about the semantics of aspect over the phone and in front of the Faculty building.

Heartfelt thanks also go to Marina Grubišić and Marija Kraljević, my dear office mates, who often sacrificed themselves by stepping into the breach so that I could fully dedicate myself to writing the thesis. I hope to return the favour soon. An additional thanks to Marija for our insightful discussions about the intricacies of aspect in Croatian.

Many thanks go to Peter Petré for initiating me into the hoary world of diachronic corpora and helping me to get started with the research. I am also thankful to Eline Zenner for being my best friend in Leuven and for all her practical help during my stay in Belgium.

I also wish to thank my colleagues Irena Zovko Dinković for her supportive advice, Nina Tuđman-Vuković for sharing all her know-how in the technicalities of dissertation writing, Mate Kapović for our interesting conversations about Proto-Germanic and Proto-Indo-European etymologies, David Mandić for our discussions of Old Church Slavonic examples, Renata Geld for our valuable conversations about aspect, Ivan Lupić for furnishing me with articles that were difficult to obtain in Europe, as well as Ivan Laćan for scanning and mailing me the literature that was available only at Berkeley.

I am very grateful to Ray Fletcher for his proofreading of the manuscript and Stephen Dickey for his enthusiasm to discuss theoretical matters of aspect by e-mail. Thanks also to Michiko Ogura, Maxi Krause and Anna Zbierska-Sawala for posting their work to me.

My friends deserve a big thank you for helping me in a number of ways: Ivana Simeon for explaining to me how aspect functions in Russian and for comforting me whenever I was plunged into a PhD crisis, Tvrtko Černoš for his translation expertise that helped me shape some good sentences, Nebojša

Topolščak for his computer skills that can solve any problem, Ivana Sekol for being the most important member of my PhD support group and Ivana Juriša-Acheré for instructing me in French when needed.

Finally, I heartily thank Patricio Alejandro Agüero, Lea Lasić, Andrea Marić and Ana Tonković-Dolenčić for all their moral support over the years, for putting up with my moody behaviour, as well as for distracting me during my long gestation of the dissertation.

VB

Abstract

This monograph examines preverbs and post-verbal particles expressing aspectuality in early English. Preverbs are also known as verbal prefixes such as *ge-* in the Old English verb *gegladian* 'cheer up' or *ā-* in the verb *āstreccan* 'stretch out', whereas post-verbal particles are preposition-like adverbs that come after a verb and thus comprise a phrasal verb, such as the particle *up* in Modern English *cheer up* or the particle *out* in Modern English *stretch out*.

The discussion starts from the hypothesis that English has several well-developed systems of aspect, one of which is expressed by preverbs and post-verbal particles. Besides investigating how English expressed aspect by means of preverbs that have died out, the aims also include revisiting aspect and expanding the current analysis of aspectual systems in English and with contrastive insights in relation to Croatian.

The approach taken in this book is eclectic. In order to account for the phenomenon of aspect, a wide range of theories have been combined such as a number of aspectual theories, as well as some more recent theories such as Grammaticalization Theory and Lexicalization Theory. For the purpose of this research I have used two basic corpora. For Old English, it was *The York-Toronto-Helsinki Parsed Corpus of Old English Prose*. For Middle English, *The Penn-Helsinki Parsed Corpus of Middle English*.

According to previous research, Old English had seven prefixes that could perform an aspectual function. They were looked up in the corpus and the three most frequent prefixes (*ge-*, *a-* and *for-*) are analysed here. Their analysis gives an account how preverbs express aspect in early English and thus contributes to an understanding of aspect in diachrony. The preverbs *a-*, *ge-* and *for-* are traditionally thought to be derivational prefixes, but ample evidence in the book shows many of their inflectional properties. Their decline and loss coincides with the decline and loss of all other inflectional suffixes that were used to mark case, gender, verb person and other grammatical functions, as English was changing from a more synthetic type of language to a more analytic type.

The prefixes *a-*, *ge-* and *for-* show some typical features of grammaticalization. The investigation of their etymologies showed that once they were both content items which changed into grammatical words and then reduced to an inflectional affix. The preverb *a-* had a stronger capacity to express perfectivity than the prefix *ge-*. The preverb *ge-* is four times more frequent than the prefix *a-*, but in more than half the cases its meaning is not aspectual. The preverb *for-* was also grammaticalized as a marker of perfectivity, but only in 35% of the cases.

Contents

Acknowledgements v
Abstract vi
List of tables and figures x
Abbreviations xii
Chapter 1: Introduction 1
   1.1 Scope of the study 1
   1.2 Research questions and hypothesis 1
   1.3 Theoretical framework 2
   1.4 Structure of the study 3
Chapter 2: Aspects of Aspect 6
   2.1 The complexity of aspectual studies 6
   2.2 Aspect Defined 7
   2.3 Aspect Exemplified 9
   2.4 Origins of Aspectology 15
   2.5 Aspect vs. Aktionsart 21
   2.6 Aspect in the 20th Century 27
   2.7 In The Beginning Was Aspect 31
   2.8 Aspect in Slavic Style 34
      2.8.1 Old Church Slavonic 37
      2.8.2 Irregularities of Slavic aspect 40
   2.9 Aspect in Germanic 51
   2.10 Aspectual Categories 62
      2.10.1 Perfective 63
      2.10.2 Imperfective 65
      2.10.3 Telicity 66
      2.10.4 Ingressive 67
      2.10.5 Bounded vs. Non-bounded 70
      2.10.6 Mustanoja's categories 70
      2.10.7 Conclusion 71
Chapter 3: Previous Studies of Prefixed Verbs and Phrasal Verbs 73
   3.1 De la Cruz (1972, 1975) 73
   3.2. Hiltunen (1983) 76
   3.3 Brinton (1988) 79
   3.4 Petré (2005) 84
   3.5 Elenbaas (2007) 88
   3.6 Synchronic research of verb-particles 90
Chapter 4: Theoretical Foundations and Methodology 93
   4.1 Grammaticalization (and Lexicalization) Theory 93

- 4.2 Methodological Tools 96
- 4.3 Problems in identifying preverbs 98
- Chapter 5: An Analysis of the Preverb *a*- 99
  - 5.1 Introduction 99
  - 5.2 Etymology of *a*- 101
  - 5.3 *A*- as a perfectivizer 103
  - 5.4 Resultative and completive 108
  - 5.5 Ingressive / inchoative / inceptive 111
  - 5.6 Instantaneous / Momentous / Punctual 112
  - 5.7 Contrastive analysis 115
  - 5.8 Co-Existing Systems of Prefixes and Particles 118
  - 5.9 Prefix *a*- in Middle English 122
  - 5.10 Middle English Additions 124
  - 5.11 Conclusion 125
- Chapter 6: An Analysis of the Preverb *ge*- 127
  - 6.1 Introduction 127
  - 6.2 Previous studies 128
  - 6.3 The etymology of *ge*- 133
  - 6.4 The meanings of *ge*- 136
  - 6.5 Empty *ge*- 137
  - 6.6 *Ge*- as a past participle marker 140
  - 6.7 Ge- as a perfectivizer 140
  - 6.7. Co-occurrence with *ða* 141
  - 6.9 Stylistic functions of *ge*- 142
  - 6.10 Lexicalization Cases 143
  - 6.11 *Ge*- in Middle English 145
  - 6.12 Conclusion 149
- Chapter 7: An Analysis of the Preverb *for*- 151
  - 7.1 Introduction 151
  - 7.2 The meanings and etymology of *for*- 152
  - 7.3 Perfectivizing *for*- 153
  - 7.4 Lexicalizing for- 160
  - 7.5 *For*- in Middle English 162
  - 7.6 Conclusion 164
- Chapter 8: Conclusion 165
- References 168
  - Dictionaries 184
- Appendix I: Old English Corpus 185
- Appendix II: Middle English Corpus 190

List of tables and figures

Table 1 Non-progressive vs. progressive aspect in English 9
Table 2 Aktionsarten in Croatian 21
Table 3 Agrell's subdivision of aspect 22
Table 4 Terms for aspect and aktionsart in the literature 27
Table 5 Vendler's verb classes 28
Table 6 Aspectual (actional) classifications 30
Table 7 Aspectual prefixes in Old Church Slavonic 37
Table 8 The tense/aspect system of Old Church Slavonic: *nes-ti* 'carry' 38
Table 9 Interaction of aspect and tense in OCS 39
Table 10 Aspectual prefixes in Croatian 42
Table 11 Central and peripheral aspectual partners of an imperfective simplex verb in Gothic 53
Table 12 Most frequent Gothic prefixes with their Old English cognates 54
Table 13 A sample from Scherer's Table 1: The Verbal Set *deð* (1958: 246) ... 60
Table 14 The interaction of Telicity with Perfectivity in French 67
Table 15 Mustanoja's aspectual categories in Middle English 71
Table 16 The functions of Old English pure prefixes 74
Table 17 A complementary perspective of Early English prefixed verbs and Modern English phrasal verbs 75
Table 18 An aspect model for English (from Brinton 1988: 53) 81
Table 19 An aktionsart model for English 81
Table 20 Corpus results for early English prefixes: initial hits vs. tokens 96
Table 21 Corpus results: types and tokens for *a-* 99
Table 22 The most frequent *a-* types in Old English 100
Table 23 Old English – Croatian verb correspondences 115
Table 24 The distribution of post-verbal particle correspondences to the prefix *a-* 116
Table 25 The most frequent *a-* types in Middle English 122
Table 26 The most frequent *ge-* types in Old English 128
Table 27 The meanings and functions of the prefix *ge-* 136
Table 29 Versions of the prefix *ge-* in Middle English 147
Table 30 The most frequent *ge-* types in Middle English 147
Table 31 The most frequent *for-* types in Old English 151
Table 32 The meanings and functions of the prefix *for-* 153
Table 33 The most frequent *for-* types in Middle English 162

Figure 1 The meanings of the Present Perfect 10
Figure 2 Aspectual distinctions in early Proto-Indo-European 33
Figure 3 The "geography" of Slavic aspect 36

Figure 4 Prefix occurrences per 1,000 lexical verbs 97
Figure 5 A map of Old English *a*-V correspondences to Modern English post-
    verbal particles.. 116
Figure 6 The meanings of *ge*- 137

Abbreviations

a	ante (before a year date)	nom.	nominative
acc.	accusative	OCS	Old Church Slavonic
aor	aorist	OE	Old English
c	circa (before a year date)	OF	Old French
c.	century	O.Fr.	Old French
conj	conjunction	OFris	Old Frisian
dat.	dative	ON	Old Norse
DOE	Dictionary of Old English (see References – Dictionaries)	ONF	Old Norman French
		OSax	Old Saxon
f.	feminine	p.	person
G	German	PDE	Present-Day English
gen.	genitive	perf.	perfective
imp	imperative	PIE	Proto-Indo-European
impf	imperfect	pl.	plural
impf.	imperfective	p.ptcp	past participle
indf	indefinite	PP	past participle
inf	infinitive	pres	present
ins	instrumental	pret	preterit
L.	Latin	pron	pronoun
Lat	Latin	ptcp	participle
m.	masculine	refl.	reflexive
ME	Middle English	sg.	singular
MED	Middle English Dictionary (see References – Dictionaries)	Skt	Sanskrit
		Subj	subjunctive
MF	Middle French	V	verb
n.	neuter		

Chapter 1
Introduction

1.1 Scope of the study

This study primarily examines prefixed verbs or preverbs expressing aspectuality in the Old and Middle English periods, but it also takes a look at the post-verbal particles in the subsequent periods of English. Preverbs are also known as verbal prefixes such as *ge-* in the Old English verb *gegladian* 'cheer up' or *ā-* in the Old English verb *āstreccan* 'stretch out', whereas post-verbal particles are preposition-like adverbs that come after a verb and thus comprise a phrasal verb, such as the particle *out* in Modern English *stretch out* or the particle *up* in Modern English *cheer up*. Prefixed verbs in Old English are said to be the functional equivalents (and predecessors) of phrasal verbs in Modern English. The most frequent Old English prefixes such as *a-, ge-* and *for-* are no longer used in English today, so different Modern English particles such as *up, out* and *away* have taken over their function.

Preverbs and post-verbal particles are characterized by a frustrating degree of polysemy. The focus of this study is on those preverbs and post-verbal particles whose meaning is aspectual, which is in itself too broad to discuss exhaustively. The discussions and analysis will inevitably touch upon meanings other than aspectual since they tend to form intricate networks. Verbal properties such as unaccusativity and ergativity have not been treated, as have not been Old English modal verbs as preterit perfects, since this domain of verbal aspect is not expressed by prefixes.

One of the aims of this study is to consider how various Old English prefixes such as *a-* and *ge-,* which are no longer productive, were used in the past to express aspect when attached to verbs and which post-verbal particles perform their function in Present-Day English.

Other aims include revisiting aspect and expand the current analysis of aspectual systems in English, both diachronically and synchronically and with contrastive insights in relation to Croatian, which is a Slavic language with a morphologically marked aspect. Old English is typologically closer to Croatian than to Modern English.

1.2 Research questions and hypothesis

There are several research questions that the present study addresses. The key question could be phrased as follows:

How did English express aspect by means of preverbs that have died out?

This question leads onto a number of secondary questions that are also tackled in this discussion, which are worth mentioning here.

Does English have aspect? How did a system or systems of aspect evolve in English? Why are aspectual studies so complex? Why are attitudes towards aspect so dramatically different among linguists? Why is there such a proliferation of aspectual categories? Why did aspect originate in the studies of Slavic languages? Should Slavic languages be regarded as "an absolute standard" or merely "an idiosyncratic example" in terms of their structure of aspect? Does a contrastive analysis of aspect between a Slavic and a Germanic language help to account for the characteristics of both languages? Which preverbs were used in early English to mark aspect? Which aspectual categories are there in early English? Why is the basic rule of perfectivization not universally applicable in early English? Why are there so many cases of verbs without a prefix denoting perfective actions as well as prefixed verbs denoting imperfective actions? Do preverbs exhibit properties of grammaticalization, lexicalization or both?

The central hypothesis of this study is that English has several well-developed systems of aspect, one of which is expressed by preverbs and post-verbal particles. The aspect system of preverbs was abandoned during the Middle English period, parallel to which a new aspect system was emerging – that of post-verbal particles. This transition was part of the development of English from a more synthetic type of language to a more analytic one.

Furthermore, it is hypothesized that by and large Old English preverbs expressed aspect in a similar way as they do in Slavic languages even though many scholars tried to prove otherwise. It is proposed that aspectual preverbs are grammaticalized rather than lexicalized. Even though they appear before the verb stem, they act more like inflectional rather than derivational prefixes.

The exceptions to the basic principles of marking aspect are accounted for by other functions of preverbs and other syntactic markers of aspectuality, as well as by examining how aspect really functions in Slavic languages.

1.3 Theoretical framework

The approach taken in this discussion is essentially eclectic. In order to account for the phenomenon of aspect in the diachrony of English, a wide range of theories need to be combined.

There is no single theory, school or movement in the field of aspect. Studies on aspect have their traditions, as for example Slavic or Anglo-American, but even these traditions feature a number of widely differing angles, interpretations or methods in dealing with the linguistic phenomenon of aspect. Therefore, many individual approaches springing from different traditions need to be discussed in order to elicit their theories and ideas. Some of these theories are surprisingly old but they have been evolving and improving for centuries, thus showing a fascinating example of maturation of linguistic thought. All these theories could be called theories of aspect, but it is important to stress that they are not characterized by adherence to any central positions or principles.

There are other theories that can shed light on aspectual phenomena. They have also been taken into consideration in this study. These include Grammaticalization Theory, which has been expounded in several textbooks (e.g. Hopper and Traugott 1993) and Lexicalization Theory (as expounded in Brinton and Traugott 2005). Both Grammaticalization Theory and Lexicalization Theory could be subsumed under a more general theoretical framework, which is that of Cognitive Linguistics. Again, Cognitive Linguistics is not a theory but an approach to language that places meaning in focus, blurs the boundaries between grammar and lexicon, as well as the boundaries between pragmatics and semantics. It studies cognitive mechanisms and principles of human categorization that in turn account for a wide range of linguistic phenomena.

1.4 Structure of the study

This introduction set the topic of the study, defined its scope and research questions. It also briefly stated the hypothesis and theoretical frameworks used.

Two avenues of research converge in this discussion; one is that on aspect, and the other is on verbal prefixes and particles. Chapter 2 deals with the former, while Chapter 3 with the latter, presenting a brief, selective and critical overview of previous research in both fields. The second chapter addresses the complexity of aspectual studies, comments on several definitions of aspect as a semantic category, shows some examples how aspect can be expressed morphologically and syntactically in a wide range of world languages, outlines the history of studying aspect, discusses aspect in Slavic and Germanic, as well as the aspectual categories used in the analysis.

The third chapter is a survey of previous studies of preverbs and particle verbs, evaluating the works of De la Cruz (1972, 1975), Hiltunen (1983), Brinton (1988), Petré (2005) and Elenbaas (2007). It also presents a short overview of synchronic research of verb-particles.

The fourth chapter discusses theoretical foundations other than aspect-related theories, as well as the methodology of the study.

The fifth chapter analyses the aspectual properties of the preverb *a-*, whereas the sixth and seventh chapters analyse the preverbs *ge-* and *for-* respectively. For each of these three preverbs, there is a discussion of etymology, followed by a corpus-based analysis of semantic and syntactic features with numerous examples. The bulk of analysis focuses on Old English, but for each prefix there is a section that also deals with Middle English.

1.5 Why preverb?

The term 'preverb' is traditionally used in Indo-European linguistics to denote morphemes that appear before a verb and form a close semantic unit with that verb. Fortson defines it as "an adverbial particle that modifies the meaning of a verb and often appears attached to the verb as a prefix" (2004: 475).

This term is not widely accepted in English historical linguistics, but there is a significant number of authors (Bloomfield 1929, Mossé 1938, Pilch 1953 and 1955, Lindemann 1965, Fraser 1975, West 1982, Booij and Van Kemenade 2003) who use it to refer to what the majority call a verbal prefix.

Like many terms in linguistics, the notion of *preverb* has received many interpretations in the literature. In this book it is understood as a verbal prefix, which in English, and in particular in its early stages, is a bound morpheme, i.e. inseparable from the verb. It can have a grammatical function, representing a case of grammaticalization as hypothesized in this study, or it can have a lexical function with a non-productive word-formation pattern, representing a case of lexicalization or even petrification or fossilization. It needs to be stressed that one and the same preverb can have both grammaticalized and lexicalized meanings (cf. Van der Auwera 1999).

And finally the term neatly allows expressing the idea of a 'verbal prefix' in one word. Quite often in the literature, the adjective 'verbal' is omitted and only 'prefix' is used, which may give rise to confusion as prefixes can also be nominal or adjectival. Indeed, more often than not, the very same prefix can also be attached to nouns and adjectives. Furthermore, the term 'preverb' is used in Indo-European linguistics and points to a developmental continuity that can be traced back to Proto-Indo-European (PIE).

In Vedic Sanskrit, which is considered to be the closest attested language we will ever come to PIE, preverbs were freely detachable from the verb and could take any position in the sentence. The following examples show the Sanskrit preverbs *út* 'up' and *ví* 'out' in different sentence positions – left-adjacent to the verb as in (1) or at the very end of the sentence as in (2).

(1) *tán no   mahā́m̐   úd   ayā́n   devó   aktúbhiḥ*
    it we.ACC great.NOM up.PREVERB extend.AOR.3.P.SG. god.NOM twilight ray.INS.PL
    'The mighty god has proffered it to us with twilight rays.'

Rigveda IV, 53 (352)[1]

(2)   *áprathatam   pr̥thivī́m mātáraṃ   ví*
         spread (√*prath*).IMPF.2.P.DU earth.ACC mother.ACC out.PREVERB
         'you two spread out mother earth'

Rigveda VI, 72, 2

The preverb can also be coalesced and univerbated with the verb, as in the combination of the preverb *ā́* with the verb *aprās* in example (3). The function of the preverb *ā́* is intensifying and sometimes reversing the meaning. On a formal level, this combination of verb and preverb is the same as the Old English *afyllan* or Gothic *us-fulljan* 'fill up', but Sanskrit and Old English *ā́* are not considered to be cognates.

(3)   *ā́prā*   *rájāṃsi*   *diviyā́ni*   *pā́rthivā*
            up.PREVERB+fill (√*prā*).AOR.3.P.SG fairy space.ACC.PL heavenly.ACC.PL earthly.ACC.PL
            'He has filled the dark regions, heavenly and earthly'

Rigveda IV, 53 (356)[2]

In Classical Sanskrit, as codified by the grammarian Pāṇini, the syntax of preverbs was no longer as free as in Vedic Sanskrit, so the position of preverbs was fixed in the position immediately preceding the verb or compounded with the verb. In other words, postponing the preverb to the end of the sentence as in example (2) was no longer possible. Many aspectual functions of the preverbs in Sanskrit are discussed in Gonda (1962: 225-250).

It should be noted that some authors regard *preverbs* as a cover term for verb particles and prefixes (cf. McIntyre 2003: 119), which points to the common

---

[1] Adapted from Slocum, J. and Thomson, K. (2006). *Ancient Sanskrit Online*
[2] Adapted from Slocum, J. and Thomson, K. (2006). *Ancient Sanskrit Online*

origin of verb particles, verb prefixes and prepositions. It also explains why so many of them have a similar appearance in English today, as well as in many other present-day Indo-European languages. Preverbs are said to follow the grammaticalization path (Booij and Van Kemenade 2003: 4):

independent preverb > left member of verbal compound > prefix > (zero)

One may find it paradoxical to consider particles in English as preverbs since they come post-verbally and not preverbally, but that is a consequence of the syntactic development of the English language. Due to the loss of the OV order in Middle English, the position of particles is "no longer on the left of the verb" (Van Kemenade and Los 2003: 87), i.e. it moved from a preverbal to a post-verbal position.

To summarize, whether one defines preverbs as autonomous constituents which were predecessors to prefixes or as a cover term for any verb particles and prefixes, or verbal prefixes as they are called in this study, they all have one conceptual link in common: preverbs usually appear before the verb, as their name suggests (Lat. *pre-* 'before'), they form complex predicates in combination with verbs and they form a lexical unit with the verb that they modify, typically contributing to the aspectual properties of the derived verb.

Chapter 2
Aspects of Aspect

This chapter examines different aspects of aspect in ten thematic subsections. It starts with a discussion of the complexity of aspectual studies and reviews several definitions of aspect in the literature. This is followed by exemplifying explicit forms of encoding aspectual meaning in Modern English, as well as in other languages in the world. Then it briefly outlines the history of studying aspect, which is important in order to understand the problems of differences in opinions and interpretations of this challenging linguistic issue. Furthermore, the distinction between aspect and aktionsart is explained in section 2.5. There is also a short insight into the theory of *chronogenesis* which accounts for the development of tense and aspect systems in Indo-European languages.

The current chapter also takes a closer look at aspect in Slavic languages which gave rise to many aspect theories and play a significant role in the studies of aspect. A brief look is taken at Old Church Slavonic, followed by an in-depth look at the "irregularities" of aspect in Croatian as an example of a Slavic language. This section is important because of the contrastive analysis carried out in the subsequent chapters, as well as the hypothesis that Old English aspectual preverbs in many ways resemble Modern Slavic verbal prefixes. The next subsection contains a discussion of aspect in Germanic languages, starting with Gothic which is contrasted with Old English in a few examples. Finally, there is a discussion of aspectual categories relevant to the present analysis.

2.1 The complexity of aspectual studies

Linguistic scholarship on aspect is without doubt the most prolific and diverse area of linguistics. The topic is simply inexhaustible and its theoretical proposals too numerous to mention in this book.

One can often hear statements like *English is not an aspect language* or *Dutch is not an aspect language.* What does that mean? English is not an aspect language in the traditional sense, where aspect plays an equal role like tense (or in some languages an even more important role). However, both English and Dutch are perfectly capable of expressing aspectual nuances by means of the tense system in combination with other interpretational cues, such as arguments or adverbials.

Aspectual systems differ fundamentally across languages and consequently this area of research has produced such a vast literature, very possibly more than on any other topic in linguistics.

In order to contribute something fresh to the field of *aspect,* which has always been notoriously difficult to treat and describe, the writing of this study was preconditioned by a careful scrutiny of classical works on aspect whose ideas shaped my research such as Pollak (1960), Comrie (1976), Dahl (1985),

Binnick (1991), Smith (1991), Bache (1995a) and, Michaelis (1998), Dickey (2000) to name but a few in chronological order, not to mention a number of significant, widely cited articles such as Vendler (1957), Sasse (2002) and Declerck (2007). In fact, the vastness of this area of research and the extent of literature written on aspect, and consequently the daunting prospect of becoming engaged in this research can best be shown by viewing the bibliography compiled by Binnick. Professor Robert Binnick from the University of Toronto at Scarborough has compiled and annotated a bibliography of more than 6,600 works in *Contemporary Research in Tense, Aspect, Aktionsart* and related areas, which can be downloaded as four pdf-files, each of 100 pages. It is not a hyperbole to say that it would take a lifetime to access all the items from this list and several more lifetimes to read them.

The study of aspect has been compared with

> "a dark and savage forest full of obstacles, pitfalls and mazes which have trapped most of those who have ventured into this much explored but poorly mapped territory."
>
> (Macaulay 1978: 416, quoted after Binnick 1991: 135)

Macaulay's reference to the phrase *selva oscura* from the opening of Dante's *Inferno* is a vivid metaphor that perfectly illustrates the complex nature of this linguistic phenomenon, namely the semantics of time. Using the same conceptual metaphor to comment on the immensity of research in this field of linguistics, Sasse (2002: 199) refers to "an impenetrable thicket of definitions, theories, and models."

How does one enter this savage forest without becoming trapped? Why is there so much confusion and controversy surrounding this subject? What is it about this linguistic category that has drawn so much attention, produced such extensive scholarship and led scholars to develop radically different understandings? This chapter is merely an attempt to address these questions and will sketch only the main outline of the notion of aspect which is relevant to the issue of aspect expressed by verbal prefixes and particles.

2.2 Aspect Defined

As with many concepts or categories in linguistics, there are numerous definitions of the term aspect, none of which has come to be universally accepted. Until recently, different ideas have been subsumed under the notion of aspect. However, even though the scope of study is still disputable, there is *some* general agreement about the concept today. Kruisinga (1931: 221) suggested that aspect shows the distinction between two possible perceptions of an action – in its entirety or with reference to a particular part of it – whereas Jakobson (1957: 130) saw aspect as dealing with temporal values that are inherent in the activity or state itself.

Some authors base their definitions on Holt (1974)[3], among them Comrie (1976: 3) who says that:

> "Aspects are different ways of viewing the internal temporal constituency of a situation".

Dickey (2000: 2) defines aspect within the cognitive linguistic approach:

> "aspect profiles the contour of a situation in time"

This definition makes use of Langacker's term *profiling* which refers to conceptual foregrounding or highlighting boundaries of a particular phenomenon. In this case, the boundaries correspond to the contour and aspect is defined as a linguistic structure that reflects our conceptual organization of situations (or events) as they unfold in time.

Michaelis (1998: 1), who also works in the cognitive paradigm, defines aspect as

> "the disposition of the situation through time: aspectual marking locates the situation denoted within a reference interval, which can but need not be identified with the time of speaking. Aspectual marking indicates whether the situation obtains throughout the reference interval, culminates within that time, or begins at that time".

This is a very accurate definition, but regrettably violates the principle of brevity. Rothstein (2004: 1) puts it more simply but in fact quite aptly by saying that

> "aspect is concerned with the structural properties of the event itself."

Ferrell (1951: 112) gives a very thorough definition that also touches upon a fundamental question addressed in this study – whether English expresses aspect with preverbs and post-verbal particles.

> "Aspect is a general linguistic phenomenon that can convey any number of meanings or any number of combinations of meanings. It can express repetition of an action, duration of an action, commencement or termination of an action. This does not begin to exhaust the list of possible aspect relationships. Moreover, these differences in action can be shown in several ways. They can be shown by morphological changes in the stem or ending of the verb, they can be shown by particles or auxiliary verbs, they can be shown by separate words. When a language shows these changes in a systematic fashion, that language is said to have aspect."

This quote is taken from an article by James Ferrell that deals with the meaning of the perfective aspect in Russian. It may be somewhat surprising that at that time a linguist, particularly of Slavophile persuasion, would have such an open-minded view on what constitutes aspect. Even today, there is a tendency among Slavists to think that only Slavic languages have real aspect and that all other aspect systems are merely pale shadows of the Slavic system. As long as

---

[3] Holt (1943: 6): "les manières diverses de concevoir l'écoulement du procès même", ('different ways of conceiving the flow of the process itself') (translation by Comrie 1976: 3)

changes of an action's distribution in time are manifested in a systematic fashion in any language, we can safely assume that we are dealing with aspect.

This discussion is based on Comrie's definition, but Ferrell's idea about aspect plays an important role. Additionally, a distinction should be made between aspect as a semantic category and the expression of aspect in the morphology and/or syntax. All languages have aspectual meaning, but not all of them have explicit (i.e. grammaticalized) means or forms to encode it. Aspect can be conveyed in all languages.

2.3 Aspect Exemplified

When we say aspect in English, what is usually meant is the progressive / non-progressive opposition which cuts across all tenses, as the table 1 shows:

NON-PROGRESSIVE (SIMPLE)	PROGRESSIVE (CONTINUOUS)
John walks.	John is walking.
John will walk	John will be walking.
John walked.	John was walking.
John has walked.	John has been walking.
John had walked	John had been walking.

Table 1
Non-progressive vs. progressive aspect in English

English is the only Germanic language with the exception of Icelandic that developed this aspectual opposition which runs through the entire tense system. Other Germanic languages exist perfectly well without this opposition. Dutch has a periphrastic construction to express progressive: *aan het* + infinitive (literally 'at the' + infinitive)[4], which is grammaticalized, as we can see in the following example taken from Booij (2008: 82).

(4) *Jan is aan het fiets-en*
 John is at the cycle-INF
 'John is cycling'

However, this construction cannot be regarded as a member of an aspectual opposition, as it does not have a correlate pair. It is not a member of a grammatical paradigm in the sense that English progressives are, as presented in table 1. Furthermore, the Dutch *aan het* progressive has certain restrictions which can be revealed in a contrastive analysis with English. They include passivization, habitual meaning or using stative and achievement verbs as in:

---

[4] German has a typologically similar construction (*am/beim* + infinitive) but it is not considered to be as grammaticalized as in Dutch. The German construction is regarded as a stylistic variant, whereas the Dutch construction is used obligatorily.

(5) She was living in London at the time
    *Ze was in Londen aan het wonen (from Boogaart 1999: 175)

The French Imperfect is often said to be equivalent to the English progressive and in a number of cases one is used to translate the other:

(6) *Il s'amusait.*
    He was having fun.

However, these two categories are not completely identical, so in a number of cases the French Imperfect is to be translated with the Simple Past, as in

(7) *Il quittait le travail tous les jours à 5h.*
    He left work every day at 5.
    *He was leaving work every day at 5.

(8) *Il n'avait pas le temps pour une éventuelle maîtresse.*
    He never had time for mistresses.
    *He was never having time for mistresses.

Besides the progressive aspect, Modern English has two more systems although their status in terms of aspect has been the subject of much debate.

The first is the Present Perfect, whose status has often shifted from tense to aspect and back again, depending on the author. Žic Fuchs (2009) has shown that the Present Perfect exhibits a dual nature, with two of its meanings belonging to aspect and the other two to relative tense:

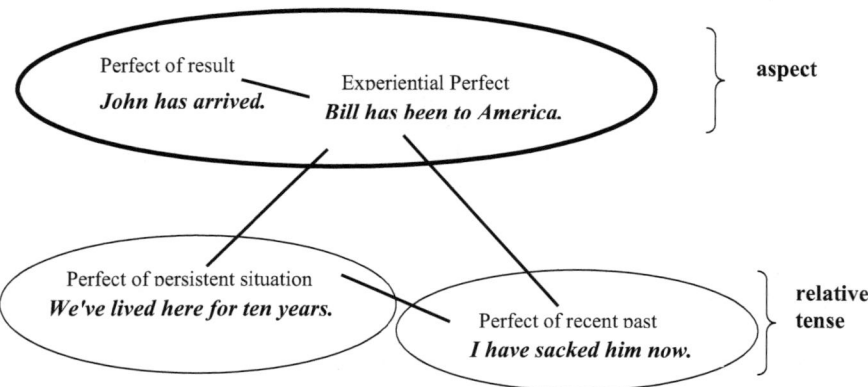

Figure 1
The meanings of the Present Perfect
(adapted from Žic Fuchs 2009: 201)

The progressive and perfect aspects in English are in many ways intertwined with tenses, which is why the Present Perfect has often been conflated with tense for pedagogical purposes. Even though the main subject of this study is aspect in English from a diachronic perspective, aspect as expressed by the progressive and the perfect forms fall outside the scope of this research. They have been dealt with at length in Ziegeler (2006).

There is a further system of aspect in Modern English having the status of a 'grey area'. That is the system of particle verbs or phrasal verbs and is one of the topics investigated in this study. It is generally considered that particles express aspect but not in a systematic manner. Since phrasal verbs or their particles are not perceived as a structured system, they are typically labelled as lexical rather than grammatical aspect. The original meaning of particles is spatial, but in many cases they have grammaticalized into aspectual markers. The following three sentences contain different phrasal verbs but with the same particle. However, this particle is aspectual in only one of these three sentences:

(9) *John went up to his room.*

(10) *John threw up in his room.*

(11) *John cleaned up his room.*

In number (9) we see the particle *up* in its literal sense, so the meaning of the phrasal verb is spatial – or directional, to be more precise. John literally went to his room which was upstairs.

In number (10) the meaning of the particle *up* is lexicalized because the meaning of the phrasal verb *throw up* 'vomit' is not entirely predictable from the sum of its parts. This does not mean that *up* is not motivated by its primary spatial (and directional) meaning, driven by a specific metaphor in which John's stomach is the agent of throwing. The particle *up* has modified the simplex verb *throw* in such a way that it radically changed its lexical meaning. Therefore, we can say that the particle *up* has a lexicalizing function in this case. Here the particle *up* contributes to the meaning of the whole phrasal verb in a way that falls outside the productive rules of grammar, which is why this is a case of lexicalization.

Example number (11) features the particle *up* expressing aspect. Here the particle *up* has only slightly modified the meaning of the verb, but in a very predictable manner which signifies completion or result. The sentence can be rephrased as *John finished cleaning the room* or *John cleaned the room completely*. This use of the particle *up* is a very productive rule in English, which means that it can combine with a wide array of other verbs and thus produce slightly modified meanings according to a very predictable pattern. In other words, this is a case of grammaticalization, not only because this phrasal verb's meaning can be accounted for by a regular grammatical rule, but also because the particle expresses aspect, which is a grammatical category.

The above sets of examples (progressive, perfect, particles) show that English expresses aspect on the level of syntax, rather than morphology as in languages such as Slavic. Slavic languages have formal markers of aspect – special morphemes whose function is primarily aspectual, but Modern English expresses aspectual meaning through the interaction of different linguistic devices whose principal function is not aspectual such as tenses, particles, verbal constructions and adverbial phrases[5] (cf. Freed 1979: 12). Early English also used to have morphological marking of aspect by means of preverbs or verbal prefixes, which will be analysed in this study. However, the English language abandoned this system, as it underwent an important structural change – the shift from OV to VO word order during the Early Middle English period.

Based on a survey of the literature on aspect, scholars agree about only one aspectual opposition in English today – progressive vs. non-progressive in the tense system. All the other instances of aspectual marking in English, both synchronic and diachronic, have been dogged by controversy.

In many languages throughout the world there is no grammatical category of tense, so aspect is the only way to express the information about the temporal flow of action. Such is, for example, Mandarin Chinese, a language with more native speakers than any other language in the world. As it does not have any inflectional morphology, aspect in Chinese is marked only through particles and word order. There are two perfective or punctual particles, *le* and *guo,* and two imperfective or durative particles, *zhe* and *zài*. The following two examples show how Chinese lacks the temporal deictic reference that Indo-European languages normally express through tense:

(12) *wŏmen chī fàn le*
    we   eat rice POINT IN TIME, SITUATION
'We have eaten rice' or 'Now we eat rice'.   (from Egerod 1994: 290)

(13) *wŏ chī zhe   fàn*
    I eat ONGOING rice
'I am eating rice'. (from Egerod 1994: 298)

In the first example we have a situation which is rather ambiguous in the absence of more context. The only temporal reference in the sentence is the particle *le,* which does not tell us whether the action took place in the past, the present or the future but "refers to a point in time where something happened, or happens, was accomplished, began or ended, or will end." (Egerod 1994: 288)

Another language which does not express aspect morphologically but syntactically is Samoan, a Polynesian language. It makes use of a range of preverbal particles such as *na* for expressing terminative past or *sā* expressing stative past or habituality:

(14) *sā alofa*
    PAST love
'loved' (taken from Sasse 1991: 40)

(15) *na alofa*
    PAST love
'fell in love' (taken from Sasse 1991: 40)

These particles belong to a system of tense-aspect-mood markers. In isolating languages such as Samoan, all these three categories are expressed with separate words and not by verb inflection.

---

[5] Sapir (1921: 108) already noted that "aspect is expressed in English by all kinds of idiomatic turns rather than by a consistently worked out set of grammatical forms."

In an agglutinative language such as Hungarian, aspect is expressed by means of verbal prefixes and object noun phrases. Aspectual prefixes in Hungarian can also appear in post-verbal position. The prefix *meg-* can express a range of aspectual meanings, such as resultative (e.g. *megír* 'write'), instantaneous (e.g. *meglebben* 'flutter') or inceptive (e.g. *megszeret* 'begin to love'). The following two sentences exemplify the simplex vs. compound verb *tud* 'know':

(16) *Tudta   az igazságot.*
     know.3.P.SG.PAST the truth.ACC
     'He knew the truth.'

(17)   *Megtudta   az igazságot.*
       meg.PREFIX+know.3.P.SG.PAST the truth.ACC
       'He came to know the truth.' (from Kiefer 1994: 188)

The perfectivizing prefix *meg* is often mentioned as an example of a purely aspectual prefix (cf. Comrie 1976: 94).

As can be seen, the category of aspect can be expressed at different levels of language, with cross-linguistic incompatibilities present even between closely related languages. If one contrasts the prototypical aspectual oppositions between English and Slavic, one will see that the English progressive / non-progressive opposition does not have much to do with the Slavic perfective / imperfective opposition. For example, all instances of progressives in English will be translated with an imperfective verb in Croatian, but not vice versa. In certain contexts English progressive forms do help to translate the Slavic imperfective, but this similarity is only superficial and appears randomly. English progressive / non-progressive is restricted to finite verb forms, whilst Slavic aspect is expressed and obligatorily marked in all tenses including imperatives, in all non-finite verb forms such as infinitives, participles and even in verbal nouns.

I will now give a thumbnail sketch of the formal properties of aspect in Croatian in order to show how aspect functions in Slavic languages.

Aspect in Slavic languages is morphologically marked or coded. Every verb in Croatian (as well as in any Slavic language) has two complete sets of forms – perfective and imperfective. The distinction between perfective and imperfective is an obligatorily marked category of a verb. All verbs have their aspectual pair or partner. In other words, every imperfective verb has its perfective counterpart and vice versa.

For example, the verb *jesti* 'to eat' is imperfective. In order to create its perfective pair, the prefix *po-* is attached to the verb stem, as in (18). Other verbs take different prefixes such as *na-* or a few others, as can be seen in the examples (19) to (23). For every verb there is only one prefix that changes only its aspectual meaning without affecting the lexical meaning of the verb. There is no rule or predictable pattern which prefixes come into combination with which verbs in order to only change the aspectual meaning. One verb can come in combinations with several prefixes, but only one prefix changes its aspect exclusively. Other prefixes change the lexical meaning of the verb in addition to assigning the perfective aspect.

According to the basic rule of perfectivization in Slavic (Silić 1978: 49), when prefixes are attached to imperfective verbs, they act as perfectivizers. The following examples illustrate this basic rule.

(18) *jesti* 'to eat'   -   *pojesti* 'to eat up'

(19) *pisati* 'to write'   -   *napisati* 'to write (something) to completion'

(20) *čitati* 'to read'   -   *pročitati* 'to read completely, read through'

(21) *grijati* 'to warm'   -   *zagrijati* 'to warm up'

Translating the aspectual pairs in isolation is very tricky. Sometimes the English post-verbal particle *up* does the job of a rough equivalent because it also has a perfectivizing meaning in Modern English. However, there are many examples where it is difficult to find an adequate distinguishing translation, such as the following:

(22) *brojiti*   -   *prebrojiti* 'to count'

(23) *činiti*   -   *učiniti* 'to do'

It has always been a matter of great debate whether this kind of prefixation is an inflectional or a derivational process. Formally it looks more as belonging to the derivational domain. Spencer (1991: 197) argues that this is "an example of what appears at first sight to be inflectional morphology behaving like derivational morphology". For Bybee (1985: 81-110), the distinction between inflection and derivation is in the amount of semantic content of a morpheme.

Nonetheless, aspect is considered to be a grammatical category in Croatian (as with all other Slavic languages), so if prefixation only affects the aspect of the verb, the process is thought to be inflectional. Those who see it as an inflectional category ultimately believe that an aspectual pair of verbs are two forms of the same word – or the same lexeme, whereas those who see it as a derivational category basically see an aspectual pair of verbs as two different words (or lexemes) even though there is difference only in their aspectual meaning. This in turn suggests that they see aspect as a lexical rather than a grammatical category (cf. Gojmerac 1980: 27-28).

To express aspect, Slavic has another word-formational process apart from prefixation, and that is suffixation. This kind of process is in fact considered to be purely grammatical because the inflectional status of the aspectual suffix has never been questioned, as its semantic content never licenses any lexical modification. The most common aspectual (non-terminal) suffix is *-va-*[6] and it acts as an imperfectivizer:

(24) *dati* 'to give' -   *davati* 'to be giving'

(25) *kupiti* 'to buy' -   *kupovati* 'to keep buying'

This suffix can also be added to prefixed verbs, thus creating new words with slightly different aspectual meanings:

(26) *pisati* → *zapisati* 'to write down' - *zapisivati* 'to be writing down'

---

[6] The allomorphs of this suffix are *-ova-, -ava-, -iva- or -a-*. In Croatian linguistic literature, it is also sometimes labelled as an infix.

(27) *pisati* → *prepisati* 'to copy'   - *prepisivati* 'to be copying'

When attached to the imperfective verb *pisati*, the prefixes *za-* and *pre-* changed the lexical meaning of the verb in addition to perfectivizing them. The perfectivization in this case is only its secondary effect – *zapisati* is not an aspectual pair of *pisati* but an example of lexical derivation of that verb. However, such newly derived verbs can create their aspectual pairs, as the above examples show.

There is another suffix, *-nu-* which is a perfectivizer and serves to express so-called single, instantaneous actions (also known as 'semelfactive aktionsart'):

(28) *vikati* 'to yell / scream'   - *viknuti* 'to cry out; to scream once'

(29) *doviknuti* 'to shout to'   - *dovikivati* 'to be shouting to'

This brief exposition of the morphological means to mark aspectuality only foreshadows the complexities of aspect in Slavic languages for the purpose of understanding the formal incompatibility of Slavic aspect with aspect in non-Slavic languages. A more detailed survey of aspect in Slavic is presented in section 2.8

2.4 Origins of Aspectology

In order to understand why this field of study is so controversial and why there is so much confusion not only in terminology but also in the scope of the phenomenon under investigation, it is very important to give a brief outline of the history of the concept and the term of aspect in linguistics.

Aspect was first discussed by the Indian linguist Pāṇini in his descriptions of Sanskrit verb morphology and then by the Greeks in the fifth century BC. Aristotle and Plato were aware that in addition to tense, Greek marked a second type of distinction, that of aspect.

The Roman grammarian Marcus Terentius Varro (116-27 BC) divided the Latin tenses into two aspectual categories: *infectum* and *perfectum* (Gray 1939: 205-206). *Infectum* included the present, the imperfect and the future, whereas *perfectum* included all the perfect tenses. In Aelius Donatus's *Ars grammatica*, which was the standard Latin grammar throughout the Middle Ages, the primary verbs such as *dico* were called *formae perfectae,* as opposed to derived verbs such as *dictito (formae frequentativae)* and *fervesco (formae inchoativae)* (Gojmerac 1980: 10).

In an early 17th century Russian grammar book by Meletiy Smotritskiy the term *vid* ('viewpoint') appears for the first time as a loan translation of the Greek cognate word εἶδος. However, it did not refer to the binary perfective / imperfective opposition but was used in the sense of 'type', 'kind', 'category' or 'species', just as the term εἶδος was previously used in Greek grammars to denote two kinds of word formational categories for verbs *and* nouns: the primary and the derived. Smotritskiy also coined the term *sovershennyj vid* ('completed viewpoint') as a translation for the Latin term *formae perfectae*, but did not use it in the present-day sense of the term.

It took another century before Mikhail Lomonosov gave the term *sovershennyj* a more modern sense of the term in his 1755 grammar book[7]. He distinguished three basic types of verbs, one of which was *sovershennyj* that denoted the verbs derived by prefixation. Interestingly enough, Lomonosov did not make use of the term *vid*. According to Gojmerac (1980: 11), the German grammarian Johann Severin Vater interpreted Lomonosov's data and singled out the category of aspect in 1808. According to Newman (1976: 35, 47), Vater merely published a complex classification of verbs according to the infinitive, which only stimulated others to call for a revision of Lomonosov's classification. Newman (1976: 42) suggests that it was Lomonosov who captured the semantic distinction between the imperfective and perfective aspect, but that it was not clearly visible as he classified verbs into tenses. Based on his ten tenses, Vater proposed three morphological groups: *imperfectum, simplex* and *perfectum* and called the category *vid* or εἶδος (Gojmerac 1980: 11).

This still did not place aspect in the domain of grammar but continued to denote a type or kind of different semantic classes of the verb. So, for example, in 1827 Nikolai Greč wrote a grammar that identified six aspects in Russian based on their semantic features and calls them "circumstances of the verb". A few years later, Greč's *Practical Russian Grammar* was translated into French by the slavicist Carl Philipp Reiff, who rendered the term *vid* as *aspect*[8]. Szemerényi (1987: 2) notes that this was "a happy misunderstanding", as only its basic meaning was translated and not its classificational meaning which it had at the time in Russian grammatical terminology (cf. Gojmerac 1980: 12). Kravar (1976: 291) believes that the French translation *aspect* introduced vagueness and an impression of some kind of 'viewing' or a subjective attitude of the speaker towards the course of verbal action, so understanding 'aspect' changed from objective and concrete to abstract and subjective.

The term 'aspect' was soon borrowed by English from French. It was first attested in 1853 according to the Oxford English Dictionary. The modern concept of Slavic aspect that consists of the perfective / imperfective opposition in morphologically linked pairs of verbs first appeared in Miklosisch's *Vergleichende Grammatik der slavischen Sprachen* (1868-74). However, it was not until the early 1930's that the present-day concept of the binary opposition was firmly established with the work of Jakobson (1932) (Binnick 1991: 140).

Even though the "discovery" of aspect is now credited to Russian linguistics, it must be noted that grammarians of other Slavic languages also worked on the establishment of aspect as a grammatical category.

In 1603 the Slovak scholar Benedikt Vavřinec von Nudožer wrote *Grammaticae Bohemicae*[9], one of the first grammars of the Czech language. He pointed to a complementary nature of verbs, distinguishing prefixed from

---

[7] M. V. Lomonosov, *Rossijskaja grammatika*

[8] According to Tichy (2000: 115), a more accurate rendering would be the Latin word *genus* 'kind', 'species'.

[9] The full title is *Grammaticae bohemicae ad leges naturalis methodi conformatae et notis numerisque illustratae ac distinctae libri duo.*

simplex verbs which, according to Pollak (1960: 30) he called perfective and imperfective.

According to Brlobaš (2007: 264), there are two basic models of treatment of aspect in the grammars of Croatian. Starting with the first Croatian grammar written by Kašić in 1604 until Starčević in 1812, there was only an implicit description, where grammarians did not observe or define the category of aspect but made only latent references to it when they described the system of verbal tenses. The first explicit description of aspect appeared in Ignjat Alojzije Brlić's *Grammatik der illyrischen Sprache* in 1833 where it was clearly described as one of the fundamental characteristics of the Croatian verb. The name of the category was established and the members of the aspectual oppositions were explicitly defined as perfective and imperfective.

Due to such a clear-cut binary morphological distinction between opposites of almost every single verb, Slavic aspect is often considered to be "the prototypical exemplar of aspectual systems" (Binnick 1991: 136). Much of the confusion arose when the concept of aspect was imported from the study of Slavic grammar into the Western grammatical tradition. This was the beginning of a long debate about the universality of aspectual categories (Binnick 1991: 139). Scholars such as Jespersen (1924: 286) regard Slavic aspect as fundamental to all languages.

Jacob Grimm was the first Germanic linguist to extend the concept of aspect from Slavic languages to Germanic languages in 1824 in the preface to his translation of Vuk Karadžić's *Grammar of Serbian*:

> "Es ist nicht unmöglich die spuren eines die slavischen sprachen so durchdringenden unterschiedes auch in der deutschen aufzufinden. Composita mit -ver, -be, -hin, -durch etc. (wie im slavischen mit -po, -do, -na etc.) böten etwa perfectiva dar, unzusammengesetzte dagegen imperfectiva."[10]
>
> (Streitberg 1891: 77)

It is not just a resemblance on formal grounds that Grimm noticed between the prefixed verbs in Slavic and the prefixed verbs in other Indo-European languages. Such oppositions of simplex and prefixed verbs that Grimm compared actually do point to a difference in aspect on the morphological level without any implications of tense, as the following often quoted example from German shows (Leskien 1909: 216, Verkuyl 1972: 3, Bache 1985a: 10, Binnick 1991: 141, Labeau 2005: 56):

(30) *jagen* 'chase, hunt' vs. *erjagen* 'catch'

Jagen is not a completed action and is inherently imperfective, while *erjagen* denotes a resultative (successful), completed action. One of the quick aspectual tests is the adverbial 'all day', which is semantically incompatible with perfectives, thus showing the aspectual status of this verb pair:

---

[10] "It is not impossible to find in the Germanic languages also the traces of a distinction which so permeates the Slavic languages. Composites with *ver-*, *be-*, *hin-*, *durch-*, etc. (as in Slavic with *po-*, *do-*, *na*, etc.) perhaps represent perfectives, uncomposed verbs on the contrary imperfectives" (translation from Binnick 1991: 141)

(31) *sie jagten den Hirsch den ganzen Tag*
  'they chased the stag all day'

(32) **sie erjagten den Hirsch den ganzen Tag*
  *'they caught the stag all day'

In this transfer of the category of aspect from Slavic to Germanic, we can see history repeating itself. In the same manner that the grammar of English was distorted to fit the mould of Latin until well into the 18th century, now starting in the 19th century we have another language (or group of languages) that have a supposedly "neatly" organized grammatical system.

It did not take long for linguists to start considering attempts to transfer the category of aspect from Slavonic to Germanic as futile (Mitchell 1985: 364) and the comparison with Slavic to be "overstated and unjustified" (Hewson & Bubenik 1997: 64). The Dutch linguist Zandvoort (1962: 19) said that

> "the attempt to transfer the category of 'aspect' from Slavonic to Germanic, and from there to Modern English grammar, strikes one as an instance of misdirected ingenuity".

In addition to the basic perfective – imperfective opposition, during the 19th century a number of other aspectual distinctions and oppositions were proposed, such as accomplished – unaccomplished, durative – nondurative / momentous, semelfactive –frequentative / iterative, many of which were based on dubious semantic criteria. These categories will be discussed in a separate subchapter on aspectual categories (2.10).

After extending the concept of aspect to German, other languages soon came into play, further complicating aspectual terminology. In 1852 the German scholar Georg Curtius wrote his *Griechische Schulgrammatik* ('School Grammar of Greek') in which he translated the term aspect with the German compound *Zeitart* ('kind of time') which he contrasted with *Zeitstufe* ('tense'). He believed that the perfective / imperfective opposition of Slavic corresponded to the opposition of the imperfect and the aorist in Ancient Greek. Besides *dauernd* ('durative; continuous') and *eintretend* ('entering'), Curtius proposed *vollendet* ('complete') as the third member of the *Zeitart* category, which in turn correlate to the Greek present, perfect and aorist stems (Gonda 1962: 18-20).

In 1885 the Indo-Europeanist Karl Brugmann objected to the terms *Zeitart* and *Zeitstufe* because the word *Zeit* in these two compounds does not mean the same thing. With *Zeitstufe* it means actual, physical time, whereas with *Zeitart* it may lead to confusion because both the aorist and the imperfect refer to the past, but the difference is in the aspect. Therefore, Brugmann proposed a new term: *Aktionsart*[11] ('kind of action') as well as the Latinate triad *imperfektiv – perfektiv – perfektisch* to replace Curtius's *dauernd – eintretend – vollendet*.

---

[11] The German term 'aktionsart' is widely used in linguistic literature written in English. However, many authors italicize it to show that it is a foreign word and even capitalize the first letter to follow the original German spelling convention. Authors like Comrie and Brinton do not follow this practice and conform to the English conventions of spelling loanwords – retaining the etymological spelling, but without capitalizing and italicizing. Such practice has also been adopted in this book, except in quotes by other authors.

"Aktionsart ist, im Gegensatz zu Zeitstufe, die Art und Weise, wie die Handlung des Verbums vor sich geht.[12] "

(Brugmann 1904a: 492-493).

It should be stressed that at this point, and for another 30 years, the term aktionsart was still only a translation for Slavic *vid* or French *aspect*.

In 1891 Streitberg adopted Brugmann's term aktionsart in his book *Perfective und imperfective Actionsart* [sic!] *im Germanischen*. This work became well known in Germanic and Slavic aspectology. Strongly influenced by Grimm, Streitberg wanted to establish a connection between Slavic and Germanic languages. He studied the Gothic prefix *ga-* in an attempt to show that the perfective / imperfective aspect was preserved in Gothic. However, it is known that the perfective / imperfective distinction in binary opposition for every verb is not something that Slavic inherited from Proto-Indo-European, but is an innovation developed independently at a later stage (Hewson and Bubenik 1997: 84).

Streitberg compared Wulfila's Gothic translation of the Bible with the Greek original, arguing that Gothic verbs with the prefix *ga-* (as well as *us-, at-, bi-, dis- in-* and *du-*) are perfective opposites of their simplex imperfective versions.

For example, Streitberg contrasted *slepan* (German *schlafen*) with *gaslepan* (German *entschlafen*) 'to fall asleep'. *Slepan* is 'durative' or 'continuative', referring to an action which endures through time, whereas *gaslepan* refers to something instantaneous or momentaneous, taking place instantly without duration.

Traditionally, the Old English prefix *ge-* is thought to be fulfilling a variety of aspectual roles, including expressing a resultative and a completed action (Lindemann 1970: 2-6). However, Streitberg's theory was challenged by several linguists, such as Krause (1953) who claimed that *ga-* does not alter the aspect but the meaning of the basic verb, giving the following examples:

(33) *sitan* 'sit' but *ga-sitan* 'sit down'

(34) *bairan* 'carry' but *gabairan* 'give birth'

(35) *standan* 'stand' but *ga-standan* 'stand fast, remain' (Szemerényi 1996: 306)

Even if Streitberg was wrong to think that Gothic was the only Germanic language that had 'the fundamental' aspect as in Slavic, the counter-examples seem slightly exaggerated.

Verbal prefixes are famous for their polysemy, and certainly a handful of examples where *ga-* changes the meaning and not the aspect of the verb can be accounted for. In Slavic languages, some prefixes change the meaning of the verb completely, while others only change aspect, as the prefix *po-* illustrates in the following sets of examples:

(36) *kazati* 'to say'   - *pokazati* 'to show'

(37) *reći* 'to tell'   - *poreći* 'to deny'

---

[12] 'The manner in which an action or situation develops or proceeds in particular circumstances' (translation by Forsyth 1970: 19)

as opposed to the aspectual pairs:

(38) *trošiti* 'to use / spend'   - *potrošiti* 'to use up'

(39) *jesti* 'to eat'   - *pojesti* 'to eat up / finish eating'

In (36) and (37) the prefix *po-* changes the meaning of the verb in unpredictable ways, whereas in (38) and (39) the same prefix perfectivizes the verb according to a productive grammatical rule.

It was only in 1908 that the two synonymous terms, aspect and aktionsart, were first differentiated in the doctoral dissertation of the Swedish Slavist linguist Sigrud Agrell, *Aspektänderung und Aktionsartbildung beim polnischen Zeitwort*. He narrowed down the concept of aspect only to the main category of verbal opposition in Slavic – perfective and imperfective, whereas all the other composite verbs which describe the way in which an action takes place were labelled as 'aktionsart':

> "Unter Aktionsart verstehe ich . . . nicht die beiden Hauptkategorien des slavischen Zeitwortes, die unvollendete und die vollendete Handlungsform (das Imperfektivum und das Perfektivum) — diese nenne ich Aspekte.
>
> Mit dem Ausdruck Aktionsart bezeichne ich bisher fast gar nicht beachtete— geschweige denn klassifizierte — Bedeutungsfunktionen der Verbalkomposita (sowie einiger Simplicia und Suffixbildungen), die genauer ausdrücken wie die Handlung vollbracht wird, die Art und Weise ihrer Ausführung markieren."[13]

Agrell 1908: 78

Agrell follows his basic distinction with a discussion and listing of twenty types of aktionsarten in Polish. It took some time before other scholars accepted Agrell's subdivision of aspect (understood broadly) into aspect (in the narrow sense) and aktionsart, but by the 1930's it gained ground. Basically, this distinction set apart grammatical aspect, which Slavic expresses with inflectional morphology, from lexical aspect, expressed by derivational morphology. In other words, aktionsart is lexicalized aspect restricted only to lexicalization achieved by derivational morphology, in Slavic typically by prefixation.

Before we continue, we shall briefly discuss this new distinction, its implications and its impact on modern linguistic research.

---

[13] "I do not use the term Aktionsart to mean the two main categories of the Slavic verb, the imperfective and the perfective - these I call aspect.
My use of the expression Aktionsart denotes the hitherto unconsidered, and much less classified, semantic functions of verbal compounds (as well as of some simplexes and suffixed forms), which express more precisely how an action is performed and signal the manner of its execution." (the translation is mine)

2.5 Aspect vs. Aktionsart

In order to better understand what Agrell had in mind when he came up with this influential subdivision, it is perhaps a good idea to see how his aktionsart classifications work in a related Slavic language. These categories are supposed to work in all Slavic languages, so Silić applied Agrell's theory and classification to Croatian, supplying Croatian examples. The morphological markers have been underlined (adapted from Silić 1978: 50-53):

Ingressive	*progovoriti* 'to begin to speak'
Completive	*dograditi* 'to build an addition to'
Totalizing	*odslužiti* 'to serve out'
Attenuative	*primiriti se* 'to calm down for a bit'
Intensive	*razigrati se* 'to get carried away playing'
Cumulative	*nabacati* 'to throw into a pile'
Majorative	*nadvladati* 'to overpower'
Distributive	*porušiti* 'to tear down one after another'
Diminutive	*pjevušiti* 'to hum'
Augmentative	*drmusati* 'to shake violently'
Semelfactive	*skoknuti* 'to drop in'
Serial	*kapati* 'to drip (all night)'
Determinate	*voziti* 'to drive'
Indeterminate	*nosati* 'to carry'
Resultative	*napisati* 'to write (to completion)'
Inchoative	*gasnuti* 'to extinguish'
Stative	*spavati* 'to sleep'
Relational	*pripadati* 'to belong'
Evolutive	*šetati* 'to walk'

Table 2
Aktionsarten in Croatian

As we can see, most examples feature derivational prefixes and occasionally suffixes. Some of the examples do not work for Croatian, as they do not exhibit any morphological modifications.

Such morphological patterns can sporadically be found in German, as in *lieben* 'to love' and *liebeln* 'to love superficially', or *lachen* 'to laugh' and *lächeln* 'to smile' which can be classified as attenuative or diminutive aktionsart. The cognate English morpheme can be identified in the examples such as *spark* and *sparkle, suck* and *suckle, wag* and *waggle.* (cf. Binnick 1991: 145 and Filip 1999: 194)

The only other Modern English morphological feature existing in English that would meet the aktionsartal criteria set by Agrell is the suffix *–en* which signifies inchoative or resultative aspect, as in the following verbs (cf. Jespersen 1928: 76):

(40) *blacken, brighten, broaden, dampen, darken, deafen, fatten, flatten, freshen, gladden, harden, lighten, loosen, moisten, quicken, quieten, redden, ripen, roughen, sadden, sharpen, shorten, sicken, slacken, smarten, soften, stiffen, straighten, sweeten, thicken, tighten, toughen, weaken, whiten, widen*

Agrell established two subsystems in aspect and again this happened on the basis of the description of a Slavic language. But one of his chief contributions is the explanation that grammatical aspect can cut across aktionsarten – one can work independently of the other, as the following example shows:

(41) *Ispijao je svoj čaj.*
'He was drinking up his tea.'

Imperfective aspect is compatible with telic[14] aktionsart, so the imperfective verb ***piti*** 'to drink' is perfectivized by the prefix ***iz-*** 'from, out of', forming an aktionsartal rather than aspectual pair of the verb ***piti***[15]. The newly derived perfective verb ***ispiti*** can in turn be imperfectivized into ***ispijati*** 'to be drinking up'. The above English translation happens to work well purely by chance in this particular example, as the progressive tense renders the imperfective notion of the verb and the particle ***up*** corresponds to the prefix ***iz-***. In most cases there is little morpho-syntactic correspondence between the two languages.

The distinction between aspect and aktionsart has been followed by many scholars to this day, with an incredible number of articles and book chapters featuring the opposition of aspect and aktionsart in the title, such as van Wijk (1928), Goedsche (1934), Bache (1982), Brinton (1985b), Sasse (1991).

According to this distinction, there are only two aspects (perfective and imperfective), i.e. only one aspectual opposition, but there are many aktionsarten. With the introduction of this distinction, aspect came to be considered a matter of the speaker's viewpoint or perspective on a situation, whereas aktionsart is lexical, or as Comrie calls it (1976: 41-51), *inherent* or *semantic* aspect. Table 3 illustrates the properties of this subdivision.

ASPECT	AKTIONSART
grammatical	lexical
morphological	semantic
inflectional	derivational

Table 3
Agrell's subdivision of aspect

---

[14] The original term was *non-durative*, as *telic* was coined by Garey in 1957.
[15] The true aspectual pair of *piti* 'to drink' is *popiti*.

Most traditional Slavic linguists stick to this division, such as Kravar (1976) or Gojmerac (1980). A large number of non-Slavic linguists also subscribe to this view, as for example Gonda (who says that disregarding this terminological and notional distinction is "much to be regretted" 1962: 29) and Brinton, ("it is a useful distinction of long standing", 1988: 3). They see the difference between aspect and aktionsart in terms of contrasts 'grammatical' vs. 'lexical' and 'subjective' vs. 'objective':

> "Aspect is grammatical because, broadly speaking, it is expressed by verbal inflectional morphology and periphrases, aktionsart by the lexical meaning of verbs and verbal derivational morphology. Aspect is subjective because the speaker chooses a particular viewpoint, whereas aktionsart, since it concerns the given nature of the event and not the perspective of the speaker, is objective."
>
> (Brinton 1988: 3)

But it needs to be repeated, neither aspect nor aktionsart originate in the study of Germanic. Both were used to denote non-tense distinctions in Slavic languages. Comrie (1976: 6-7) proposes avoiding the term aktionsart because it is open to so many interpretations. He subsumes both 'types' of aspect under one category:

> "In the present book we shall speak of semantic aspectual distinctions, such as that between perfective and imperfective meaning, irrespective of whether they are grammaticalized or lexicalized in individual languages."
>
> (Comrie 1976: 6-7):

Lyons also objects to using the term aktionsart, but he does not deny the importance of the concept that the term covers. He proposes the term *aspectual character* instead:

> "The aspectual character of a verb, or more simply its character, will be that part of its meaning whereby it (normally) denotes one kind of situation rather than another. For example, 'know' differs from 'recognize' in English, as 'kennen' differs from 'erkennen' in German or 'znatj' from 'uznatj' in Russian, by virtue of its aspectual character. 'Know' (like 'kennen' or 'znatj') normally denotes a state, whereas 'recognize' (like 'erkennen' and 'uznatj') normally denotes an event. It is generally accepted nowadays that any discussion of aspect from a semantic point of view must also take account of what we are referring to as the character of particular verbs. [...] Aspect and character are interdependent in this way because they both rest ultimately upon the same ontological distinctions"
>
> (Lyons 1977: 706).

Lyons disapproves of the distinction between aspect and aktionsart because it has not always been consistently applied – sometimes it is based on the difference between inflection and derivation, other times between grammaticalization and lexicalization.

On the basis of Comrie's and his own insights, Sasse (1991: 32) comes to a very important conclusion that

> "From a cognitive point of view, *aspect* and *aktionsart* [...] are actually one and the same thing, the difference being a matter of individual lexicalization and grammaticalization processes. [...] It is methodologically problematic to define *aktionsart* as a universal lexical category because we do not know where the exact borderline between lexicon and grammar is. We cannot predict, on a universal basis, what kind of meaning will be lexicalized, and what kind will be grammaticalized."

This becomes particularly evident in cross-linguistic comparisons, as we have seen in one of the previous sections. Moreover, if we stick to this rigid aspect vs. aktionsart distinction, we would actually have to conclude that all Slavic aspect which is formed through prefixation is actually aktionsart[16] (cf. Dahl 1995: 27). In another paper Sasse says in a footnote that

> "the term "aktionsart" was invented to indicate a strict division between lexicon and grammar (or lexicalization and grammaticalization), which was coupled with the assumption that the two constitute different (and in a way unrelated) compartments of language, each of which was associated with their distinct semantic characteristics."
>
> (Sasse 2002: 203)

The area of prefixes and particles is one of the language features which shows that lexicon and grammar are not two distinct compartments of language. Placing meaning in focus rather than form is in fact one of the basic tenets of cognitive linguistics. This is what Sasse's claims are based on:

> "There is no meaningful distinction between grammar and lexicon. Lexicon, morphology, and syntax form a continuum of symbolic structures, which differ along various parameters but can be divided into separate components only arbitrarily."
>
> (Langacker 1987: 3)

Sasse's cognitively-minded treatment of aspect is only a logical conclusion. In fact it solves many problems that previous movements in linguistics such as structuralism did not know how to deal with.

Verbal prefixation has traditionally been considered as a process of lexicalization, but recently prefixed verbs have been looked upon as constructions (Petré 2005, Petré & Cuyckens 2008), which shows them as belonging to the domain of grammaticalization rather than lexicalization. Kemenade and Los (2003: 104) have also suggested that Old English prefixes are in an advanced state of grammaticalization.

In 1985 Brinton published an article entitled "Verb Particles in English: Aspect or Aktionsart?" where she suggested that certain particles serve as markers of perfective aspect, whereas others are markers of telic aktionsart. Three years later, in her seminal book on the aspectual systems in English, she claimed that all phrasal verbs (i.e. verb particles) belong to the aktionsart, and not aspect.

---

[16] There are in fact some linguists who think that only suffixation is a legitimate process in forming aspectual pairs such as Karčevski (1927) and Maslov (1959) (Mlynarczyk 2004: 152).

According to Brinton (1988), there are two well-developed aspectual systems in English:
1) primary – aspect – grammatical
2) secondary – aktionsart – lexical

In other words, the primary system of aspect marking in English is that represented by formal variation of the main verb, which can be modified by the *progressive* (or *continuous*) aspect, the *perfect* (or *completed*) aspect or both (Comrie 1976). For Brinton, the primary system also includes grammaticalized forms such as 'begin', 'continue' and 'stop', which collocate with infinitives or participles and thus express distinctions in aspect, an area of aspect in English first discussed elaborately by Freed (1979).

Brinton's secondary system is aktionsart, which is semantic[17], i.e. lexical aspect, as opposed to grammatical (being the primary system). What Brinton sees as belonging to aktionsart is the verb-particle combination better known as the phrasal verb. When particles are added to simple verbs, they can express different aspectual distinctions such as perfective meaning (e.g. *up* as in *clean up* or *out* as in *fade out*) or continuative meaning (e.g. *on* as in *carry on* or *away* as in *chat away*). Even though they are extremely productive and show grammaticalizing properties, Brinton does not grant Modern English phrasal verbs the membership of the primary aspectual category, but relegates them to the secondary aspectual category, that of aktionsart or lexical aspect. In a similar fashion, when using the term *aspect* in the context of phrasal verbs in English, Bolinger (1971:98) notes that it "should probably be replaced by *Aktionsart*, to reserve *aspect* for deeper and more systematic phenomena such as the progressive and the perfect tenses". Filip (1999: 206-207) also argues that English prefixes and verb particles express lexical aspect rather than grammatical like Slavic prefixes.

Nevertheless, for want of a better word, as with other scholars before her, Brinton (1988: 4) chooses the denominal adjective *aspectual* as a cover term to encompass both aspect and aktionsart. Originally, the cover term 'aspectuality' is credited to Bondarko (1967: 18-31) and is often adopted in the literature (e.g. Verkuyl 1993: 11 and Boogaart 1999: 8). However, it needs to be pointed out that the term 'aspectual'[18] is ambiguous, as it can refer both to aspect in the narrow sense and to aspectuality.

There will be a further discussion of Brinton's view of aspect systems in English in section 3.3, but there is an objection that I would like to raise against Brinton's categorization of aspectual systems.

Brinton subsumes analytic verb constructions such as *begin* to do something, *stop* or *continue* doing something and *used to* do something under primary rather than secondary aspectual system, on the grounds that they have been

---

[17] There seems to be a terminological problem with the word 'semantic' as used by a number of authors. By saying that aspect is "semantic, i.e. lexical" suggests that aspect expressed by grammatical means is not semantic, which is of course a false assumption. 'Semantic' in this context refers to the inherent meaning of the verb.

[18] For this reason it was also used in the title of this book (and dissertation), as at the beginning of my research I was not certain what kind of aspect my data analysis would show.

grammaticalized, that is, verbs such as *begin, stop* or *continue* have a quasi-auxiliary status. If we apply the same logic (or principle) and use grammaticalization as a criterion with phrasal verbs as Brinton does for the above aspectualizing constructions, then it may occur as a paradox that particle verbs do not belong to the same group. Many scholars agree that the particle *up,* the most frequent and the most productive particle in English phrasal verbs, has grammaticalized and is referred to in the literature as the 'completive' *up*[19] or 'aspectual' *up*[20], then it falls within the domain of grammar, not lexicon. If this is the premise, then we can conclude that particle verbs do not express lexical aspect or aktionsart, but rather grammatical aspect or *aspect* proper.

Notwithstanding many objections to using the German term aktionsart, it has gained wide acceptance in Slavic, Germanic and Romance linguistic literature denoting lexical aspect. However, there is a slight difference between the use in the Slavic tradition and the other two, which is a result of formal typological differences. In Slavic languages aktionsart refers to lexical aspect expressed by morphological modifications of verbs, whereas in other languages it has been generalized and typically refers to aspect inherent in the meanings of verbs.

Agrell's division of aspect into the grammatical and lexical dimension had powerful reverberations in aspectual theories of the twentieth century. Sasse calls the approaches of theoreticians who adhere to this division *bidimensional* (2002: 202), even though there are significant differences in such approaches in terms of conceptual relatedness of these two dimensions. The approaches where this distinction is disregarded (the present study included) are called *unidimensional* and they proceed

> "from the assumption that there is only one set of aspect-relevant semantic primitives, a single conceptual dimension in terms of which aspectual phenomena on all representational levels can be analyzed and described. In their strongest form, they employ the same set of categories with the same labels on all levels or, in a different version, assume only one level (the sentence) where aspectual distinctions manifest themselves."
>
> (Sasse 2002: 202)

Apart from such categorization of aspect into two broad approaches, Sasse also proposes new terms for aspect in the narrow sense of the term and aktionsart (2002: 203). He refers to the former as ASPECT$_1$ and the latter as ASPECT$_2$, listing a wide array of terms that have been used to label these two basic categories. This list has been complemented with other terms found elsewhere in the literature and adapted into table 4:

---

[19] Lindner 1983: 150, Denison 1985: 37, Cappelle 2005: 413
[20] Jackendoff 2002: 76, Hampe 2002: 182

ASPECT₁	ASPECT₂
aspect	aktionsart
aspect proper	situational aspect
aspect in the narrow sense	procedurals (Forsyth 1970)
viewpoint (Smith 1983)	aspectual character (Lyons 1977)
perspective point aspect	actionality (Bertinetto 1997)
outer aspect	inner aspect
	vendlerian aspect
	event structure
	situation type (Smith 1991)
	eventuality type (Bach 1986, Filip 1999)

Table 4
Terms for aspect and aktionsart in the literature

2.6 Aspect in the 20th Century

With the arrival of structuralism, aspects were established as a system, much like tenses. The binary nature of Slavic verbs and the bipartition of aspect into grammatical and lexical (aktionsart) simply lend themselves to the theory of oppositions which is fundamental to structuralist thought. Roman Jakobson and the Prague School of linguists were particularly active in this field. The bulk of Slavic aspectology is based on the structuralist tradition of defining categories by means of oppositions.

German structuralists such as Porzig were also influenced by Jakobson. He also believed that aspect was a binary category and that it can only be expressed by verbal morphology:

> "Der Aspekt ist also seinem Wesen nach streng polar, d.h. wir nennen nur einen solchen Unterschied innerhalb der Verbalbedeutungen Aspekt, der die Vorgänge unter den Gesichtspunkt "Verlauf" und "Ereignis" bringt.
>
> Ob es in einer gegebenen Sprache den Aspekt gibt, ist nur zu erkennen durch die Morphologie; denn jede Bedeutungskategorie muss morphologisch fassbar sein."[21]
>
> Porzig 1927: 152

---

[21] 'Aspect is, therefore, by its very nature strictly polar, i.e. we only call aspect the kind of difference within verbal meanings that marshals occurrences into the dual perspective of "progress" and "event".
As every semantic category must be morphologically realized, the existence of aspect in a given language can only be identified through morphology,.' (the translation is mine)

Porzig was, unfortunately, not alone in this erroneous belief that aspect exists only if it is morphologically overt. This would suggest that only Slavic languages have aspect as a category. Such thinking has been expressed by other authors on many occasions, as will be mentioned again in the subsequent subchapters. Soon Germans came to understand that aspect in German *does* exist but that it is expressed by syntactic means. Renicke's (1961) paper entitled "Deutsche Aspektpaare" applies the Slavic concept of aspectual pairs to German, but rather than listing pairs of verbs, Renicke listed pairs of sentences. Gradually, the morphological pre-requisite was abandoned and research on aspect turned in a different direction.

The Anglo-American response to the Central and Eastern European aspect theory started in the mid-20th century with attempts to organize classes of situations according to their inherent temporal characteristics with respect to duration, boundedness and so on. This approach is also known as time-schema approach, the most influential of which is that of Vendler (1957), whose classification is still often taken as a point of departure in studies on aspect in English and many other languages. Vendler's time-schema theory is said to be an adaptation of Aristotle's who is "generally credited with the observation that the meanings of some verbs necessarily involve an 'end' or 'result' in a way that other verbs do not" (Dowty 1979: 52). Aristotle distinguished between actions that are goal-directed (*kinesis* 'movements') and actions which are not goal-directed (*energeiai* 'actualities').

Vendler's (1957) four classes are intended to "describe the most common time schemata implied by the use of English verbs" (Vendler 1957:144), as can be seen in the examples presented in table 5.

STATES	*know, desire, want, have, own, love, hate, dominate*, etc
ACTIVITIES	*run, walk, sleep, dream, swim, push a cart, think about*, etc
ACCOMPLISHMENTS	*run a mile, paint a picture, grow up, recover from illness*, etc
ACHIEVEMENTS	*recognize, reach the summit, lose, win the race, start/stop/resume*, etc.

Table 5
Vendler's verb classes

The differences between these four classes are based on their inherent temporal properties – continuity and homogeneity. Both activities and accomplishments involve "periods of time", but only accomplishments also require being "unique and definite" (Vendler 1957:149). Only achievements "occur at a single moment, while states last for a period of time" (Vendler 1957:147). The fact that only activities and accomplishments are "processes going on in time" makes them compatible with the progressive tenses, while states and achievements are not (Vendler 1957: 146).

Most of modern aspectology is an elaboration of Vendler's categories, which Sergej Tatevosov (2002: 320-1) organized into a table, giving an excellent overview and comparison of aspectual classifications.

Vendler 1957/67

states	activities	accomplishments	achievements

Comrie 1976

stative	dynamic		
	durative		punctual
	atelic	telic	

Mourelatos 1978/1981

states	occurrences		
	processes	events	
		developments	punctual occurrences

Moens 1987

states	processes	culminated processes	point	culminated point

Smith 1991, 1995, 1996

states	events			
	activities	accomplishments	semelfactives	achievements

Dik 1989, 1994

situation (position/state)	event (action/process)	
	activitity/dynamism	accomplishment/change

Bach 1986

states		non-states		
		processes	events	
			protracted	momentaneous
dynamic	static			happenings	culminations

Padučeva 1995, 1996

static		dynamic		
atemporal properties	inherent states	nonterminative	terminative	
		(activities/ atelic processes)	actions proper / telic processes	achievements/happenings

Chung & Timberlake 1985

states	inception of state	atelic process	telic process

Bache 1985b, 1995a, 1995b

-actional	+actional		
	simplex (vs. complex)		
	durative		punctual
	atelic	telic	

	directed	self-contained		

Durst-Andersen 1992, 1994, 2000

states	activity	action	
stative		dynamic	
simplex		complex	

Klein 1995

0-state	1-state	2-state

Verkuyl 1972, 1993, 1999

+ADD TO	-ADD TO

Filip 1999

same as Bach 1986 plus α quantized predicates

Johanson 1996

nontransformative		transformative	
		fini-transformative (vs. initio-transformative)	
-dynamic	+dynamic	-momentaneous	+momentaneous

Breu 1994

totally static	inceptively static	activity	gradually terminative	totally terminative

Table 6
Aspectual (actional) classifications
(from Tatevosov 2002: 320-1)

All these time-schemata refer to ASPECT$_2$ or aktionsart, as they classify verbs according to their intrinsic semantics, i.e. lexical meaning. Timberlake does not think that Vendler's verb categories do much for Slavic languages, even with adaptations, noting that "the insights are modest" (2004: 411). However, Dickey points to a number of studies in Slavic that use this approach (2000: 13).

This section is only a very brief outline of the development of linguistic thought on aspect. It is not necessary to go deeper[22]. The only important point presented here is the evolution of the understanding that aspect is not only a morphological category, which was more or less accepted by the end of the 20th century. Sasse's conclusion summarizes this as follows (2002: 263):

> "The international research on aspect over the past 50 years or so has shown that the goal of cross-linguistically adequate theory of aspect should be the investigation of aspectual phenomena on the sentence (or, rather, clause) level in connection with the investigation of the role of the lexicon,

---

[22] The best overview of recent research on aspect is Sasse (2002).

conventionalized grammar, and discourse in the constitution of these phenomena."

The nature of aspectual meaning is compositional. It is not expressed by the verb alone but in the predication – even in Slavic (where it is morphologically marked) in a significant number of cases. Aspectual meaning is the property of an entire verb phrase. Objects and complement of the verb can change the inherent meaning of the verb from one aspectual category to another.

2.7 In The Beginning Was Aspect

In Indo-European languages, the principal marker of temporality is tense. Comrie defines tense as 'grammaticalized expression of location in time' (1985: 9). Tenses are structurally salient and are highly grammaticalized, which is why it took a long time for European linguists to understand that there was another system of marking temporality, that of aspect. It also took them a long time to finally separate tense from aspect, as it was not so overtly expressed in the languages which were first being described. Only when Western grammarians looked at non-Indo-European languages did they become aware of the pervasiveness of aspect, rather than tense.

Both tense and aspect are grammatical categories as well as semantic categories. Thus both tense and aspect are a pairing of the morpho-syntactic form with meaning (cf. Declerck 2006: 94). However, their main conceptual difference is in the way they refer to temporality or in their representation of time.

The twentieth century saw some interesting theories as to the development of these two categories. They are still rather speculative, but as in any other field of science, there is no progress without speculation. The evolution of tense and aspect systems in these theories is called *chronogenesis,* whose idea was first proposed by Guillaume (1929, 1945) and later refined by Hewson and Bubenik (1997) within a cognitive framework. They look upon tense and aspect as mental systems based on bodily experience as propounded in *The Body in the Mind* by Mark Johnson (1987).

Their studies are based on the Indo-European language family and are an attempt to reconstruct verbal systems of more than ten representative languages during the course of four thousand years, tracing them back to Proto-Indo-European.

According to the idea of chronogenesis, the development of child language follows a similar pattern as the diachronic development of linguistic systems. The way we encode time in language does not – and cannot – correspond to actual or real time (as with other concepts) but reflects the way in which we perceive it. Our experience and representation of time is based on personal consciousness, which is influenced by our perception. Consciousness is fundamentally threefold and is represented as follows:

memory < ----- sensory experience -----> imagination

(Hewson and Bubenik 1997: 3)

These three elements of consciousness are the immediate past, the moment of immediate experience and the immediate future; in other words corresponding to the past, the present and the future. The past is memorized, the present is experienced and the future is imagined.

The first verbal elements that an English speaking child learns are the following:

1) the infinitive *(to) sing*, by which the event is represented as conceived in the imagination, a complete whole

2) the present participle *singing*, by which the event is represented as an activity that takes place in the immediate sensory experience

3) the past participle *sung,* by which the event is represented as recorded in the immediate memory, just completed[23]

(adapted from Hewson and Bubenik 1997: 5)

These three representations make the foundation of the development of tense and aspect systems. Here they were exemplified in English, but similar basic items can be found in other Indo-European languages.

Once we have established these three rudimentary elements of consciousness, we see that there are two ways of interpreting the passage of time, something that was also discussed by Fillmore (1975), Traugott (1978) and Lakoff & Johnson (1980): upward and downward progression of time. Hewson and Bubenik explain these two progressions of time as follows:

> "With the downward progression of time, in Descending Time, imagination becomes experience, and experience in turn becomes memory. With the upward progression of time, in Ascending Time the event that is already recorded in the memory as having begun eventually comes to completion at some point that is now in the future."
>
> (Hewson & Bubenik 1997: 4)

The double experience of time in English can be observed in the expressions such as

In the weeks ahead of us... (future)

That's all behind us now... (past)

As opposed to

In the following weeks... (future)

In the preceding weeks... (past)

---

[23] The expression *all gone* is reported to be one of the first expressions that an English child utters, which indicates the child's awareness that the event is complete and now stored in its memory (Hewson & Bubenik 1997: 5-6).

These examples, taken from Lakoff & Johnson (1980: 41), point to two different perceptions of the how time passes. In the first two examples, we are those who are moving whilst time is standing still. In the other two examples, it is time that is moving, while we are standing still (Lakoff & Johnson 1980: 44).

Chronogenesis is a stratified system consisting of three stages: the quasi-nominal mood, the representation of Universe time and the indicative. In the first stage, the 'quasi-nominal mood', the three elements of consciousness give rise to a system of three aspects: the Imperfective (which represents time as passing), the Perfective (which represents events as complete) and the Retrospective (which represents events as leaving a lasting result).

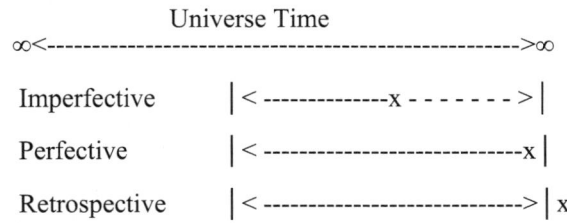

Figure 2
Aspectual distinctions in early Proto-Indo-European
(from Hewson & Bubenik 1997: 352)

Hewson and Bubenik propose that this "original three-aspect system" developed into two basic tense systems, which in turn evolved in their own directions in different languages, depending on the prevalence of the view of how time progresses. In other words, one group of languages such as Greek, Sanskrit, Armenian, Slavic, Albanian, and Tocharian view it as Descending Time, so in their verbal systems the imperfective evolves into the present and the imperfect tense, the perfective aspect is re-analysed as the aorist tense and the retrospective as perfect.

Languages such as Germanic and Hittite make another group which views the progress of time as Ascending Time. In these languages, the present tense develops from the imperfective aspect, while the past tense from the perfective aspect. These languages have only two basic tenses – the present and the past (a preterit, which is a merger of the original aorist and the perfect).

There is a third group of languages, Italic, Celtic and Baltic, whose tense systems combine both Descending Time and Ascending Time, and as a result have a mixed system with three tenses.

One fact that seems to give credence to this theory is the correspondence of ablaut in the system of strong verbs in Germanic languages to ablaut in the aspectual pairs of Slavic languages. According to the theory of *chronogenesis,* the original imperfective and perfective aspects of Proto-Indo-European developed into the Germanic present and the preterite tense respectively. The similarity of patterns found in ablaut alternations between the tense forms of Germanic and the aspect stems of Slavic is striking:

(42) Croatian *skakati* 'to jump' (imperfective) *skočiti* (perfective)

Croatian *voziti* 'to drive' (impf.) *odvesti* 'to drive away' (perf.)
(43) English *stand* (present) - *stood* (preterit)
English *blow* (present) - *blew* (preterit)

Germanic strong verbs are considered irregular today, as the pattern of forming the past tense with the dental suffix is more productive. In a similar way, some of the most frequent verbs in Slavic languages form their aspectual pairs according to such irregular patterns. These patterns are in fact considered to be irregular just from a synchronic point of view. From a diachronic point of view, they are not irregular. They are believed to have formed a rule, but are now regarded rather as an exception.

This is my observation, based on Hewson and Bubenik's proposal that the three aspect system of Proto-Indo-European became the Germanic two tense system. However, this is not the area of aspect that is the main topic of this discussion, so it is merely a suggestion for further research. In a similar vein, many of Hewson and Bubenik's proposals need further elaboration, as they are not completely foolproof. Thus, for example, Sasse (2002: 259-262) criticizes Hewson and Bubenik's book for not being philologically informed enough, for being generally sloppy in the treatment of data and for taking hardly any notice of other recent Indo-European aspect research.

Other authors also discuss the earliest developments of tense and aspect in Germanic, but do not go into such depth. For example, in his book which deals with the earliest reconstructable stages of the prehistory of English, Ringe (2006: 25) briefly mentions how aspect systems evolved in Indo-European languages. Some languages like Greek preserved the inherited system of aspect, Armenian, Albanian and Old Church Slavonic preserved the imperfective / perfective opposition, but Germanic restructured it into a tense-based system. This means that as imperfective and perfective verb stems were reanalysed into present and aorist stems, their functional opposition broke down (Ringe 2006: 157).

Harbert (2007: 272-273) explains that Proto-Indo-European had an articulated aspect/tense system "which simultaneously localized events in time and indicated something about the shapes of those events". Germanic reduced this aspect/tense system to a simple tense system with only one opposition: present / past. He also gives three examples from the Bible in Gothic and contrasts them to Greek, which has a distinct tripartite system. In these examples the Greek imperfect, aorist and pluperfect correspond to the Gothic simple past.

But since the earliest substantial documents, we have seen Germanic languages grammaticalizing all other tenses - periphrastic constructions with auxiliary verbs for perfect and pluperfect, future and their combinations. English also developed two aspectual systems – the progressive and the perfect.

2.8 Aspect in Slavic Style

The existence of the category of aspect has often been refuted for English (cf. Zandvoort 1962: 19-20) for the simple reason that it was not morphologically marked. The aspectual system in English, both synchronically and diachronically, is not as clearly articulated and evident as in Slavic languages, which are for some reason idealized as the only languages that have "true aspect". In traditional Slavic linguistics, the term 'aspect' is reserved only for the grammatical category of the opposition between perfective and imperfective aspect. Even outside Slavic linguistics, many linguists such as Zandvoort (1962: 20) think that aspect in Slavic languages should be taken "as an absolute standard":

> "The plain statement 'Aspect is a conception which does not exist in English grammar' may be hard to digest for some linguists who, like Mossé, refuse to take the character of aspect in Slavonic as an absolute standard. But what is the use, also from the standpoint of general linguistics, of a term which in the Germanic languages 'means something entirely different from what it means in the Slavonic languages'?"

It seems that Zandvoort has a pre-conceived idea about aspect in Slavic languages. What is worse, the expression "absolute standard" is unwarranted. There are no absolute standards in languages, particularly from a cross-linguistic perspective.

The purpose of this chapter is to dispel such notions as Zandvoort's and to show that Dahl (1985: 69) is much closer to the truth when he says:

> "if one looks at Slavic aspect from a typological perspective, it becomes clear that the Slavic systems are in fact rather idiosyncratic in many ways".

In order to better understand not just aspect in the diachrony of English but also aspect in general, it is worth taking a closer look at how this "true aspect" actually works – is it merely "idiosyncratic" or is it "absolute standard"? As a matter of fact, it was Dahl himself who suggested that this would be a worthwhile endeavour, as English post-verbal particles resemble Slavic verbal prefixes in many ways[24]:

> "From a cross-linguistic point of view, it would have been valuable to make a comparison with the Slavic languages, where the corresponding morphemes (verbal prefixes) are commonly taken to play a role in the aspect system."
>
> (Dahl 1990: 118)

Studies in verbal aspect are considered to be one of the most important contributions of Slavic linguistics to general linguistic theory (Comrie & Corbett 1993: 10). Slavic languages are also known for a plethora of other fascinating linguistic phenomena that have been researched, but still need further extensive exploration.

About two thirds of all speakers of Slavic are speakers of Russian, so it is little wonder that, in addition to other historical reasons, the majority of linguistic research on aspect focuses on Russian. As a consequence, Russian is

---

[24] Bybee et al. (1994: 87) also point to the similarity between the Slavic system of verbal prefixes and the English system of post-verbal particles: "In these [Slavic] languages adverbs, comparable to English *up, down, over* and *through,* for example, with originally locative meaning, pair with verbs to create a sense of completion, or, in Dahl's terms, "attainment of a limit"."

taken as the prototypical example of Slavic languages in the linguistic literature. However, linguists of other Slavic-speaking countries are catching up, so recently a number of important works have been published on aspect that have either described aspect in cross-linguistic terms contrasting English with another Slavic language, such as Kabakčiev (2000) for Bulgarian, or applied cutting-edge theoretical frameworks to describe aspect such as Dabrowska (1996), Tabakowska (2003) and Mlynarczyk (2004) for Polish and Filip (1999) for Czech, to name but a few.

Since Russian has commonly been presented as the paradigmatic example of the aspectual system in Slavic, it is largely assumed that there are no major differences between aspectual systems of different Slavic languages (Dickey 2000: 1). There is quite a lot of variation in morphology, syntax and semantics of aspect even between closely related Slavic languages. However, most of the description of the aspectual system in Croatian offered in this chapter is also applicable to other Slavic languages. Perhaps the reason for this is the special position of Croatian on the map of Slavic aspect. The following figure shows the division of Slavic into aspectual zones as established in Dickey (2000)'s study.

West	Transitional	East
	Polish	Russian
Sorbian		Belarusian
Czech		Ukranian
Slovak		
Slovene		Bulgarian
	Serbo-Croatian	Macedonian

Figure 3
The "geography" of Slavic aspect
(taken from Dickey 2000: 5)

This aspectual isogloss does not coincide entirely with the main three branches of the Slavic languages. The South Slavic languages have been divided between the eastern group and the western group. The macro-western group happens to correspond to what is known as *Slavia Romana*, which uses the Latin alphabet, whereas the macro-eastern group happens to correspond to *Slavia Orthodoxa*, which uses Cyrillic script, although the overlap of the aspectual isogloss with that of script and religion is merely coincidental.

Based on Dickey's aspectual isoglosses, which primarily concern use rather than morphology, Croatian and Polish belong to the Transitional group. This means that they share certain properties with both the macro-western group and the macro-eastern group. This justifies taking Croatian as the paradigm example of Slavic in the short description of Slavic aspect in this study. But before taking a look at aspect in Croatian, it is worthwhile to discuss aspect in the earliest attested Slavic language.

2.8.1 Old Church Slavonic

The oldest extant Slavic language, codified in the late ninth century translations of the gospels by the Saints Cyril and Methodius, the 'Apostles of the Slavs', is known as Old Church Slavonic. It was largely based on the South Slavic of the Bulgarian-Macedonian area, but it is also thought to be a near equivalent of Late Common Slavic, which was intelligible throughout the Slavic world at the time.

The first attested languages of both Slavic and Germanic were translations of the Bible from Greek, so both are thought to be heavily influenced by Greek syntax. However, this factor is usually taken into consideration in diachronic studies, depending on the linguistic phenomenon under investigation. Aspect in Old Church Slavonic is not thought to have been affected by Greek (as opposed to Gothic, for which some scholars thought that it was influenced by Greek).

It is commonly assumed that the aspectual system in Old Church Slavonic is in principle the same as the one we have in Modern Slavic languages (cf. Senn 1949: 402, Scherer 1954: 212), although Comrie (1976: 89, 126) and Matasović (2008: 276) say that the systematic perfective / imperfective opposition was not completely established. The following short discussion serves to illustrate that the aspectual system in Slavic was already well developed twelve centuries ago and that all subsequent changes were only minor adaptations in individual languages.

In Old Church Slavonic, verbs were already marked for perfectivity and imperfectivity. Perfectivity was marked by prefixation, but also by suffixation, albeit to a much lesser extent (the non-terminal suffix –nǫ-, as in *krik-nǫ-ti* 'shout' cf. Croatian -*nu*- as in *kriknuti*). There were 20 verbal prefixes in Old Church Slavonic (Lunt 2001: 82), which can assume many different roles including aspectual. They are presented in the table 7.

do- 'to',	*prě-* 'before',
iz- 'from, out of',	*prědъ-* 'in front of, before',
mimo- 'by, past',	*pri-* 'at the time',
na- 'on',	*pro-* 'through',
nadъ- 'upon, over',	*raz-* 'apart',
nizъ- 'down',	*sъ-* 'with, away, for the extent of'
o(b)- 'round, about',	*u-* 'at, in'.
ot(ъ)- 'from, away',	*vъ-* 'in',
po- 'under, below',	*vъz-* 'up, for',
podъ- 'under, beneath',	*za-* 'for',

Table 7
Aspectual prefixes in Old Church Slavonic

These prefixes are thought to have developed from spatial prepositions and continued to co-exist with their correlate prepositions, except for *pro-* and *raz-*.

Imperfectivity can only be marked by suffixation. For example, the perfective verb *pasti* (<pad-ti) 'to fall' is imperfectivized by adding the suffix -*a*-, as in *pad-a-ti* 'keep on falling'. The attachment of this suffix is sometimes accompanied by the lengthening of the root vowel, as in *let-ěti* 'fly' vs. *lět-a-ti*

'keep on flying'. The third imperfectivization process involves adding the suffix -*i*- along with ablaut in the root syllable, as in *nes-ti* 'carry' vs. *nos-iti* 'carry around' or the suffix -*a*- along with ablaut in the root syllable, as in *roditi* 'give birth' vs. *raždati*.

Based on the proposal of Hewson and Bubenik (1997: 86) and their idea of *chronogenesis,* Old Church Slavonic had three aspects, as shown in table 8.

	Imperfective Aspect	Perfective Aspect	Retrospective Aspect
Non-Past	*nes-ǫ* (Pres) 'I carry'		*nes-lъ jesm-ь* (Perf) 'I have carried'
Past	*nes-ěaxъ* (Impf) 'I was carrying'	*nes-oxъ* (Aor) 'I carried'	*nes-lъ běaxъ* (Plqpf) 'I had carried'

Table 8
The tense/aspect system of Old Church Slavonic:
***nes-ti* 'carry' (imperfective verb)**
(adapted from Hewson and Bubenik 1997: 86)

According to the idea of *chronogenesis,* the imperfective aspect represented passage of time without a boundary and was reanalysed as the Present and the Imperfect Tense. The perfective aspect represented events as complete and developed into the aorist tense. The retrospective aspect was expressed analytically with the present or imperfect form of the auxiliary verb 'to be' in combination with the resultative participle and developed into the Perfect and the Pluperfect Tense. Hewson and Bubenik (1997: 13fn) devised the term 'retrospective' as a replacement for the traditional term 'perfect', which often causes considerable confusion with 'perfective' in aspectology.

The following example shows the perfective verb *posъlati* 'send (away)' (cf. Croatian *poslati*) whose imperfective pair is *sъlati* (cf. Croatian *slati*). This verb's prefix *po-* is purely aspectual and does not alter the meaning of this verb stem in any other manner but aspectual. The prefix *po-* is still one of the most productive verbal prefixes in all Slavic languages with one of its main functions as a marker of perfectivity (cf. Dickey 2007: 329ff). With other verb stems, this prefix can also change the lexical meaning of the newly derived verb along with making them perfective, as is the case with all modern Slavic languages.

(44) *I tъgda bo Gospodь mę   bě   posъlalъ*
and then for Lord.NOM I.ACC be.3.P.SG.AOR *po*.PREFIX+send.P.PTCP.ACT.II
kъ   tebě.
to you.DAT
'So then Lord had sent me to you.'

Codex Suprasliensis, Gregory 5.2

The next sentence features four imperfective verbs in the imperative form. The first verb *počivati,* which contains the suffix –*va*- which is an imperfectivizer.

(45) *Počivai,   jaždъ,   pii,   veseli   sę.*
    rest.2.P.SG.IMP. eat.2.P.SG.IMP drink.2.P.SG.IMP be merry 2.P.SG.IMP REFL.PRON.ACC
'Rest, eat, drink and be merry.'
                                               Zographensis, Marianus; Luke 12.19

The perfective of *počivati* is *počiti* (present *počьj-e-*) and corresponds to present-day Croatian *počinuti,* which contains the perfectivizing suffix *-nu-* that signifies semelfactive actions. Here the function of the prefix *po-* is not aspectual (grammatical) – it does not signal perfectivity, but is entirely lexicalized. This verb stem has not been attested without a prefix *(*čiti, *čivati),* although there is the adjective in Croatian *čio (m.), čila (f.)* 'the one who got rest' which seems to be derived from the past participle of that verb.

The other three verbs, *jesti, piti* and *veseliti se* do not have an imperfectivity marker, but are inherently imperfective, conforming to one of the basic rules of Slavic aspect according to which most simple unprefixed verbs are imperfective. The respective perfective partners of those three verbs are *poěsti, popiti* and *vъzveseliti sę.*

In Old Church Slavonic, as in Modern Bulgarian, perfective verbs are used both in the Imperfect Tense (past non-completed tense) and in the Aorist Tense (past completed tense) – just as imperfective verbs are used both in the Imperfect Tense and in the Aorist Tense. The situation is quite different in Croatian where only imperfective verbs can be used in the Imperfect Tense and only perfective verbs in the Aorist Tense, two past tenses which are now considered archaic and obsolete. It is interesting that the situation in both languages is quite symmetrical.

Furthermore, the fact that imperfective verbs are used in the Aorist Tense and perfective verbs in the Imperfect Tense might appear as an oxymoron or a semantic paradox. Nevertheless, all sorts of combinations have been noted in Old Church Slavonic texts. Migdalski (2006: 21) reports on a study by Dostál (1954) with statistics related to the interaction of aspect and tense in a corpus of Old Church Slavonic, whose calculation results are presented in table 9:

Aspect / Tense	Imperfective Aspect	Perfective Aspect
The Imperfect Tense	99%	1%
The Aorist Tense	40%	60%

Table 9
Interaction of aspect and tense in OCS
(Adapted from Migdalski (2006: 21) from Dostál (1954: 599-600)

Such examples of seemingly contradictory categories in the corpus show the complexity of the Old Church Slavonic aspect and tense system. Migdalski (2006: 21) concludes that "because of this complexity, the language could express very intricate temporal relations".

The following example (adapted from Huntley 1993: 151) illustrates the complexity of aspectual use when it comes into play with tenses such as combining the perfective aspect with the Aorist and the Imperfect Tense:

(46) i   ěviše   sę   prědъ nimi ěko bledi
    and appear.3.P.PL.PERF.AOR REFL.PRON before they.INS as pale.NOM.PL
    glagoli   ixъ   i   ne   iměaxǫ   imъ   věry
    words.NOM they.GEN and not have.3.P.PL.PERF.IMPF they.DAT faith.GEN
    'And their words appeared to them to be nonsense and they would not believe them.'

Zographensis, Marianus; Luke 24.11

The perfective aorist is used to express the immediacy of the action, whereas the perfective imperfect is used in order to present the event as an ongoing process. According to Huntley, the form *iměaxǫ* is a perfective imperfect. However, it is more likely to be an imperfective imperfect of the verb *iměti* 'to have, take', and thus interpreted as a multiple event. Then the event interprets as if they did not believe those words on many occasions. Moreover, according to the statistics in the charts above, the likelihood that this form would be a perfective imperfect is only 1% as opposed to 99% of chances being an imperfective imperfect.

This case proves how difficult it is to determine the aspect of individual verbs in a dead language, as there are few formal criteria that can be relied on, and there are no native speakers who can confirm our educated guesses. To make matters worse, variation is often found in the original texts, which is typically ascribed to scribes coming from different regions and subsequent periods. Lunt (2001: 87) also points to frequent disagreements among modern scholars including native speakers of Slavic languages on determining the aspectual forms of certain Old Church Slavonic verbs.

2.8.2 "Irregularities" of Slavic aspect

The systems of aspect and tense in Slavic languages are intertwined, although Senn claims native speakers to be "more tense-conscious than aspect-conscious" (1949: 404)

As noted earlier, Slavic is said to have a duplicate set of forms for all verbs. This duality of expression or bipartition of perfective and imperfective aspect is usually given as an illustration of the formal set-up of aspect in all Slavic languages. It is undeniably the most important feature of Slavic verbal aspect. However, it is far from regular, as we shall see in the description of exceptions.

Many grammars try to explain the morphology of aspect by stating the general rule according to which the presence of a prefix automatically makes a verb perfective (Silić 1978: 49). This is in keeping with another rule according to which all simplex verbs are imperfective by default. These two rules probably work in a large number of cases, but it is doubtful whether they help learners as there are far too many exceptions. The thumbnail sketch of aspect in Croatian in the introductory chapter presents the system of morphological mechanisms how verbal pairs can be formed. It is only an idealized model for those with no knowledge of any Slavic language. Those who speak a Slavic language are immediately aware of that. If it was not presented as a set of some basic rules, it would not be experienced as a system. The existence of such a system is something that both linguists and speakers of Slavic languages believe in deeply.

The following examples are just a few that show that the basic rule of perfectivization is not always applicable, i.e. that the presence of a prefix is not always indicative of the verb's aspect. Just because there is a prefix, it does not mean that the verb is perfective, as the following imperfective verbs show:

(47) *prenositi* 'to carry across'
razmatrati 'to consider, look over'
odvajati 'to separate'
poduzimati 'to undertake'
napuhavati 'to blow up'
izvoditi 'to perform'

There are numerous such verbs which remain imperfective even though they are prefixed with prefixes which have the perfectivizing force with other verbs. The following list of verbs show the very same prefixes in combinations with other verb stems that do conform to the "basic rule of perfectivization".

(48) *pregledati* 'to check'
razbiti 'to break'
odseliti 'to move (away)'
podgrijati 'to warm up'
narasti 'to grow up'
izgubiti 'to lose'

Sometimes a verb stem is differently affected by prefixes. The following examples show one and the same verb stem that in one case remains imperfective even though a prefix is attached to it, while in another case it is perfectivized (Silić 1978: 49):

(49) *prethoditi* 'to precede' (impf.) but *pohoditi* 'to pay a visit' (perf.)

(50) *sadržati* 'to contain' (impf.) but *podržati* 'to support' (perf.)

(51) *izgledati* 'to appear' (impf.) but *pogledati* 'to have a look' (perf.)

The reason why the above examples on the left are not affected in terms of aspect, while those on the right are affected, may be historical and have its origins in a lexicalization process. However, from a synchronic point of view, we can only observe them as irregular in terms of 'the basic rule of perfectivization'. They have a prefix and yet they are not perfective.

In other words, the presence or absence of a prefix does not determine which aspect a verb belongs to. It is not the semantics of prefix that determines whether the verb as a whole will be perfective or imperfective, but an interplay of factors in the relationship between the verb stem and the prefix.

Grammar books rarely point out that if a verb contains both a prefix (which can but need not perfectivize) and a non-terminal imperfectivizing suffix (such as *-a-, -va-, -iva-* or *-ava-*), the imperfectivizing suffix cancels out the perfectivizing effect of the prefix. This suffix is sometimes difficult to detect, but in fact it is present in the above examples like *napuh-ava-ti*. It is also present in the examples *odvaj-a-ti* and *razmatr-a-ti* in addition to ablaut (their perfective pairs are *odvojiti* and *razmotriti*).

In other words, even though aspect is said to be morphologically marked, this system of marking is not wholly transparent because there is no single unique morphological marker for perfective or imperfective verbs (cf. Timberlake 2004: 399). It may be really difficult to tell them apart on the basis of their morphology.

This is a very important point for the analysis of Old English prefixes, as very often the meaning of the verb seems to remain imperfective even though it is prefixed and the other way round. Many times an Old English prefix does not alter the aspectual meaning of the verb, which is why some linguists were quick to say that (Old) English does not have an aspectual system.

Furthermore, when one starts thinking in terms of grammaticalization and lexicalization theories, one is likely to regard the examples *prethoditi, sadržati* and *izgledati* as instances of lexicalization where the meaning of prefix is less transparent, or its semantic motivation seems to have weakened, as opposed to *po-* which has partly grammaticalized as a *préverbe vide* or semantically empty prefix. However, this would not be the case with *pohoditi* and *podržati,* as its spatial sense is still preserved in some way, and to a lesser extent in *pogledati* too.

Slavic languages have a whole array of verbal prefixes which have a perfectivizing force. In Croatian there are 18:

do- 'to, up to'	*pre-* 'over, across'
iz- 'from, out of'	*pred-* 'in front of, before'
mimo- 'by, past'	*pri-* 'near, by'
na- 'on, above'	*pro-* 'through'
nad- 'upon, over'	*raz-* 'apart'
o(b)- 'round, about'	*s(a)-* 'with, away, down from'
od- 'from, away'	*u-* 'into, at, in'
po- 'along, over, by'	*uz-* 'up, along'
pod- 'under, beneath'	*za-* 'for, behind'

Table 10
Aspectual prefixes in Croatian

It goes without saying that the English translations are only rough approximations based on the Croatian prepositional meanings.

There is no semantic regularity according to which one can know how the meaning of a prefix changes the meaning of the verb. For every verb there is usually only one of these prefixes which acts as a pure perfectivizer without adding any additional meaning to it, but the choice which of these prefixes performs that role for which verb is rather idiosyncratic. However, in a post-hoc analysis, it is possible to find the motivating link why a certain prefix expresses grammatical meaning (i.e. aspect) and thus is treated as inflection, while in combination with other verbs it expresses lexical meaning and is thus treated as derivation.

Verbs derived with prefixes that also added lexical meaning are traditionally called aktionsarten ('modes of action') in Croatian. Forsyth calls them *procedurals* for Russian 1970: 20), the term that has already been discussed in section 2.5. As a result of so many by-product effects of prefixation, some Slavic linguists think that the only "true" aspectual pairs may be formed by suffixation, which is why they distinguish aspect from aktionsart. According to Mlynarczyk (2004: 48), aktionsart seems to function "as a dustbin for all those prefixes which did not really derive a new verb, but which also involved a slight modification of the way an event was presented." To explain this phenomenon, Gojmerac (1980: 49) uses the Neogrammarian term *Systemzwang* ('system pressure' or 'system coercion'): there is *Systemzwang* on every simplex verb (most of which are imperfective) to find a perfective pair. If this is not possible to achieve with a suffix, the verb resorts to borrowing from an adjacent subsystem – the system of prefixed verbs, which are besides aspect also marked for their aktionsart.

In order to give an illustration of grammatical vs. lexical prefixation, the imperfective verbs *pisati* 'write' and *čitati* 'read' can serve as examples of which prefix makes them "truly aspectual" rather than "merely aktionsartal". To keep things simple, only two prefixes have been chosen (*na-* and *pro-*) which give four possible combinations with these two verbs. Depending on the verb stem that it is attached to, one and the same prefix can be grammaticalized or lexicalized. The imperfective verb *pisati* can be prefixed with any of the 18 listed prefixes (except for *mimo-, pred-, s-* and *uz-*), resulting in new meanings together with perfectivization.

pisati - napisati. The meaning of *na-* is grammatical - purely aspectual – perfectivizing.
- ***propisati.*** The meaning of *pro-* is lexical, giving a completely new meaning to the verb stem of the newly derived verb – 'to prescribe' (which itself as a loan from Latin can be morphologically analysed into equivalent elements). The prefix's secondary effect is also that of perfectivization.

čitati pročitati. The meaning of *pro-* is grammatical - purely aspectual – perfectivizing.
- ***načitati se.*** The meaning of *na-* is both lexical and grammatical. We say that it is lexical because it changes the meaning of the verb stem. The newly derived verb is reflexive and it means 'to read enough', but there is an adjective derived from the past participle *načitan* meaning 'well-read'. We may also argue that it is grammatical not only because of its perfectivizing property, but also because of its constructional property. The prefix *na-* is very productive in combining with other verb stems, changing their meaning in such a way that the action denoted by the basic verb comes to mean that it is performed to a great degree, very often becoming reflexive.

In other words, *na-* is used as a means of forming an aspectual pair for *pisati* and in this case it is treated as an 'empty morpheme' or 'hijacked morpheme' (Mlynarczyk 2004: 17), semantically bleached of its original spatial meaning and in this case employed for aspectual purposes. In the same manner, *pro-* is used as a means of forming an aspectual pair for *čitati*. However, I would like to argue that the meaning is not entirely bleached, as the literal spatial relationship can still be remotely felt in both *napisati* and *pročitati*. The prefix *na-* means 'on', suggesting a kind of surface on which the action of writing takes place. What we have here is a metonymy in which this surface stands for the result of the action of writing – because the final product of writing will always be on some kind of surface.

Compared with English, this would be the particle *down* in the phrasal verb *write down*, where *down* also suggests the surface where we write. The construal is somewhat different, probably arising from where the surface of writing is in relation to the eyes.

Such semantic motivation can also be interpreted for *pročitati*. The prefix *pro-* means 'through' and its correlate preposition is *kroz,* which are not cognates. The metaphor involved is probably the same as when one says in English that you go through some material. In order to explain its meaning, we could say that the notion of path is evoked along which the eyes run. In the case of reading, this path stands for the lines or the pages of a text that eyes run through until they reach the end. When the eyes come to the end of their path, the action of reading the book is finished. Such explanations could be worked out for any prefix that we consider 'purely aspectual' in order to account for the motivation of the choice of prefix. There will always be some meaning in the prefix that will suggest how the action is performed to completion, so the meaning is not entirely bleached (cf. Forsyth 1970:38-39). The question "whether such prefixes are ever truly lexically neutral is one of the controversies in current Slavonic aspectology." (Comrie & Corbett 1993: 12)

Another important word-formational process is secondary imperfectivization. This is an inflectional process since it does not have any effect on the lexical meaning of prefixed verbs. All verbs that have been derived with prefixes that besides perfectivizing also changed the lexical meaning of the simplex verb can be imperfectivized again by suffixation. Mlynarczyk (2004: 51) notes that this is a good test for checking whether a certain prefix is a true aspectual pair or if it also affected the lexical meaning of the verb. So, for example

(52) *pisati* → *napisati* → **napisivati* but
→*zapisati* 'to write down'→ *zapisivati* 'to be writing down'
→*opisati* 'to describe' → *opisivati* 'to be/keep describing'
→*prepisati* 'to copy' → *prepisivati* 'to keep/be copying'
→*upisati* 'to enroll' → *upisivati* 'to be enrolling'

The above examples *napuhavati* and *razmatrati* also belong to secondary imperfectivization, which cancels out the perfectivizing effect prefix.

Prefixes can also be stacked (as in Old English), giving rise to morphologically complex examples like the following:

(53) *pisati* → *prepisati* → *prepisivati* → *isprepisivati* 'to keep copying thoroughly'

(54) *baciti* 'to throw' → *izbaciti* 'to throw out' → *izbacivati* 'to keep throwing out' → *poizbacivati* 'to keep throwing out one after another'

If all the morphological complexities of aspect do not leave an impression of a system susceptible to major irregularities, then the following list of exceptions definitely will.

1) Pairless verbs. There are many verbs which do not enter into aspectual pairs. These are divided into two types:
   a) *imperfectiva tantum* – those which are exclusively imperfective
   b) *perfectiva tantum* – those which are exclusively perfective

Those of the first type, *imperfectiva tantum,* are more frequent, as there are many verbs that have inherent durative meaning, so they have no corresponding perfectives. Some examples include:

(55) *ovisiti* 'to depend', *nadati se* 'to hope', *sastojati se* 'to consist of', *znati* 'to know', *moći* 'can', *smjeti* 'to be allowed to', *imati* 'to have', *izgledati* 'to appear', *hodati* 'to walk', '*voljeti* 'to love', *mrziti* 'to hate', *bojati se* 'to be afraid', *razlikovati se* 'to differ', verbs of movement such as *ići* 'go', *plivati* 'swim'

Those of the second type, *perfectiva tantum*, include examples such as:

(56) *ruknuti* 'to crash, to blow', *smesti* 'to confuse', *razmaziti* 'to spoil', *živnuti* 'to perk up', *obudovjeti* 'to become a widow(er)', *prolupati* 'to lose one's marbles', *svisnuti* 'to break down', *kosnuti* 'to affect'

2) Biaspectual verbs. Hundreds of verbs in Slavic languages are biaspectual, meaning they are both perfective and imperfective. They are never actually both at the same time but rather aspectually neutral, as their contextual environment and syntactic structure will always show that they are either perfective or imperfective. This is a very popular topic in Slavic aspectology (e.g. Janda 2007: 83ff). It must be noted that in this regard, the differences across the individual Slavic languages are substantial.

Many biaspectual verbs are loanwords (with the suffix *-irati, -izirati*), borrowed from languages without aspectual opposition, such as the following:

(57) *telefonirati* 'to telephone', *komunicirati* 'to communicate', *organizirati* 'to organize', *financirati* 'to finance', *izolirati* 'to isolate', *montirati* 'to mount, assemble'

Many verbs of eating are also biaspectual, such as

(58) *večerati* 'to have dinner', *ručati* 'to have lunch', *doručkovati* 'to have breakfast'

There are also quite a few frequently occurring native verbs such as

(59) *vidjeti* 'to see', *čuti* 'to hear', *savjetovati* 'to advise', *uzrokovati* 'to cause', *žrtvovati* 'to sacrifice', *krstiti* 'to baptize', *imenovati* 'to appoint'

The aspect of such verbs is never morphologically distinct but can only be determined in context, as the following two examples show:

(60) *Kad večeramo, uvijek imamo i desert.* (imperfective)
    'When we are having dinner, we always have desert'.

(61) *Kad večeramo, gledat ćemo film.* (perfective)
    'When we have had dinner, we will watch a movie'.

Sometimes speakers add perfective morphemes and thus create perfective pairs to make them more transparent in communication (Silić-Pranjković 2007: 49), but these forms are considered colloquial:

(62) *večerati* → *povečerati* 'to have dinner'
ručati → *poručati* 'to have lunch'

There is one subgroup of biaspectual verbs which have one meaning in perfective and another meaning in imperfective (Babić et al. 1991: 670)

(63) *roditi* (perfective) 'to give birth to (a child)'
roditi (imperfective) 'to bear fruit'

(64) *tužiti* (perfective) 'to sue'
tužiti (imperfective) 'to express sorrow'

From a morphological point of view, biaspectual verbs can be regarded as an example of zero-derivation (Gojmerac 1980: 50).

There are some verbs in which the accent is the only distinctive feature of aspect (Grubišić 1995: 127). Even though grammar books do not traditionally consider them biaspectual, they could be classified as another subgroup of biaspectual verbs for two reasons. Firstly, marking accents is not mandatory in Croatian and is very rarely done in practice. Secondly, a substantial number of speakers of Croatian (Kajkavian dialects including Zagreb) follow the Germanic principle of pronouncing verbs, so they never stress the prefix but the root. In other words, Croatian speakers from Zagreb would pronounce the following pairs as homophones.

(65) *ràzgledati* 'to finish watching' (perfective)
- *razglédati* 'to observe' (imperfective)

(66) *ràskidati* 'to cut off' (perfective)
- *raskídati* 'to be cutting off' (imperfective)

3) Irregular perfective. The perfectives of a few verbs are formed from a different root (suppletive), not with a prefix, such as

(67) *reći* 'to tell'   *govoriti* 'to say'
naći 'to find'   *nalaziti* 'to be/keep finding'
doći 'to come'   *dolaziti* 'to be/keep coming'
otići 'to go away'   *odlaziti* 'to be/keep going away'

According to some grammars, such as Grubišić (1995: 129), this list can be complemented with the pairs such as the following

(68) *čuti* 'to hear'   *slušati* 'to listen'
vidjeti 'to see'   *gledati* 'to watch'

However, it is arguable whether it is really only aspect in which these 'pairs' differ.

4) Primary perfectives. There are many verbs which are perfective by nature without having a prefix.

(69) *baciti* 'to throw', *dati* 'to give', *platiti* 'to pay', *kupiti* 'to buy' *reći* 'to say', *riješiti* 'to solve', *staviti* 'to put', *roditi* 'to give birth, *pasti* 'to fall', *stati* 'to stop', *stići* 'to arrive', *pustiti* 'to let', *javiti* 'to inform', *vratiti* 'to return', *leći* 'to lie down', *spasiti* 'to save'

5) Irregular patterns. Many verbs have unpredictable patterns in the formation of secondary iteratives, as the following list illustrates.

(70) *predložiti* 'to suggest' (perfective) vs. *predlagati* (imperfective)
skočiti 'to jump' (perfective) vs. *skakati* (imperfective)
oprostiti 'to forgive' (perfective) vs. *opraštati* (imperfective)
okupiti 'to gather' (perfective) vs. *okupljati* (imperfective)
vratiti 'to return' (perfective) vs. *vraćati* (imperfective)
steći 'to acquire' (perfective) vs. *stjecati* (imperfective)
poslati 'to send' (perfective) vs. *pošiljati* (imperfective)
izabrati 'to select' (perfective) vs. *izabirati* (imperfective)
posuti 'to sprinkle' (perfective) vs. *posipati* (imperfective)
pomoći 'to help' (perfective) vs. *pomagati* (imperfective)

It is difficult to find the right aspectual pair for every verb, so even native speaker linguists offer dubious combinations as aspectual pairs. For example, Silić (1978: 56) suggests that *ubiti* 'kill' is the aspectual pair of *biti* 'beat', as the prefix *u-* 'in' (cf. the English phrasal verb *do in*) has a purely aspectual (i.e. grammatical) meaning. I would argue that *u-* is completely lexicalized and speakers would not use it productively. They have no idea how the prefix *u-* contributes to the whole. Many speakers in fact are not even aware that this is a prefixed verb and typically analyse it as a single morpheme. Another example is Geld & Zovko Dinković (2007: 118) and the aspectual pair *bacati* / *nabacati* 'throw', which actually does not follow the same pattern as *pisati* / *napisati* but the perfective pair of *bacati* is *baciti,* whereas *nabacati* is a newly derived verb with a change of lexical meaning (*na-* suggests throwing onto a pile in this case) and its perfective pair is *nabaciti.*

In terms of use and syntax, aspect in Slavic shows proportional oddness. Imperfectives are not always used to signal imperfective meaning and the same is with perfectives. For example, when you want to ask someone if they have seen a certain movie or read a certain book, implying that the action is finished, as it is expected that they have seen it in its entirety or read the book from the beginning to the end, you use imperfective.

(71) *Jesi čitao "Zločin i kaznu"?*
'Have you read Crime and Punishment?'

(72) *Jučer sam gledao Avatara.*
'I saw *Avatar* yesterday.'

The verbs *gledati* 'to watch, see' and *čitati* 'to read' are used in their imperfective form and there is no suggestion that the action has not completed. The imperfective aspect in combination with the Perfect Tense is used to talk about one's experience in general, whereas the perfective aspect in the same sentences would imply asking if the action was performed on a specific occasion or if it was performed in its entirety:

(73) *Jesi pogledao Avatara?*
'Did you see *Avatar*?'

(74) *Jesi pročitao "Zločin i kaznu"?*
'Did you read *Crime and Punishment*?'

According to Comrie (1976: 112-113) and Gojmerac (1980: 67), imperfective verbs can be used to denote perfective actions, but not the other way round. In order to explain this, they apply Jakobson's concept of markedness[25]. Jakobson (1957:[1971: 137]) describes the perfective aspect as semantically marked ("concerned with the absolute completion"), while the imperfective aspect is semantically unmarked ("noncommittal with respect to completion or noncompletion"). In other words, imperfective verbs, being semantically unmarked, can be employed in certain situations to express perfective actions, which Gojmerac illustrates with the following example (1980: 41):

(75) *Tko je slikao ovu sliku?* (imperfective form for perfective meaning)
'Who painted this picture?'

A similar situation exists in Spanish and Italian which grammaticalize the progressive aspect like English. But unlike English, the progressive aspect in Spanish and Italian is semantically marked. This means that the non-progressive forms are the unmarked members of the aspectual opposition and can be used to cover both the progressive and the non-progressive meaning, making the use of the progressive form optional, as in the following example from Spanish (cf. Comrie 1986: 112):

(76) *Estoy escribiendo mi tesis.* (semantically marked)
'I am writing my thesis'

(77) *Escribo mi tesis.* (semantically unmarked)
'I write my thesis' but also 'I am writing my thesis'.

In Present-Day English, the progressive form in the present tense is not optional because the non-progressive form cannot denote the progressive meaning, according to Comrie (1986:112). However, this has not always been the case in the history of English. A famous example from Shakespeare's *Hamlet* demonstrates that in Early Modern English the present simple form is semantically unmarked and can take a progressive reading (just as in Modern Spanish or Italian):

(78) POLONIUS: *What do you read, my lord?*
HAMLET: *Words, words, words.*

Hamlet, II.2.191-192

---

[25] Markedness theory refers to a relation of asymmetry between elements of linguistic or conceptual structure. Originally, the structuralist Trubetzkoy applied it to phonology, but soon it was extended to morphological, syntactic, semantic and lexical oppositions. An unmarked form is the default form. In lexical opposites, for example, the unmarked tiger can refer to a male or female, while tigress is marked since it can refer only to females.

Furthermore, a progressive form in English can exhibit non-progressive meaning, as the following example shows (cf. Declerck 2007: 53):

(79) *You are red in the face. Have you been running?*

One of the meanings of the present perfect progressive is to explain the result of an action that was recently performed and has its consequences in the present. A question like that would be typically asked when one can see the consequences of the action, such as redness in the face, sweating or breathing rapidly. It is evident that the person who is red in the face is not running at the moment of speaking. Therefore, the progressive form does not denote an action taking place at the moment of speaking. The action of running was completed before what we have in (79) was uttered. In other words, the *perfect* aspect in combination with the progressive does not always result in a meaning that is progressive.

The concept of semantic markedness is a very important observation that can shed light on all the cases in Old English where simplex rather than prefixed verbs are used in perfective meaning. Declerck also noted that a "nonprogressive verb form can sometimes be used in a sentence receiving a progressive interpretation" while "a sentence receiving a nonprogressive interpretation may sometimes make use of a progressive verb form" (2007: 53)

In Croatian, the use of aspect in the Present Tense is also quite problematic. The imperfective has two basic meanings in the Present Tense, as can be seen in the following two examples:

(80) *On čita novine svaki dan.*
'He reads newspapers every day.'

(81) *On sada čita novine.*
'He is now reading newspapers.'

The imperfective in the Present Tense is used to denote habitual situations (80), but also to denote the actions in progress (81). In other words, Slavic is "aspectually indifferent" when it comes to the progressive / non-progressive opposition in the Present Tense. The only way to signify a difference between the habitual and the progressive meaning is by using an appropriate time adverbial. On the other hand, English has grammaticalized this aspectual opposition so it uses the simple form for the former and the progressive form for the latter.

In Croatian, the usage of perfective in the Present Tense is restricted. It is used for hypothetical situations, in clauses and sometimes (especially in dialects) to refer to the future. In Russian, its main use is to express futurity (Russian *napišu* means 'I will write'). In Croatian it sometimes has functions similar to subjunctive in other languages. Spanish is given here by way of illustration.

(82) Croatian: **Sutra   napišem pismo.*
    Russian: *Zavtra   'napishu pis'mo.*
    tomorrow write.PF the letter
    'Tomorrow I will write the letter.'

(83) *Možda sutra **napišem** pismo.*
'Perhaps tomorrow I (will) write the letter.' (perfective)

(84) *Rekao mi je da sutra **napišem** pismo.*
'He told me to write the letter tomorrow.' (perfective in the subordinate clause)

(85) Spanish: *Cuando escribo una carta, me gusta usar tinta violeta.*
(*escribo* – indicative present)
Croatian: *Kad pišem pismo, volim korisititi ljubičastu tintu.*
(*pišem* – imperfective present)
'When I write a letter, I like using purple ink.'

(86) Spanish: *Cuando escriba la carta, la llevaré a la oficina postal.*
(*escriba* – subjunctive present)
Croatian: *Kad napišem pismo, odnijet ću ga na poštu.*
(*napišem* – perfective present)
'When I write the letter, I will take it to the post office.'

In Slavic languages the specific use of a certain aspectual form is sometimes considered to be a stylistic preference rather than a grammatical rule. The usage of aspect may convey the attitude of the speaker. For example, there is a difference in the degree of politeness in the imperatives, as the following examples show:

(87) *Zatvaraj vrata.* (imperfective) vs. *Zatvori vrata.* (perfective)
'Close the door.'

The use of the imperfective form is less polite than the use of the perfective form. The imperfective form suggests that the speaker is slightly annoyed that the door was open. One could also interpret it as if the speaker insists that the door should be closed not just on this occasion. This is in keeping with Galton's (1976: 233) observation that the imperfective "seems more insistent, since it dwells on the action."

Gojmerac also discusses the stylistic markedness of the imperative (1980: 97) illustrating it with the following example:

(88) *Uđi.* (perfective) vs. *Ulazi.* (imperfective)
'Come in.'

The perfective form is more commonly used and is spoken to a guest or visitor with a wish for the action to be performed in its entirety. The imperfective form can be used with a friend, or as a command in the army or police, but also with a wish for the action to be performed in its entirety.

On the other hand, there are situations in which the imperfective is the more 'polite' option:

(89) *Dolazim sutra.* (imperfective)   vs. *Dođem sutra.* (perfective)
'I am coming tomorrow.'

The imperfective present is the more formal and more polite way of announcing one's arrival than the perfective present, which is rather informal and colloquial.

It is interesting to note that the Russian use of aspect in the imperative is completely opposite. The imperfective is used as a more polite version, as opposed to the perfective which tends to be used in strong orders and commands (cf. Kravar 1976: 309):

(90) *Vhodite.* (imperfective).   vs.   *Vojdite.* (perfective)
'Come in.'

Such a marked difference in the choice of the aspectual form in related languages such as Russian and Croatian is an example that defies any logical explanation.

In conclusion, we can say that there are no hard-and-fast rules with aspect in Slavic languages. Hardly any foolproof claims can be made about its use, its morphology, semantics or syntax, as there will always be counterexamples to every example put forward (cf. Janda 2004: 474). Yet, in spite of this significant amount of irregularities and exceptions, nobody disputes the existence of an aspectual system in Slavic languages.

This discussion of aspect in Slavic showed that all these "irregularities" should also be taken into consideration in the analysis of aspect in early Germanic, which most opponents of Streitbergian hypothesis neglected. The only principle that they applied from the aspect of Slavic languages is the basic rule of perfectivization – which does not always work even in Slavic.

2.9 Aspect in Germanic

Studies of aspect in Germanic languages started when Wilhelm Streitberg (1891) elaborated Jacob Grimm's ideas and developed a theory that the Gothic language had a system of prefixed verbs similar to that of Slavic languages.

Gothic, the language of the Visigoths and the Ostrogoths, is the oldest attested member of the Germanic family which belongs to the eastern branch with no modern descendants. Our only substantial record of Gothic is a fragmentary translation of the Bible by the Visigoth archbishop and missionary Wulfila ("Little Wolf") from the fourth century AD. It serves as a basis for reconstructing Proto-Germanic, as it precedes other Germanic texts by 300 or 400 years (Lehmann 1994: 19).

Even though Gothic does not belong to the same branch as English and German, it is often taken as their ancestor in diachronic studies of Germanic languages. Such practice is justified by the fact that all Germanic languages were still mutually intelligible in the time of Wulfila, and this is the only record available of an early Germanic language. The interest in studying Gothic started in the 19th century with the rise of Indo-European linguistics and the development of the comparative method.

The most notable scholar in the field of Gothic studies was Wilhelm Streitberg, whose work is still regarded as standard in Germanic linguistics, but his authority was challenged many times in the 20th century. In his lengthy article on aspect in Gothic, Streitberg tried to prove that the Germanic languages had a developed system for expressing aspect:

> "Das gotische kennt den unterschied zwischen perfectiver und imperfectiver actionsart ebensowohl wie das slavische, entbehrt aber der iterativa.

> Die perfectiva werden durch zusammensetzung des verbs mit praepositionaladverben aus den imperfectiven simplicia gebildet."[26]

(Streitberg 1891: 176)

According to Streitberg's theory, the prefix *ga-* is the most frequent perfectivizing preverb, as the following examples of aspectual pairs selected from Krause (1987) show:

(91) andjan   ga-andjan 'end'
     arman   ga-arman 'pity'
     dailjan   ga-dailjan 'share'
     dauþjan   ga-dauþjan 'kill'
     digan   ga-digan 'form'
     drigkan   ga-drigkan 'drink'
     taujan   ga-taujan 'do'
     waljan   ga-waljan 'elect'

Streitberg proposed a theory that has remained a controversial subject until this day, generating two kinds of work on aspect in Gothic: those who refuted it (e.g. Beer 1915, Mirowicz 1935, Goedsche 1940, Krause 1953, Pilch 1953, Scherer 1954, Lindemann 1970, Szemerényi 1987) and those who accepted it (e.g. Rice 1932, Hirt 1934, Pudić 1956, Lloyd 1979, West 1982, Krause 1987, Coleman 1996, Leiss 2000).

The Czech scholar Beer (1915) disputed Streitberg's analysis of the Gothic Bible by counting all the instances where the prefix *ga-* does not perfectivize. Beer claimed that 66% are exceptions and that Wulfila only added the prefix *ga-* to imitate Greek compound verbs. The Serbian linguist Pudić (1956: 391) rejects Beer's claim that Wulfila used the prefix *ga-* at whim in his lengthy analysis, showing that the prefix *ga-* did act as a perfectivizer.

Some of the opponents of Streitberg's theory expressed their views so vehemently and engaged in fierce debates with the proponents in the form of articles such as Szemerényi 1987 with a reply in Lloyd 1990. Szemerényi dismisses Streitberg's view as "erroneous and untenable" (1987: 4), concluding his very brief discussion with the following words:

> "Aspect was certainly not a morphological category in Gothic and it is beyond all doubt that Streitberg's thesis is simply not tenable. This negative verdict applies to the other Germanic dialects also."

Szemerényi (1987: 4fn) also refers to Mirowicz (1935: 48) who quoted Trnka's statement that the theory of aspect in Germanic is "die größte wissenschaftliche Fiktion" ('the greatest science fiction').

In Szemerényi's opinion Lloyd's treatment of a single aspectual pair *wrikan* 'pursue' – *gawrikan* 'punish' is sufficient evidence that proves the theory's untenability. In his reply, Lloyd (1990: 129), explains that Szemerényi mistranslated the verbs as 'pursue' and 'punish', rather than translating them as

---

[26] "The Gothic language distinguishes perfective and imperfective aspect much like Slavic, but lacks iteratives. Perfectives are formed by compounding of prepositional adverbs with imperfective simplexes." (the translation is mine)

'persecute' and 'avenge' respectively, which Lloyd himself "categorized as a somewhat doubtful case" (ibid.). At the same time, Szemerényi ignored "hundreds of indisputable pairs" that Lloyd listed. Lloyd believes that the evidence for aspect in Gothic is

> "overwhelming, and, on the basis of (to be sure far less conclusive) remnants of what appears to be a similar system in Old High German, at least worth considering for Germanic as a whole."
>
> (Lloyd 1990: 130)

According to Leiss (2000: 120), the current linguistic discussion on this topic is whether Gothic operates with a sufficient number of aspectual pairs in order to establish aspect as a category, reminding us that the corpus of Gothic texts is too limited to find an aspectual pair for every verb. This brings us back to the theoretical question of what constitutes aspect and whether a binary system is a criterion that must be met. Perhaps Coseriu's view (1980: 16) comes closer to the truth, as he believes that aspect is a collection of "possibilités universelles du langage qui peuvent être réalisées dans les langues", or "an open-ended "system", from which the languages choose some, and never realize others" (translation by Szemerényi 1987:9).

Leiss (2000: 122) believes that the prefix *ga-* is the prototypical perfectivizer, whereas the other prefixes such as *us-* and *bi-* express additional meaning, although verbs with other prefixes can also function as aspectual partners. Leiss applies Lehmann's (1988) idea of 'peripheral aspectual partners' to Gothic verbs, elaborating the central and peripheral aspectual and *Aktionsart* partners for one Gothic verb. The difference in font size is intentional (Next page, Table 11). The larger the font size, the more central the perfective pair of the simplex verb.

	and-saihvan	'look at'; 'consider'
	at-saihvan	'look at'; 'look after'
	bi-saihvan	'look upon'; 'look around'
saihvan 'see'	*ga-saihvan*	'see'; 'perceive'
	us-saihvan	'look up'; 'look at'
	in-saihvan	'look at'; 'look upon'; 'regard'
	þairh-saihvan	'look through'; 'see in the mirror'

Table 11
Central and peripheral aspectual partners
of an imperfective simplex verb in Gothic
(adapted from Leiss 2000: 123)

In this table, *ga-saihvan* represents the semantically most neutral aspectual partner, whereas, depending on the context, other less central or more peripheral verbs can act as aspectual partners for the Gothic verb *saihvan*.

A frequently occurring problem was the authenticity of the Gothic idiom in the only Gothic text that we have available. It has often been noted that this is a rather literal translation from Greek, so Greek influence has been observed in syntax (Lehmann 1994: 34), as well as in numerous loanwords and calques. How much was the translator influenced by the choice of compound words then? Were they translated word-for-word into Gothic? This question was investigated by Rice (1932), who examined all the prefixed verbs in Gothic in order to show that Wulfila did not imitate Greek in the selection of preverbs. The crux of his analysis is a chart spread over two pages (Rice 1932: 124-125) in which he cross-referenced every single occurrence of a prefixed verb with its corresponding Greek original. The conclusion that arises from a look at that chart is that the use of preverbs in Gothic is quite authentic because one prefix corresponds to up to 17 different prefixes in Greek and there are numerous cases where there are no correspondences.

For example, the preverb *us-* has a Greek prefix correspondence in 62.9% cases, and corresponds to a simplex verb in Greek in the remaining 37.1% cases. Its most frequent correspondence is to the Greek prefix ἐκ- with 22.5%, followed by ἀνα- and other 11 prefixes.

According to Rice (1932: 126), Gothic combines 28 different prefixes with 448 different simplex verbs to give a total of 5,948 prefixed verbs, whereas Greek combines 18 different prefixes with 320 different simplex verbs giving a total of 4,047 occurrences of prefixed verbs.

This study is very valuable for the present research, as the number of occurrences can be cross-referenced with the figures for the Old English data. Table 12 (next page) features the seven most frequent Gothic prefixes out of the total of 28 prefixes. The prefixes *ga-* and *us-* outnumber the rest in frequency to such an extent, which suggests that they were more grammaticalized than others, as their use was over-extended. Rice (1932: 126) also notes that these two prefixes are "most often called upon by the Gothic for figurative use."

Gothic prefix	Number of occurrences	Old English cognate	Gothic example	Old English cognate
ga-	2,516	*ge-*	*ga-laubjan* 'believe'	*gelȳfan*
us-	905	*a-*	*us-hlaupan* 'spring up'	*āhleāpan*
and-	465	*and-, ond-*	*and-waurdjan* 'answer'	*andswarian*
fra-	329	*for-*	*fra-letan* 'let go'	*forlǣtan*
ana-	231	*on-*	*ana-biudan* 'command'	*onbēodan*
bi-	228	*be-*	*bi-niman* 'take away'	*beniman*
af-	222	*of-*	*af-slahan* 'kill, slay'	*ofslēan*

Table 12
Most frequent Gothic prefixes with their Old English cognates

Recently the question of grammaticalization of the prefix *ga-* was discussed by Niwa (2008). He examines why the prefix *ga-* does not appear in the Gothic past participles. He presents the past participles in Gothic, Old English and Modern German in a rather simplified way:

(92) Gothic *saih-ans.* PP of *saihwan* 'see'
    OE   *ge-sew-en.* PP of *seon* 'see'
    G   *ge-seh-en.* PP of *sehen* 'see'

(from Niwa 2008: 13)

This suggests that Old English had already grammaticalized the prefix *ge-*, when in fact this prefix was optional but became fully grammaticalized only in Middle English. *Gesewen* could also be the past participle of the verb *geseon*, just as the past participle of the verb *seon* could be *sewen* or *sawen*. Perhaps putting parentheses would solve the problem in the way he presents it:

(93) Gothic   *qumans* PP of *quiman* 'come'
    Old English   *(ge-)cuman* PP of *cuman* 'come'
    German   *ge-komm-en* PP of *kommen* 'come'

Niwa suggests that the prefix *ga-* did not appear in past participles at all because the past participle was indicated by rich inflectional morphology. In Gothic, the past participle behaved like the adjective, so it had two sets of inflections: strong and weak, as can be seen in the verb *giban* 'give':

(94) Strong: m. *gibans* f. *gibana* n. *giban, gibanata*
    Weak: m. *gibana* f. *gibanô* n. *gibanô*

(from Braune 1883: 52)

Due to so many different inflectional endings from the adjective paradigm, the past participle was always clearly marked. With the attrition of these case and gender endings, the past participle was losing its morphological distinctness, so the prefix *ge-* took over the function of the past participle marker. In terms of the grammaticalization theory, Niwa concludes that "Gothic is a start, West-Saxon a way, German a goal" (2008: 16).

In Old English, the prefix *ge-* was not obligatory in past participles, but was frequently used, as will be shown in Chapter 6. Though it was phonologically reduced to *y-* or *i-* in Middle English, the prefix *ge-* was completely bleached of its lexical meaning and served only as a marker of past participles in more or less the same way it does in Modern German or Dutch. Dutch exhibits an even higher level of grammaticalization than German, as German makes exceptions with weak verbs ending in *-ieren* (borrowings from French or Latin), whereas Dutch consistently applies the rule:

(95) German: *organisiert, reorganisiert, studiert, repariert, manipuliert, telefoniert, kommuniziert, applaudiert, desorientiert*

(96) Dutch: *georganiseerd, gereorganiseerd, gestudeerd, gerepareerd, gemanipuleerd, getelefoneerd, gecommuniceerd, geapplaudisseerd, gedesoriënteerd*

When verbs with inseparable prefixes are used in the past participle form in Modern German or Dutch, the inflectional prefix *ge-* is not used:

(97) Dutch
    doordenken 'think through' *gedoordacht – *doordacht* 'well thought out'
    ontdekken 'discover' - *geontdekt - *ontdekt*
    verliepen 'expire' - *geverlopen – *verlopen*

(98) German
    bedenken 'consider'- *gebedacht – *bedacht*
    erzählen 'tell' – *geerzählt – *erzählt*
    zerstören 'destroy' *gezerstört – *zerstört*

The existing prefix overrules the prefix *ge-* on the grounds of redundancy. This in turn strongly suggests that these inseparable prefixes already have a perfectivizing force in a similar way as they do in Slavic languages.

Let us consider a few examples from Gothic and compare them with the situation in Old English[27].

(99) Gothic
    jah anaks   insaihwandans   ni þanaseiþs ainohun
    and suddenly look round.PRES.PTCP.NOM.PL no any more one.INDF.PRON
    ***gasehwun**, alya Iesu   ainana miþ   sis.*
    see.3.P.PL.PRET except Jesus.ACC alone.ACC with REFL.PRON.DAT

    Old English
    And sona ða hi   besawon, hi nanne hi mid him ne
    and soon when they around-looked they none one with them not
    ***gesawon**, buton ðone Hælend sylfne mid him.*
    ge-saw.3.PL but the saviour self with them
    'And suddenly, when they had looked round, they saw no man
    any more save Jesus only with themselves.'
                                                              St. Mark 9.8

In the above two examples we have the Gothic verb *saihwan* and the Old English verb *seon* prefixed with *ga-* and *ge-* respectively, both used in a situation that was completed in its entirety in the past. There is no reason to doubt that *ga-* and *ge-* in this case signal perfectivity.

The next example features several prefixed verbs which could all function as markers of aspectuality.

(100) Gothic
    ***ushofun**   þan þana   stain   þarei   was.*
    lift.3.P.PL.PRET then that.ACC stone.ACC where be.3.SG.PRET
    *Iþ Iesus   **uzuhhof**   augona iup jah qaþ:*
    and Jesus lift.3.P.SG.PRET eyes.ACC up and say.3.P.SG.PRET
    *atta,   awiliudo   þus,   unte   **andhausides** mis*
    father, thank.1.P.SG.PRES you.DAT that.CONJ hear.2.P.SG.PRET I.DAT

    Old English
    *Ða dydon hig aweg ðone stan. Se Hælend **ahof** his Eagan up,*
    then did they away the stone the saviour **a-lifted** his eyes up

---

[27] These examples have been selected from Bosworth's edition of *Gospels in Gothic and Old English* (1865).

and cwæþ, Fæder, ic do þancas ðe, forðam ðu **gehyrdest** me.
and said   father   I do thanks you because you **ge-heard** me
'Then they took away the stone from the place (where the dead was laid).
And Jesus lifted up his eyes, and said, Father, I thank you that you have
heard me.'

John 11.41

We see that Wulfila used the same verb for taking the stone away (lifting it)
and for lifting up the eyes, whereas in Old English a phrasal verb was used in
the first case (*don aweg*, literally *do away*) and the cognate verb *ahebban* in the
second case. In the second case both Gothic and Old English verb are re-
inforced by the particle *up* which indicates direction, whereas *uzuh-* in Gothic
and *a-* in Old English could both be markers of perfectivity. The verb
andhausjan is a prefixed verb just like the Old English verb *gehiran*, both
meaning 'to hear'. Their simplex versions *hausjan* and *hiran* mean 'to listen'. If
we attach a prefix to this simplex verb, we could argue that we are changing its
aspect, more precisely its resultativity.

The following example also shows a verb which is perfectivized with the
prefix, cognates both in the prefix and the stem.

(101) Gothic
  Biþeh þan   **usþwoh**   fotuns   ize,   jah   nam
  so   then **us-wash**.3.P.SG.PRET feet.ACC their.GEN and take3.P.SG.PRET
  wastjos   seinos; anakumbjands   aftra,   qaþ   du   im
  garments.ACC their set down.PRES.PTCP.ACC.PL again say.3.P.SG.PRET to they.DAT

Old English
  Syððan he hæfde hyra fet **aþwogene**, he nam his reaf; and ða he sæt,
  after he had their feet **a-washed** he took his robe and then he sat
  he cwæþ eft to him
  he said again to them
'So after he had **washed** their feet and had taken his garments and had
seated himself again he said to them.'

John 13.12

It is very likely that the Gothic verb *us-þwahan* 'wash' was the perfective
pair of *þwahan* and its Old English corresponding verb *aþwean* (in the past
participle form) is its cognate both in the prefix and the stem. The fact that the
prefix *a-* in the verb *aþwean* 'to wash' was understood as an inflectional
(grammatical) rather than a derivational (lexical) prefix can be confirmed by an
extract from Aelfric's Grammar where Latin verb paradigms are presented along
with a translation into Old English:

(102) *lauo ic ðwea, laui ic ðwoh, lautum a**ðwogen**, sume cweðað lotum oððe*
    lavo I wash lavi I washed lavatum ***a*-washed** some say lotum   or
  lauatum
  lavatum

ÆGram 139.3

In other words, the Latin verb in the present tense *lavo* 'I wash' corresponds
to Old English *ðwea*, the Latin perfect tense *lavi* 'I washed' corresponds to the

Old English preterite *ðwoh* and the past participle forms *lautum, lotum* or *lavatum* correspond to *aðwogen*, in which case the prefix *a-* was added, rather than the prefix *ge-*.

The following example contains verbs that are interesting from the perspective of aspect.

(103) Gothic
*Yah **anaaiauk**   sandyan þridyan iþ   eis yah þana*
and continue.3.SG.PRET send.INF   third and they also he.ACC
*gawondondans, **uswaurpun**.*
wound.PTCP.PL.   *us-*cast.3.PL.PRET

Old English
*Đa sende he þriddan, ða **wurpon** hig **ut** ðone gewundodne.*
then sent he third   then **cast** him **out** the wounded
'And again he sent a third: and they wounded him also, and cast him out.'
Luke 20.12

The translations into Gothic and Old English are somewhat different – the Gothic text contains the verb *anaaukan* 'continue', whereas in Old English the construction *ða... ða...* ('when... then...') is used. The verb *uswairpan* is a cognate of Old English *aweorpan*.

The Old English verb *sendan* is used without the prefix *a-*, which would make it imperfective. However, it is possible that the context gives it a perfective reading, as will be discussed in Chapter 5. As aspect was also a matter of syntax, the structure *ða... ða...* sets a frame whose verbs can only have a perfective meaning. Another interesting feature of this example is that *weorpan* is also not used with the prefix *a-* (*aweorpan* normally means to 'cast out') but is used with the particle *ut* 'out' instead. The prefixes *ga-* and *ge-* are both added in the past participle form, re-inforcing its resultative meaning.

A few lines later in the text, we have the verb *uswairpan* 'cast out' again, but this time the Gothic verb is in the past participle form, whereas the Old English one is in the preterit, and vice versa for *usquiman* and *ofslean* 'to kill':

(104) Gothic
*Jah **uswairpandans**   ina   ut us   þamma weinagarda **usqemun**.*
and **cast out**.PRES.PTCP.PL he.ACC out from   the.DAT vineyard kill.3.P.PL.PRET

Old English
*And hig hine of ðam win-gearde **awurpon**, **ofslegene**.*
and they him of that vine-yeard **a-**cast   kill. PTCP
'So they cast him out of the vineyard, and killed him.'
Luke 20.15

The context demands a perfective reading for both verbs and therefore prefixes are attached in the above example.

One of the scholars who doubted the existence of aspect in Germanic languages was Goedsche. He criticized Streitberg's followers in their efforts to find a way of explaining that prefixes play a role in verbal aspect. For Goedsche, word-formational processes in Germanic languages such as prefixation and suffixation can only change aktionsart and never grammatical aspect:

> "If we call *tropfen* iterative, *zappeln* frequentative, *ermüden* inchoative, *schälen* privative, etc. we do nothing to further the study of aspect. We only set up classifications on the basis of lexical meanings. And if we translate Goth. *sitan* by 'to sit' and *gasitan* by 'to sit down,' *fraihnan* by 'to ask' and *gafraihnan* by 'to find out,' then we give expression to the semantic function of *ga-* just as we express differences in meaning by other prefixes, e.g., *trinken*: *betrinken, vertrinken, ertrinken,* etc. The investigation of such prefixes belongs in the field of semantics."
>
> (Goedsche 1940: 191)

Goedsche seems to violate a principle of logic here. He categorizes the four German examples into aspectual categories based on their inherent lexical meaning, rightfully relegating them to the study of lexical semantics rather the study of language structure. But the prefix *ga-* in his examples points to an essential and frequent pattern in the structure of the Gothic language, so it cannot merely be a matter of lexical semantics. Furthermore, by saying that prefixes belong to the field of semantics, Goedsche implies that aspect is not a semantic but a morphological category, which is utterly unacceptable from the present-day point of view, as aspect is considered a fundamentally semantic category that is paired with morpho-syntax. Semantics is a prerequisite in any discussion of aspect. Once the semantic criterion has been established, we see a wide array of differences from one language to another whether determining temporal interpretation is achieved by morphological, syntactical or lexical means – and quite frequently there is an interplay of all three.

However, Goedsche deserves credit for rightfully pinpointing an insurmountable problem:

> "Because of the abstract nature of verbal aspect we shall always be tempted to read a preconceived notion into the grammatical forms of a dead language."
>
> (Goedsche 1940: 196)

I am in absolute agreement with Goedsche in this regard. We can hardly come to terms with semantic categories as abstract as aspect in living languages. Many scholars have devised diagnostic tests such as Dowty (1979) that help us determine what kind of aspect a certain verb or predicate expresses, but such tests can only be conducted with native speakers. They can be of little use for diachronic research, as nobody can be a competent judge for compatibility tests such as Vendler's (1957: 101) *for/in* adverbials as in *John walked for/in an hour* in Old English. All we can do is take an educated guess.

Not long after Goedsche, there was another scholar who took it upon himself to prove that there is no aspect in Germanic. In the 1950's, Philip Scherer wrote a series of three studies with an aim of disproving the existence of aspect as a grammatical category in Germanic. In his first paper (Scherer 1954) he dealt with Gothic, his second paper (Scherer 1956) with Old High German (9th century) and his third paper (Scherer 1958) with the late 10th century Wessex translation of the Lindisfarne Gospels[28].

---

[28] Scherer confused two different translations of the Bible. The Lindisfarne Gospels were translated into the Northumbrian dialect and there is another translation in the West Saxon dialect.

The problem with Scherer's method is that he focuses on only one text which is a translation, rather than choosing several texts. He starts from the assumption that *ge*-prefixed verbs express aspectuality more than the other prefixes, so he groups the verbs into three categories: simplexes, *ge*-compounds and prefixed compounds. Furthermore, his method is only contrasting a handful of verb forms with their equivalents in Latin in five tables, three of which also have their Greek equivalents, and one table with equivalents in Old Church Slavonic. His intention was to show that Old English was "indifferent to aspect" by listing examples in which different verb forms are used in Latin where Old English uses one and the same verb form. The following is an extract from one of his tables.

ge-Compounds	ipf-pres	*gebiddað* 'oratis' (L 11.2)	
	ipf-fut	*gebiddað* 'orabitis' (M 6.9)	*molite sę*
	pf-fut	*gebiddað* 'orabitis' (J 4.21)	*poklonite sę*
	ipf-pres	*gehyraþ* 'audiunt' (J 10.3)	
	pf-fut	*gehyraþ* 'audient' (J 5.25)	*uslyšętŭ*
	pf-ant fut	*gehyraþ* 'audierint' (J 5.25)	*uslyšętŭ*
Prefix-Compounds	ipf-pres	*asett* 'ponit' (L 8.16)	
	pf-fut	*asett* 'ponet' (M 24.51)	*položitŭ*
	ipf-pres	*ingæþ* 'intrat' (J 10.2)	
	pf-fut	*gæð in* 'ingredietur' (J 10.9)	*vĭnidetŭ*

Table 13
A sample from Scherer's Table 1:
The Verbal Set *deð* (1958: 246)

When Old English verb forms are contrasted with Latin and Old Church Slavonic in this manner, Old English is bound to lose the battle. The inflectional morphology of English verbs was already reduced, but this is still no conclusive evidence that there is no aspect in English, merely because a handful of examples do not show inflectional changes in the manner that Latin and Old Church Slavonic do. We should not apply standards of other languages solely because they exist in those languages. Furthermore, Scherer failed to check the syntax of those verbs – perhaps adverbials and objects can also serve as markers of aspectuality at the sentence level, while the prefix has a different function there. This points to his presupposition that aspect is something that can be exclusively morphologically marked. Scherer, in fact, states that openly:

> "To determine whether Gothic possessed a formally explicit aspectual system, we shall ask what, if any, were the morphological means corresponding to the aspectual contrast between intensive and extensive, and to the far fewer Pf meanings. Syntactical means we shall disregard completely."
> (Scherer 1954: 214)

Scherer proposes that verbal forms are indifferent to aspect in a Germanic language, and Mitchell (1985: 364) thinks he succeeded in demonstrating that. Mitchell was such a fervent opponent of applying the term aspect to the Germanic languages that in his large two-volume Old English Syntax he dedicates only a few short pages to aspect. He claims that this category does not exist in English and has never existed, and that "there can be no doubt that it is possible to give a coherent account of the OE verb without using the term 'aspect'" (Mitchell 1985: 364). He condemns all previous writers who discussed different aspectual categories in Old English:

> "Quirk and Wrenn are not alone in this error. Visser refers to three kinds of 'verbs of aspect' which respectively express 'ingressive', 'durative', and 'terminative' aspect."
>
> (Mitchell 1985: 366)

Mitchell does not hesitate to agree with Zandvoort quoting that

> "the attempt to transfer the category of 'aspect' from Slavonic to Germanic, and from there to Modern English grammar, strikes one as an instance of misplaced ingenuity. Streitberg's application of the notion to Gothic, which was the beginning of the trouble, is now completely discredited, and with it the endeavours of his imitators in the fields of other Germanic dialects, including Old English. But even those who admit defeat on the rest of the Germanic front still cling to the Modern English progressive ... whichever way we look at it, the conclusion seems inescapable that the question asked in the title of this paper should be answered in the negative"
>
> Zandvoort (1962: 19-20)

It is actually surprising that he quotes Zandvoort who merely discusses the ideas of other scholars and bases his "verdict" on his personal assumptions, rather than offering an analytical study.

However, Mitchell (1985: 366fn) makes mention of K.A. Tandy's dissertation *Aspect and Ælfric* (1976) which studies patterns of verbs' aspectual features in Ælfric's *Lives of Saints* and refers to his subsequent work (Tandy 1978), where he says that

> "in English aspect is not expressed overtly, in a morphological system, but covertly, in modifiers, periphrastic verb structures, and lexical meaning, and consequently aspect is accessible largely through the semantic analysis that was forbidden by formal grammarians"
>
> (Tandy 1978: 181).

Mitchell reports that this involves the study of special verbal phrasings, of lexical embedding, of adverbial modification, of phonesthemic clusters in English, and of the marking of aspect by syntactical units larger than single adverbs (Tandy 1978: 182-3). Mitchell adds in a rather apologetic way that he has "never 'forbidden' anyone to undertake such analysis" (1985: 366fn), but that he believes "that anyone doing so runs the risk of being lost in a chaos of infinite possibilities of distinction."

Mitchell admits that prefixes such as *a-*, *be-*, *for-*, *ge-*, *of-* and *to-* do have aspectual properties, but he insists that "this is not the sole function of any of these prefixes" (1985: 367). Such a claim is of little help, as marking aspect is never the only function of any prefix in any Indo-European language. Interestingly enough, Tandy's dissertation (1978) never mentions prefixes as having aspectual properties, although many aspectual syntactic patterns are described in detail.

There were scholars who defended the view that Early Germanic did have an aspect system and implied that a more detailed look ought to be taken at Slavic:

> "Those who refuse to believe in the existence, in Gothic and Old High German, of a verbal aspect system similar to the one in Old Church Slavic and Russian may be under the impression that the Slavic system is absolutely airtight and without exception, and since they do not find such absolute regularity in the Old Germanic dialects they deny the existence of such a Germanic system altogether."
>
> (Senn 1949: 407)

Senn (1949: 408) believes that German aspect system today is underdeveloped due to a strong influence of Latin on German syntax since the Middle Ages, just like he believes that Latin influence on German is comparable to the Russian influence on Lithuanian which otherwise would not have developed a mirror image of the Slavic aspectual system that Baltic languages normally would not have.

Senn even goes so far as to speculate that the Slavs borrowed the aspect system from the Goths, as the entire Slavic area was under Gothic influence and domination, which he corroborates with numerous loanwords in the Slavic languages. Furthermore, he refers to a study by Leskien on the declension in Baltic, Slavic and Germanic, which also confirms very close contacts between Pre-Germanic and Pre-Slavic. However, the only textual evidence that we have available today is the translation of Wulfila's Bible, which predates Old Church Slavonic gospel translation by 500 years.

Finally, there was an Indo-Europeanist who believed that Germanic did have aspect, but that its system should not be compared to that of Slavic since it may lead us to wrong conclusions:

> "In den historischen Zeiten ist das Germanische vom Slawischen verschieden, und es ist falsch, das Gotische auf das Prokrustesbett des Slawischen zu spannen und im Text Vermutungen auf Grund dieser Lehre einzuführen."[29]
>
> (Hirt 1934: 133-134)

Merely because there are some irregularities in the Old Germanic aspectual system, as so many have been pointed out in Slavic, cannot make us deny the existence of an aspectual system in Germanic altogether.

2.10 Aspectual Categories

A large number of papers and dissertations are written without defining or discussing the terminology used, presupposing that there is consensus on what these terms mean to everyone. Time and again this has proved to be a faulty assumption, as can be testified by many papers written with the aim of clearing

---

[29] "In historical tenses Germanic differs from Slavic and it is wrong to stretch out Gothic on the Procrustean bed of Slavic and introduce assumptions in the text on the basis of this doctrine." (the translation is mine)

up the terminological confusion such as Dahl (1981), Depraetere (1995) or Declerck (1979, 2007).

One can easily lapse into anachronistic labelling, as the tradition of studying the field of aspect is very long (older than linguistics itself) and its terminology complex and far from standardized. There are numerous cases of synonymous terms becoming distinguished at one point, which can cause considerable confusion (e.g. for Streitberg and Jakobson aktionsart are completely different concepts). New terms are coined for categories that already existed (e.g. telic replaced non-durative). Many labels for aspectual categories have been borrowed from the Slavic studies of aspect. Existing terms are filled with new content, often resulting in terminological confusion and conceptual problems. These are typical scenarios in research on aspect.

There is a good deal of overlap in terminology between aspectual categories. The categories such as perfective, completive, resultative, telic and bounded are often used interchangeably, even though many scholars fervently insist on keeping these categories distinct. Back in the 19th century, Streitberg (1891:70) used all three labels, *perfective, completive* and *resultative*, for one and the same concept. In spite of (or perhaps precisely due to) the vast literature written on the subject of aspect in the 20th century, the boundaries between certain categories are fuzzy.

This chapter will not attempt to clear up the terminological confusion, but will discuss the aspectual categories relevant for an analysis of aspect in early English. The discussion will also question the applicability of some aspectual categories to data in diachronic studies where native-speaker intuitions are simply unavailable.

Aspectual categories are typically defined in terms of pairing of certain features of meaning with certain morpho-syntactic forms (inflectional or derivational affixes, syntactic constructions or words).

2.10.1 Perfective

In most discussions of aspect, the prototypical category will be *perfective* and the prototypical distinction or opposition will be *perfective / imperfective*. This category is thought to be adopted from Slavic languages, although we have seen in section 2.4 that it did not ultimately originate from them. It took considerable time to establish the present-day sense of the opposition between *perfective* and *imperfective*. According to Dahl's typological investigation of aspect in a wide range of all human languages, this distinction ("in various disguises") appears in 45% of the languages in his sample. Dahl starts the discussion of this category in the following way:

> "Perfectivity is often taken to be 'the' category of aspect: this is a view taken in particular by many Slavists, who are often unwilling to label anything that differs in any way from the Slavic opposition between Perfective and Imperfective as aspect."

(Dahl 1985: 69)

Many scholars believe that the terms *perfective* and *imperfective* are not applicable to English. One of them was Jespersen, who said:

> "It is generally assumed that our Aryan languages had at first no real forms in their verbs for tense-distinctions, but denoted various aspects, perfective, imperfective, punctual, durative, inceptive, or others, and that out of these distinctions were gradually evolved the tense-systems which we find in the oldest Aryan languages and which are the foundation of the systems existing to-day. Scholars took this idea of aspect from Slavic verbs, where it is fundamental and comparatively clear and clean-cut, but when they began to find something similar to this in other languages, each of them as a rule partially or wholly rejected the systems of his predecessors and set up a terminology of his own, so that nowadays it would be possible, had one the time and inclination, to give a very long list of terms, many of them with two or three or even more definitions. ... Nor have these writers always distinguished the four possible expressions for "aspect", (1) the ordinary meaning of the verb itself, (2) the occasional meaning of the verb as occasioned by context or situation, (3) a derivative suffix, and (4) a tensed form"
>
> (Jespersen 1924: 286)

Jespersen concludes

> "I think it would be better to do without the terms perfective and imperfective except in dealing with the Slavic verb, where they have a definite sense and have long been in universal use. In other languages it will be well in each separate instance to examine carefully what is the meaning of the verbal expression concerned, and whether it is due to the verb itself, to its prefix or suffix, to its tense-form, or to the context."
>
> (Jespersen 1924: 288)

If we decide to agree with Jespersen, then we would have to develop new terms for a description of aspect in English, which would not really solve any problems. In fact, most linguists disregarded Jespersen's idea and decided to adopt the existing terminology. Even Langacker (1987: 254) adopts the terms *perfective* and *imperfective*, although he is aware that he basically redefined established terms that "carry too much "excess baggage"" (1987: 254fn).

Comrie also adopts these terms and defines them as follows:

> "perfectivity indicates the view of a situation as a single whole, without distinction of the various separate phases that make up that situation, while the imperfective pays essential attention to the internal structure of the situation."
>
> (Comrie 1976:16)

In a rather amusing definition of the terms *perfective* and *imperfective* in Russian, the linguist Isačenko used a very vivid metaphor of a parade on Red Square in Moscow (1960: 132-133). In this military metaphor, the parade stands for action. He said that the perfective is viewing the parade as a whole from the perspective of the grandstand like Lenin's Mausoleum, whereas the imperfective is like viewing the parade from the perspective of a participant in the middle of the parade.

In his discussion of the meaning of the perfective aspect in Russian, Ferrell (1951) examines all previous descriptions of the perfective aspect, organizing them as follows:

1) The perfective represents the completed action
2) The perfective represents action as a point
3) The perfective aspect expresses a single action considered in its completion and hence its result
4) The perfective indicates limitation in time
5) The perfective aspect expresses the result of the action.

These five basic and recurrent descriptions of the meaning of perfectivity make use of concepts that give names to other aspectual categories, such as completive and resultative. However, this does not mean that they are synonymous. It is true that there is overlap between *perfective* and *resultative*, but only partial. All resultative actions are perfective, but not all perfective actions are resultative. In resultative aspect, the focus is on the successful completion of the action (Comrie 1976: 20), basically its final stage. Perfective is a broad category that encompasses different subtypes which include resultative (the above meanings #3 and #5), completive (meaning #1), instantaneous, momentaneous, punctual or semelfactive (meaning #2) and some other categories that will be discussed later.

The distinction between these subcategories can be determined only by the lexical meaning of the verb. For example, if we say that the perfective verb *pasti* 'to fall' is instantaneous in a certain context, we think that this action takes place in an instant rather than over a period of time. The terms *momentaneous* and *punctual* are synonyms of instantaneous. Semelfactive refers to actions that happen only once; in other words, "once only" is in focus here, such as *he coughed* (Comrie 1976: 42)[30]. This means that semelfactive overlaps with momentaneous and punctual, but have slightly different things in focus.

2.10.2 Imperfective

Some features of the imperfective category were inevitably discussed in the previous section since the perfective cannot be described or defined without the contrast with the imperfective.

Just as the perfective has a number of subtypes, so the imperfective can be subdivided into habitual, continuous, durative, iterative and similar. Again, they may differ as well as overlap, depending on which feature of the action is in focus. Habitual aspect portrays a situation that extends indefinitely in time. Iterative aspect refers to repetitions of a given situation (and therefore could be the best opposite pair of semelfactive). Comrie argues that if a situation is repeated several (i.e. limited) number of times, then all these repetitions of the

---

[30] The inherent aspect of the verb *cough* can be radically changed by an adverbial. For example, in the sentence *He coughed a great deal / for weeks* we see a shift from semelfactive to durative.

situation can be regarded as a single situation (1976: 27) – in which case they actually belong to perfective aspect.

Continuous or progressive aspect is used for ongoing actions and is regarded as a subtype of imperfective. All progressive actions are imperfective, but not all imperfective actions are progressive, which is why all instances of progressives in English will be translated with an imperfective verb in Croatian, but not vice versa. Comrie explains that the progressive/non-progressive distinction can be compared with the perfective/imperfective "only if habitual meaning is excluded" (1976: 7), defining progressiveness as "the combination of continuousness with nonstativity" (1976: 12). In other words, certain linguists make a distinction between progressive and continuous, even though most English grammars regard them as synonymous.

Some authors simplify these concepts further, like Riemer who claims that progressive is "a language particular label for imperfective aspect" (2010: 315). Although there is an element of truth in this claim, it might on the other hand give rise to confusion.

2.10.3 Telicity

Telic situations are those that have an endpoint, or to quote Comrie, they involve

> "a process that leads up to a well-defined terminal point, beyond which the process cannot continue"
>
> (Comrie 1976: 45).

The coining of the term 'telicity' as an aspectual category is credited to Howard Garey in his description of aspect in French in 1957, the same year as Vendler's time schemata (and coincides with Vendler's category of accomplishments).

> "What then are the aspectual distinctions which are formally marked in French? The opposition between the imperfective and the perfective aspects is found in the morphological system of the French verb, but only in the difference between the *imparfait* and all the other past tenses. The distinction between telic and atelic verbs is not part of the formal structure of French, since it does not correlate with any formal criterion, but is rather part of the semantic structure of the language, determined as it is by a semantic trait."
>
> Garey 1957: 110

For Garey, verbal aspect is the perfective vs. imperfective opposition, which is realized in French in the opposition between *passé composé / simple* and *imparfait*. In order to account for inherent temporal properties of some verbs, or lexical aspect, Garey devises the term 'telicity' (based on Greek *télos* 'end') for "verbs expressing an action tending towards a goal-envisaged as realized in a perfective tense, but as contingent in an imperfective tense" (Garey 1957: 106). The opposite to telic verbs are *atelic* verbs, which would be those that "do not have to wait for a goal for their realization, but are realized as soon as they begin" (ibid.). In order to show that the lexical aspect opposition *telic* vs. *atelic* is different from the grammatical opposition *perfective* vs. *imperfective,* Garey presents their interaction in table 14:

	Imperfective	Perfective
Telic	*Pierre arrivait* 'Peter was arriving'	*Pierre est arrivé* 'Peter arrived'
Atelic	*Pierre jouait* 'Peter was playing'	*Pierre a joué* 'Peter played'

Table 14
The interaction of Telicity with Perfectivity in French
(adapted from Garey 1957: 106)

The perfective aspect applied to the verb *arriver* expresses the attainment of a goal that "creates the illusion that the achievement of the goal is part of the lexical meaning of such a verb" (Garey 1957: 108). The semantics of telic verbs specifies what is required for the event to culminate, so if a telic verb is used in the imperfective aspect, the culmination is dissociated.

Garey's concept or category of telicity was quickly taken over in studies of English. But it also "carried excess baggage" like imperfective/perfective that was imported from Slavic, as it was not originally devised for a description of English but French.

In a unidimensional approach, there is no difference between lexical and grammatical aspect – hence the boundedness present in the telic and perfective are conflated to the same category.

Once these two categories are conflated – the distinction between lexical and grammatical aspect is blurred and non-existent, as grammar and lexicon form a continuum. For this reason, I would like to argue that Langacker did not use the terms perfective/imperfective "confusingly", as Sasse suggests (2002: 214). One basic opposition is enough for Langacker, and it is understandable that Langacker opted for imperfective/perfective, rather than atelic/telic.

However, some authors do seem to confuse the two categories:

> "Instead of these terms [perfective and imperfective] in recent years the new terms *telic-atelic* (German *telisch-atelisch*) have gained a measure of acceptance; *telic* stresses that the verb implies completion of the action, while the *atelic* verb does not."
>
> (Szemerényi 1987: 1fn)

2.10.4 Ingressive

Ingressive aspect deserves special attention here, as the corpus analysis of Old English has found a number of verbs that denote this kind of aspect. Ingressive aspect is also known as inceptive or inchoative aspect, although in Slavic languages a distinction is made sometimes between ingressive and inchoative (e.g. Silić's aktionsarten in Table 2). However, this distinction is not overly clear, and most scholars use the three labels (ingressive, inceptive and inchoative) interchangeably in order to refer to aspect that denotes the beginning of a situation.

The biggest problem with the meaning of ingressive aspect is in its classification under the two main aspects – is it perfective or imperfective? The literature has been sharply divided in this regard, as the following quotes will show. Comrie exemplifies ingressive in English with the following example (1976: 20):

(105)*Suddenly he knew/understood what was happening.*

It is clear that *knew* or *understood* denote ingressive, even though it is not morphologically marked. The shift in aspect is actually caused by the adverbial *suddenly,* without which the sentence would have a completely different aspectual reading.

According to Comrie, ingressive aspect is a subtype of perfective aspect:

> "In many languages that have a distinction between perfective and imperfective forms, the perfective forms of some verbs, in particular of some stative verbs, can in fact be used to indicate the beginning of a situation (ingressive meaning)."
>
> (Comrie 1976: 19)

And indeed, his example quoted in (105) does exhibit a perfective meaning, rather than imperfective.

A radically different opinion is advocated by Declerck, who sees ingressive as a subtype of imperfective aspect:

> "There is ingressive ('inceptive', 'inchoative') aspect when the verb adopts a special form (suffix or auxiliary) which restricts the reference to the beginning of a situation, i. e. which represents the situation as just beginning. In English there is no special verb form (suffix or auxiliary) conveying this meaning. Instead, English makes use of an 'aspectual' lexical verb (or 'aspectualizer') such as *begin, start, commence*, which is a 'full verb' (i. e. a normal verb with a full conjugation rather than an auxiliary) placed before the verb phrase describing the situation (e.g. *She began to cry*). The fact that English needs such a separate aspectual verb means that we cannot speak of 'ingressive aspect' in English."
>
> (Declerck 2006: 31)

Many problems can be spotted in this extract. Firstly, the insensitivity to what kind of meaning in general ingressive should belong. Secondly, English *does* have a suffix that conveys ingressive aspectual meaning, although it is not an inflectional suffix. This is the suffix *–en,* which is amply exemplified earlier in number (40). Thirdly, Declerck denies the existence of ingressive aspect in English on the grounds of not having morphological markers to show it, even though scholars like Freed (1979) and Brinton (1988) showed that English does have ingressive aspect expressed syntactically by means of aspectualizers such as *begin, start, commence,* which are semi-auxiliaries and not "normal verbs" as Declerck suggests. Formally speaking, they may have morphological features of "full verbs" as they have a full conjugation, but semantically speaking they behave like auxiliaries because they require complementation by other verbs.

Another problematic categorization in Declerck is egressive aspect (2006: 31, 2007: 52), which he also subsumes under imperfective aspect. Egressive aspect refers to the end of an action as in *he finished painting*[31]. The whole problem with Declerck's conceptualization of perfective and imperfective is his conceptualization of the totality of action:

> "Following Comrie (1976), we speak of *imperfective aspect* when the speaker uses a verb form which explicitly refers to the internal temporal structure of the situation, i.e., a verb form which does not refer to the entire situation, but only to its beginning, middle or end."
>
> Declerck 2007: 53

Declerck misinterprets Comrie by saying that *imperfective aspect* is present in a verb form which refers only to the beginning, middle or end. If it refers specifically to a certain phase of action, particularly its beginning or end then we cannot speak of imperfective aspect on the grounds of logic (I am being careful about using the word logic, as we know that language is not logical, but here we are discussing language at a different level). Referring to the beginning or the end of an action, a specific point in time is conceptualized, therefore the action is perfective.

According to *Duden Grammatik*, the perfective has two subspecies: (1) inchoative or ingressive verbs, which refer to the moment of entering into a state (e.g. *erblassen* 'turn pale'), and (2) resultative verbs (e.g. *erschlagen* 'kill') (Binnick 1991: 145). However, Binnick is able to see the dual nature of ingressive aspect in English when he discusses the characteristics of perfectives in different languages, including Comrie's suggestion that there are counterexamples to all these characteristics:

> [3] Ingressive (inchoative) meaning. Often the perfective refers to the commencement of an action or state, while the imperfective views it as in progress; but it is perfectly possible to use verbs such as *begin* and *start* in the imperfective, and generally a perfective verb makes no reference to the commencement of an action.
>
> (Binnick 1991: 154)

If ingressive aspect refers to an action of entry into a state, then it has much in common with resultative aspect. This situation in semantics is reminiscent of the case of *the glass is half empty* and *the glass is half full*. Consider the following example:

(106) *The sky turned black.*

What kind of aspectual meaning do we have here? Is it ingressive, because we have a change of state, or is it resultative because the result is the sky being black? Do we refer to the beginning or the end of a situation? I would argue that it is a bit of both. But in either case, the meaning is perfective, and therefore both ingressive and resultative should be considered subtypes of perfective aspect.

---

[31] Another problem with Declerck is his telicity test with *finish/complete* (2007: 55). Besides saying that *write* is an atelic verb (when in fact telicity is the quality of situations rather than verbs), he claims that *He will finish writing tonight* is not a possible/acceptable sentence in English, thus bringing his diagnostic test into question.

2.10.5 Bounded vs. Non-bounded

The distinction or opposition between *bounded* and *non-bounded* is often used as synonymous with *telic* and *atelic* in the literature (e.g. Verkuyl 1972, Declerck 1979, Dahl 1981, Croft & Cruse 2004: 71 etc). However, Declerck (2007: 60) proposes "that these two distinctions represent two quite different parameters". He changed his mind 18 years later as he believes that telicity is lexical aspect expressed by means of verb phrases (or "situation templates" as he calls them), whereas boundedness is a matter of actualization aspect which is expressed on the level of clauses.

This way we have three different levels of aspect which all have in common some natural end-point that gives rise to the opposition. These oppositions are realized on three different levels: the grammatical level (perfective – imperfective opposition), the lexical level (telic – atelic opposition) and actualization level (bounded – non-bounded opposition). He illustrates these different levels using the example of the verb *run*, whose lexical meaning is atelic, i.e. does not involve a natural or arbitrary endpoint (Declerck 2007: 61). However, in the phrase *run five miles,* the aspectual meaning shifts from atelic to telic because *five miles* is the endpoint which alters the inherent lexical meaning of the verb. This phrase can have two different actualizations at a clausal level, as the following examples show:

(107) *Bill ran five miles. (bounded)*

(108) *Bill was running five miles. (non-bounded)*

These two examples show two different possibilities how phrase level aspect can be affected by the clause level aspect. The progressive aspect changes the lexical aspect of the phrase *run five miles.* In other words, lexical aspect turns out to be subordinate to grammatical aspect.

However, distinguishing these three levels of aspect is not important in a language that does not grammaticalize progressive aspect like Modern English does today. Therefore, distinguishing boundedness and telicity will not play a major role in an analysis of Old English since it did not have the progressive as expressed in number (108).

2.10.6 Mustanoja's categories

In his account of aspect in Middle English, the Finnish linguist Mustanoja (1960: 445-449) makes use of basically all the aspectual terminology imported from Slavic languages. He does note, however that

> "In the Germanic and Romance languages the term 'aspect' means something entirely different from what it means in the Slavonic languages, where the contrast between the imperfective and perfective aspects is a feature running through the whole verbal system. […] The idea of aspect in the non-Slavonic

languages is largely incommensurable with the idea behind the Slavonic term."

(Mustanoja 1960: 445-446fn)

This was a very clever move on the part of Mustanoja. Explaining it in this way at the very beginning spared him much of the criticism that other authors received. He does not make distinctions between grammatical and lexical aspect but is one of the few scholars who attempted to present the functions of prefixes as forming a system of aspect. His categories are presented in table 15.

Category	Description	Example
Perfective	attention on the completion of an activity; indicated by preverbs	*a-* in *awacian, arisan* *for-* in *fordon* *ge-* in *geascian* 'discover'
Imperfective or Durative	showing an activity as ongoing	simple present tense periphrasis *be* + *-inde* (*-ende*, later *-ing*)
Ingressive or Inchoative	attention on the beginning of the activity	*gin, begin, fon, wurthe*
Egressive, Effective or Terminative	attention on the moment when an activity comes to an end	*be-, for-, i-, to-* and verbs like *blin* and *cease*
Iterative	indicating recurrent and habitual activity	*used to* construction
Causative	bringing out the non-spontaneous character of the activity	*do, gan, let, make*
Intensive	expressing the emphatic, intensive character of the activity	*for-* and *of-* (*forhungred, ofhungred*)

Table 15
Mustanoja's aspectual categories in Middle English
(adapted from Mustanoja 1960: 445-449)

2.10.7 Conclusion

There is nothing wrong with adopting the terminology from descriptions of other languages, as long as one is aware of "the excess baggage" or the conceptual and formal differences between those two languages. Perfectivity is specific in Slavic, just like telicity is specific in French, where they originally come from. But still, the meaning of these concepts can be stretched in order to accommodate the phenomena found in different stages of the English language.

This is in fact my transition to the second avenue of research, that of particles and preverbs, which has also generated a substantial amount of literature.

Chapter 3
Previous Studies of Prefixed Verbs and Phrasal Verbs

This study is in many ways a follow-up to the works of De la Cruz (1972a, 1975), Hiltunen (1983), Brinton (1988), Petré (2005) and Elenbaas (2007). They have identified many areas and gaps where further research is needed. Their findings have been outlined in this chapter.

3.1 De la Cruz (1972, 1975)

Juan M. De la Cruz wrote a doctoral dissertation entitled *Origins and Development of the Phrasal Verb to the End of the Middle English Period* in 1969, which has not been published and was unfortunately unavailable to me. However, presumably his most important findings were published in a series of articles in 1972 and 1975. Scholars such as Hiltunen and Brinton, who worked on this topic a decade later, actually follow up on his work as the most important work in the field, which is evidenced by the highest number of citations in all subsequent research.

In 1972 De la Cruz published the article entitled "The Origins of the Germanic Phrasal Verb" in which he discusses how the original Indo-European Phrasal Verb coalesced into a "preverbial consolidation". In other words, particles lost their autonomy and became prefixed to the verbal stem, thus leaving a phrasal system and entering a derivative system. Germanic is specific as a new kind of phrasal system surfaced. He starts with an analysis of Gothic where a decay of preverbs and adverbial development do not take place, whereas adverbial uses are already found. He distinguishes "two major groups of particles as elements of the Germanic Phrasal Verb: A) those which are also found as preverbs and prepositions (Indo-European consolidation), B) those whose forms answer to "new developments" altogether" (De la Cruz 1972a: 80). He is of course interested more in these 'new developments', but he also examines the development of Modern Germanic prepositions, particles and adverbs seeking parallels in other Indo-European languages such as Sanskrit, Greek, Irish and Russian amongst others.

De la Cruz published the article "Old English Pure Prefixes: Structure and Function" in 1975, which was the first systematic analysis of the functions that these seven verbal prefixes perform. In this article he calls *a-, be-, ge-, for-, of-, on-* and *to-* 'Old English pure prefixes' because they are "without an etymological prepositional counterpart or with an etymological prepositional counterpart which, however, differs widely in function" (1975: 47).

The group without an etymological prepositional counterpart includes the prefixes *a-, ge-, on-* and *to-,* whereas the group with an etymological prepositional counterpart includes the prefixes *be-, for-* and *of-*.

De la Cruz claims that the prefix *on-* corresponds to Gothic *and-* (Modern German *ent-*), while *to-* corresponds to Gothic *dis-* (Modern German *zer-*), and not to the etymological counterparts of the homonymous *on* and *to,* which would be the prepositional adverbs *ana* and *du* in Gothic (Modern German *an* and *zu*) respectively.

The prefixes *be-, for-* and *of-* have etymological counterparts functioning as prepositions but they

> "have markedly isolated themselves from the latter on functional grounds. These prefixes have come to perform quite specific morphosyntactic functions. We may say that their prepositional counterparts are also 'pure prepositions' in their abstract functions of dative, genitive, and agentive, respectively."
>
> (De la Cruz 1975: 47-8)

De la Cruz distinguishes between five functions of Old English pure prefixes which are not mutually exclusive, as can be seen in the table that he presents (1975: 49):

			literal	*Aktionsart*	government	gram. particles	Specialized lex. formative
			a	b	c	d	e
1	*to-*	apart	*tohlidan*	*toswellen* (ME)			
2	*a-*	out	*arisan*	*abeodan*			
3	*on-*	against	*onsacan*	*oncnawan*			*onsælan*
4	*ge-*	together		*gebidan*	*geridan*	*gedrifen* (participle)	
5	*for-*	round about, all over		*forbærnan*	*forlicgan*	*forwakyd* (ME participle)	
6	*of-*	away from		*offylan*	*offeran*	*offered* (ME participle)	
7	*be-*	around	*bewindan*	*betimbran*	*beniman*		

Table 16
The functions of Old English pure prefixes
(from De la Cruz 1975: 49)

These functions are:
a) adding the literal spatial meaning of the prefix,
b) adding intensive/perfective aktionsart,
c) transitivization or change of object,
d) specialization as markers of past participles (mainly *ge-, for-* and *of-*).
e) specialized lexical formative (only *on-* as a reversative particle).

It should be noted that the function of adding intensive or perfective aktionsart (i.e. the aspectual function) is the only one that can be performed by all the seven Old English pure prefixes. The remainder of the article is basically a description of functions of each of the seven prefixes with countless examples.

Two important methodological contributions of De la Cruz's article should also be mentioned here, which were later elaborated upon in the work of Hiltunen and Brinton. First, De la Cruz perused different versions of the Anglo-Saxon Gospels to verify the interchangeability of prefixes. They include the following combinations (De la Cruz 1975: 77):

ge/be/Ø, ge/a, ge/Ø, for/ge, for/Ø, be/ge, a/for, a/to, Ø/ge, Ø/a/ge

Second, De la Cruz compared a Middle English text (*Ancrene Riwle*) with its translation into Modern English (by Morton from 1853) to see which particles have replaced which prefixes. The results are presented in table 17:

ge- = up / out	*i clumben / climbed up* *i streihte / outstretched up*
for- = up / away / off	*uorswoluweð / swallowed up* *uoruet / frets away* *vorworpen / cast away* *uor'keoruen / cut off*
be- = up / away / off	*bilepped 7 bihud / wrapped up* *binimen / take away* *bileauen / leave off*
to- = up /out / away / off	*to blowen / blown up* *tospret / stretches out* *tofleoted / flits away* *towarpled / shaken off*
a- = up / out / away	*adruweð / drieth up* *a cwen-chen / put out* *avleieð / driveth away* *a vleied / driven away*

Table 17
A complementary perspective of
Early English prefixed verbs and Modern English phrasal verbs
(adapted from De la Cruz 1975: 77-78)

Another article by De la Cruz is entitled "A Syntactical Complex of Isoglosses in the North-Western End of Europe" (1972) in which he rules out the theory of Scandinavian influence in regard to the similarity between the passive prepositional structures in Scandinavian and English, as well as the phrasal verb system. He rules it out on the grounds that other Germanic languages do not have this structure. Rather, he proposes the hypothesis of "a Celtic substratum common both to English and the Scandinavian languages". Prepositional verbs similar to those in English and Scandinavian do exist in Celtic, for example in relative clauses (De la Cruz 1972b: 175):

(109)*Nil leabhar agam le caint faoi.*
'I have no book to talk about'

(110)*Is leabhar deas é seo le caint faoi.*
'This is a nice book to talk about.'

Also in interrogative clauses:

(111) *Caidé atá tu ag caint faoi?*
'What are you talking about.'

In Norwegian:

(112) *Jeg hadde ingenting å lete etter i skapet.*
'I had nothing to look for in the cupboard.'

The German counterparts of this pattern are very different:

(113) *Ich habe keine Feder, um damit zu schreiben.*
'I have no pen to write with.'

(114) *Dies ist ein gutes Haus, um darin zu wohnen.*
'This is a nice house to live in.'

Hiltunen dismisses De la Cruz's suggestion that the phrasal verb derived from Celtic, even though De la Cruz's isoglosses are convincing evidence. Hiltunen claims that

> "it is essentially a Germanic development, one of which the English language has made more use than any of the related languages"
>
> (Hiltunen 1983: 44).

3.2. Hiltunen (1983)

Risto Hiltunen's *The Decline of the Prefixes and the Beginnings of the English Phrasal Verb* (1983) is the first systematic elaboration of the development of phrasal verbs in English and the decline of prefixed verbs based on a representative sample of prose texts. It presents a detailed analysis of the system of verbal prefixes in Old English which had been undergoing considerable weakening due to the lack of stress and lack of semantic content. Hiltunen also showed that parallel to this decline, a different morpho-syntactic system was emerging, the English phrasal verb. Hiltunen provides evidence that the phrasal verb was well established already in Old English.

Hiltunen shows that p-V order is more common in Old English but V-p order increases steeply from Late Old English to early Middle English. He finds the rapid decline of prefixes and sudden rise of particles in early Middle English remarkable (Hiltunen 1983: 92) but emphasizes on several occasions that phrasal verbs did not develop metaphorical and idiomatic meanings until late Middle English (Hiltunen 1983: 148-9, 190, 223).

Hiltunen considers that the shift from prefix to particle was caused by the interaction of the semantic weakening and grammaticalization of the prefixes and the availability of phrasal forms of greater expressiveness.

Hiltunen also investigates the factors that determine the position of the phrasal and prepositional adverbs in the clause. In terms of semantics, he is concerned with relational meaning between the components of phrasal constructions.

In order to put the English constructions in a chronological and genetical perspective, Hiltunen briefly discusses the corresponding constructions in some Indo-European languages such as Sanskrit, Greek, Latin, Gothic, German and Scandinavian.

Sanskrit is often taken as the best example of Indo-European background as it preserved more features of Proto-Indo-European than any other documented Indo-European language. In Sanskrit, the preverb is not the same as a verbal prefix as it can be freely detached from the verb and could take place in any position the sentence as an adverb. In fact, the preverb is thought to have an adverbial origin (Kuryłowicz 1964: 171).

Many authors assume that English borrowed the phrasal verb from Old Norse as there is a similar structure in Old Norse, or that Old Norse influenced the development of English in some way. This hypothesis is supported by the fact that Old Norse was much more advanced in the analytical phrasal constructions as well as the Viking invasions that led to large-scale Scandinavian settlements in Britain. However, no scholar has been able to prove it. The actual borrowing theory was dismissed when relevant syntactic patterns were found in early Old English texts. What Hiltunen does believe is that

> "Scandinavian phrasal constructions acted as catalysts, stimulating the development of the post-verbal type, and thereby contributed to the loss of prefixes in English".

(Hiltunen 1983: 43)

No conclusive evidence can be provided as the first Old Norse written documents appeared only two centuries later than the phrasal verb first appeared in English.

Like Lindemann (1970) and Horgan (1980), Hiltunen (1983: 55) notes that prefixes are interchangeable and dedicates most of his Chapter One to prefix variation, based on his comparison of different Old English translations of three Latin texts (*Gregory's Dialogue, The Gospel of St. Mark* and the *Anglo-Saxon Chronicle*). The most notable free prefix variation is that between the prefixes *ge-* and *a-*, as well as variation between a verb prefixed with *ge-* and the simplex verb. Hiltunen claims that the reason for this is the lack of semantic content of *ge-* and *a-*. Other prefixes do not exhibit such variation, although *ge-* alternates with other prefixes such as *be-, for-, on-* or *to-*, but not as frequently as with *a-*. Hiltunen assumes that the following rule applies:

> "one prefix can be substituted for another only if the contents of the two are not contradictory, i.e. there must be at least a partial overlap between the items."

(Hiltunen 1983: 84)

Hiltunen's Chapter Two deals with the breakdown of the Old English prefix system. This is how he describes the transition into Middle English:

> "Right from the first pages of *Ancr*, for instance, one cannot avoid the impression of the prefixes having been swept away almost overnight. The suddenness of the change is remarkable in view of the longish and stable OE period"

(Hiltunen 1983: 92)

With Early Middle English texts it was not possible to examine the interchangeability of inseparable prefixes as in Old English within one and the same text or in different editions of the same text. Not only is the Early Middle English period shorter, but the decline of the prefixes appears to be particularly uniform. Hiltunen also takes another factor into account, which is the consequence of an earlier development. It takes a while before a linguistic change also materializes in the written language, which is the more conservative medium (Hiltunen 1983: 92).

Hiltunen, much like De la Cruz, puts down the semantic weakening of the Old English prefixes to the fading of locative, aspectual and intensifying meanings.

> "It is difficult to draw a line between the locative meaning of *a-* ('out') and the lexical meaning of the verb (cf. *aberan, arisan, aseon, asmeagan* and the like). Also the fact that *a-*, along with *ge-, for-* and *of-*, is used with verbs that do not presuppose any locative meanings, points at a weakening of their content."
>
> (Hiltunen 1983: 95)

Hiltunen (1983: 95-96) discusses four examples where Latin verbs with a parallel translation into English which show that the scribes were confused as to which Old English forms to choose to translate the Latin verbs. On a superficial reading we could interpret the prefix *ge-* as expressing perfectivity, but on a closer look, *ge-* behaves like other prefixes, conveying a perfective meaning only sporadically. Hiltunen shows how the scribes had to resort to more explicit means in order to express perfectivity, such as phrasal and prepositional adverbs which often co-occurred with some prefixes, such as

(115) *quem viri Domini Fortunatus expulissit*
þe se drihtnes wer Furtunatus ær onweg adraf
þe ... ær ut adraf
(Hiltunen 1983: 98, example 20)

A similar case happens with the prefix *for-*, whose prototypical meaning is that of intensification. Hiltunen shows a variation of the prefix with a full lexical adverb *hetelice* 'hatefully, violently' in the following example:

(116) *ita ut in eum minibus excederit*
þæt he hine mid his handum forbeah
þæt he hine mid his handum hetelice beot
(Hiltunen 1983: 97, example 19)

Hiltunen concludes that

> "intensification may have had an indirect influence on the development of analytical constructions, for intensifiers have a tendency to fade after a while, and new, stronger expressions are needed to replace the faded meanings."
>
> (Hiltunen 1983: 97)

He argues that the prefix variation points to an inefficiency of a system that was bound to collapse as a new system was emerging, that of the phrasal verb.

> "In structuralist terms, the 'functional load' of the prefixes grew too heavy, and practically the whole system was replaced by another system in ME"
>
> (Hiltunen 1983: 97)

Even though this replacement process lasted throughout the Middle English period, the system of verb prefixation proved to be inadequate by the beginning of the Early Middle English period according to Hiltunen's results (1983: 97), but it took a while for the system to collapse. Hiltunen stresses that "the decay of the inseparable prefixes ties in with the overall development of English at the time"(1983: 101), namely the establishment of the SVO syntax, so it should not "be seen as an isolated process of waning and wearing out, but as part of the changing systems" (ibid.). Hiltunen sums up that

> "further research into larger corpora along these lines is needed to determine to what extent the tendencies noticed in the present material are valid in other texts, and to gain a better understanding of the manifold processes (lexical, semantic and syntactic in nature) leading to the abandonment of the OE prefix-morphology as a productive means of word-formation in subsequent stages of the English language."
>
> (Hiltunen 1983: 101)

Parts II, III and IV of Hiltunen (1983) deal extensively with a syntactic and semantic description of particles in Late Old and Early Middle English, focusing on the emergence of the phrasal verb pattern. In his treatment of the rise of the phrasal verb, Hiltunen is concerned with the interplay between element-order and the position of the phrasal adverb. He also thinks that other factors influenced the development of the phrasal verb, such as the form of the verb (tense and mood) and the verb's surrounding elements (those that come before, between and after the verb).

3.3 Brinton (1988)

Laurel Brinton's *The Development of English Aspectual Systems. Aspectualizers and post-verbal particles* (1988) is the most comprehensive work on the subject and in all probability the most important book for the present research since the aim is to investigate aspectual preverbs and post-verbal particles. Brinton examines them at length and sees them as belonging to a lexical or secondary system of aspect marking in English. Her book has received mixed scholarly reviews (Allen 1990, Dahl 1990, Declerck 1990, Diensberg 1992, Traugott 1990), as this complex topic raises a number of controversial issues, but it is nevertheless groundbreaking in terms of offering an original discussion of the systems that mark aspect in English, both from a synchronic and a diachronic point of view. It is not only a notable contribution to the theory of aspect, but also to the diachronic development of the English language.

In the preface Brinton claims that "there is a strong empirical orientation" (1988: XI) but her study is not based on a corpus, for which she has been criticized, as well as for relying on secondary sources of her data and lacking a list of the sources quoted (Diensberg 1992: 191-194).

Brinton's treatise was published over 20 years ago at a time when cognitive linguistics established itself as the most propulsive and cohesive approach in many areas of linguistics. Obviously, much related research has been done in the meantime, so this study intends to compare the later findings with Brinton's to see how some of her claims and ideas can be updated. A very important theoretical framework associated with cognitive linguistics that was emerging at the time and developed into a mature framework in the mid-1990's is construction grammar, which is also mentioned in this discussion.

At the very beginning she states that aspect is one of the most difficult grammatical categories to define and consequently the object of study includes a wide variety of different linguistic phenomena. The study of aspect is particularly problematic in English,

> "since formal markers of aspect are not predominant in the verb – English is a 'tense', not an 'aspect' language – and since lexical markers of aspect do not appear to constitute a coherent system"
>
> (Brinton 1988: 1).

It is precisely this system, or better to say systems, that she tries to make coherent. According to Brinton, there are two well-developed aspectual systems in English. One system is aspect in the narrow sense, which Brinton regards as a subjective category or "the speaker's viewpoint or perspective on a situation" (1988: 3). The other system is aktionsart, which Brinton regards as an objective category or "an indication of the intrinsic temporal qualities of a situation" (1988: 3).

To account for this differentiation, Brinton adopts Kruisinga's (1931: 230-7) contrast grammatical vs. lexical aspect, according to which aspect is grammatical because it is expressed by the inflectional morphology and periphrases of the verb, whereas aktionsart is lexical because it is expressed by the verb's lexical meaning and its derivational morphology.

Brinton insists on a sharp and crucial distinction between aspect and aktionsart, claiming that much of the confusion in the discussion of aspect was caused due to the fact that they were not kept strictly apart. I would rather argue that even more confusion is caused because different authors differently interpreted the notion of aktionsart. Moreover, the present study argues that the distinction between aspect and aktionsart is rather blurred and fuzzy rather than clear-cut, which is a fundamentally different starting-point.

After a well-organized critical review of previous research on aspect, Brinton proposes an aspect model for English, consisting of five categories (perfective, imperfective, phase, habitual and perfect) and four subcategories (the imperfective category is subdivided into progressive and continuative, and the phase category is subdivided into ingressive and egressive) (Brinton 1998: 53).

CATEGORY	SUBCATEGORY	FORMAL MARKERS
1. perfective		simple forms
2. imperfective	progressive	*be* V *-ing*
	continuative	*continue to* V, V*-ing; keep on* V*-ing*
3. phase	ingressive	*start to* V, V*-ing; begin to* V, V*-ing*
	egressive	*stop* V*-ing; cease to* V, V*-ing; finish* V*-ing*
4. habitual		*(be) used to* V*; be accustomed to* V*; simple forms*
5. perfect		*have* V*-en*

Table 18
An aspect model for English (from Brinton 1988: 53)

Brinton also proposes an aktionsart model, which she originally presents in two charts, but for the purpose of understanding it as an integral hierarchy of binary oppositions, I have fused them into one chart:

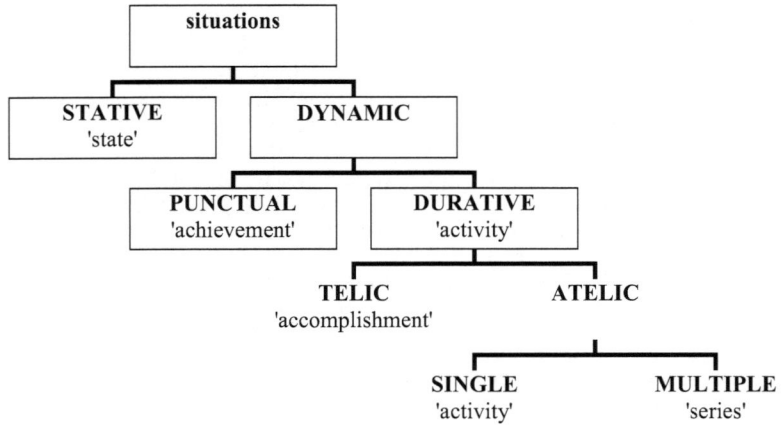

Table 19
An aktionsart model for English
(adapted from Brinton 1988: 54)

Brinton reminds us that the focus of attention in the studies of English aspect have traditionally been the progressive and perfect phrases for the simple reason that they are clear formal markers of aspect in English. But Brinton is trying to shift the focus from fully grammatical markers of aspect to partially grammaticalized markers, such as verb-particle combinations or phrasal verbs and aspectual semi-auxiliaries or aspectualizers.

In phrasal verbs, particles can add perfective meaning (e.g. *drink up, calm down*), ingressive meaning (e.g. *hurry up, lie down*) or continuative / iterative meaning (e.g. *hammer away, drive on*). Brinton claims that aspectualizers

> "form a somewhat better developed system for expressing aspectual distinctions, with ingressive forms such as *begin, start,* or *come* to do something, egressive ones such as *finish, quit, stop,* or *cease* doing something, and continuative / iterative ones such as *keep on, go on,* or *continue* doing something"
>
> (Brinton 1988: 4).

Brinton assumes that aspect studies have given little attention to aspectualizers because they have not reached full auxiliary status. She proposes that "from a semantic and functional perspective, aspectualizers should be seen as auxiliaries" (Brinton 1988: 74), although their syntactic characteristics are still not those of auxiliaries. In other words, there are two distinct trends in the studies of aspect, Brinton sums up (1988: 5),

> "one concentrates on the grammatical meaning of verbal forms, while the other concentrates on the lexical meaning of verbs and their complements".

Brinton touches upon the former in Chapter One, whereas the remainder of her book deals with the latter. Chapters Two and Three discuss aspectualizers synchronically and diachronically, arguing that they express aspect proper, while Chapters Four and Five are devoted to a synchronic and diachronic analysis of post-verbal particles, claiming that they express aktionsart. If the present study insisted on a distinction between aspect and aktionsart, it would argue that it is actually the other way round: aspectualizers express aktionsart because they do it by lexical means (employment of another verb) and post-verbal particles express aspect because they do it by grammatical means, as the meaning of particles has been grammaticalized. However, Brinton considers aspectualizers as grammatical rather than lexical to make her point that they are being grammaticalized from independent verbs into auxiliaries. She asserts that

> "the selection of particular verbs to become aspectualizers is not arbitrary, but is motivated by the spatial meanings of the verbs, the nature of the aspectual categories, and iconic principles of semantic change"
>
> (Brinton 1988: 57).

And indeed, there does seem to be a correlation between the spatial meanings of aspect categories and the semantics of the verbs that are grammaticalized as markers of aspect.

In her chapter on verb particles in Modern English, Brinton notes that particles in phrasal verbs are most commonly cited as having perfective meaning. However, she suggests that

> "the aspectual meaning of particles such as *up, down, off, over, out, through* and *away* is better understood as an aktionsart meaning – that of expressing the goal or endpoint of a situation"
>
> (Brinton 1988: 163).

In her exposition of the development from prefixed verbs to phrasal verbs in English, Brinton mainly relies on the findings of De la Cruz (1975) and Hiltunen (1983), claiming that evidence which Hiltunen provides is similar to her own, both supporting the view that phrasal verbs were well-established in Old English, although prefixes were predominant.

Brinton (1988: 190) briefly compares the accounts of the reasons for the shift from prefix to particle by Samuels (1972: 80-5, 163-5) and Hiltunen (1983: 94-8) and notes that there are some issues about the shift which neither Hiltunen nor Samuels deal with. These issues include the questions

> "why some prefixes have counterparts as particles and others do not, why new particles develop, what the meaning relationships are between prefixes and particles, and how and when non-spatial meanings develop in the prefixes and particles"
>
> (Brinton 1988: 191).

Brinton organized the following proposed explanations of the reasons for the shift from prefix to particle (1988: 189):
 a) the general analytic tendency of English
 b) the shift in word order from OV to VO
 c) the model of Old Norse, which had lost verbal prefixes at an early stage
 d) the lack of stress in the particles and subsequent loss of phonetic content
 e) the weakening of the meaning of the prefixes, their syncretism, and grammaticalization
 f) the development of adverbial functions in the particles
 g) the greater clarity and expressiveness of phrasal forms
 h) the tendency to shift meanings from literal to figurative

In the chapter dealing with semantic change in the verbal prefixes and particles, Brinton first explains bleaching and metaphor as mechanisms traditionally associated with the development of aspectual meanings in preverbs and particles. Brinton (1988: 193) believes that there are two aspects of the meaning of prefixes and particles that weaken the standard explanations of bleaching and metaphor.

The first objection is the co-existence of both concrete and non-concrete meanings in the same particle or preverb, e.g. Bolinger's (1971: 101) example *to grow up,* where *up* is both directional and perfective or De la Cruz's *ofthowed* = 'thawed away' or 'completely thawed' (1975: 56, 71, 75), where 'perfective aktionsart' co-exists with directional meaning. Brinton argues that such co-existence of meanings is not in accordance with the theory of bleaching, as there is no fading of one meaning to another.

Brinton's second objection to metaphor as a traditionally associated mechanism of semantic change seems to be unwarranted. She quotes Bolinger's conclusion that

> "phrasal verbs present a semantic gradient from highly concrete meanings of direction and position to highly abstract meanings akin to aspects"
>
> (Bolinger 1971: 110).

Brinton believes that a continuum from spatial to aspectual meanings argues against the theory of metaphorical change because, she claims that

> "metaphorical change involves a shift or transfer of meaning from one domain to another and should yield discrete meanings".
>
> (Brinton 1988: 193)

It is not clear why she thinks that a metaphorical change must result in discrete meanings. However, Brinton does find a good objection to both standard theories. They do not address the fundamental questions: how and why does the semantic change take place? These two questions on the motivation of semantic change sum up the gist of Traugott's (1982: 267) cognitively-minded questions

> "What is there about the spatial relationship of *up* that allows it to become a perfective particle? What is there about *on* that allows it to become a durative particle?"

Brinton thinks that Bolinger (1971) is on the right track to find answers to these questions by suggesting that for the particle *up*, "the primitive directional meaning was modified to the aspectual one by the direction that most physical acts of completion take" (1971: 98) and that "the purely aspectual sublimation of 'remaining in view' is 'continuation', or durative aspect, and this we find, especially with *on*" (1971: 107). Brinton (1988: 194) also says that Traugott (1978: 391-3) suggests that

> "terminative / resultative (telic) markers derive from terms denoting source (Engl. *out*, Got. *fra-* 'away', German *ver-, er-* [from Germanic **uz-* 'out'], *aus-* 'out'), goal, path (Engl. *through*, German *ver-*), and the vertical plane (Engl. *down, up, over, off*, German *auf-*), which presupposes sources and goals. Continuative or progressive markers derive from terms denoting contiguity or withinness (*in, at, on*)."
>
> (Traugott 1978: 388-90).

Basically, both views metaphorically analyse verbal events as spatial concepts, or the development of a situation corresponds to the movement of objects through space (Traugott 1978: 373).

3.4 Petré (2005)

Petré's (2005) thesis focuses on only two verbal prefixes, *be-* and *to-*, whose meanings primarily do not express aspectuality. His intention is to show how the internal structure of these prefixes has an important effect on their life span, which he does in depth by analysing this structure within the constructional framework of Goldberg (1995, 2006). His thesis is a study in morphological productivity and the factors that determine the life span of a prefix.

Petré takes issue with the traditional views that the inseparable prefixes were on the decline at the beginning of the written tradition because some of them have remained productive to this day. He notes that the question why some inseparable prefixes survived is more complex and therefore worth looking into than why others disappeared.

In this constructionally oriented approach, Petré shows prefixes as consisting of

> "networks of constructions, each of which has its own specific characteristics in terms of semantics, syntax, aspectuality and frequency. Some prefixes exhibit these characteristics more saliently. This degree of salience is directly related to the life span of a particular prefix"
>
> (Petré 2005: 1-2).

Petré argues that initially Germanic prefixes often had essentially different functions, being either like predicates, prepositions or adverbs, and in that way served different communicative or pragmatic purposes. He claims that the shift from OV to VO word order in English, or more generally, the general trend from a more synthetic to a more analytic type of language, is an external factor responsible for the breakdown of the OV-structured inseparable prefixes. He considers that

> "during this shift, it is mainly the combination of the four internal factors (semantics, aspectuality, syntax and frequency), being the result of an original difference in function, that will determine to what extent each prefix will be preserved in ME and afterwards".
>
> (Petré 2005: 5)

According to Petré, the problem with the 20th century approaches in the studies of inseparable prefixes is the tendency to look upon prefixes as a whole, while underestimating their semantic and structural differences. Petré organizes his critical evaluation of previous research into five different approaches (2005: 10-26), but stresses that it was only the last two that influenced his study:

1. External influences played a role in the decline of prefixes, such as the influence of Old French and Old Norse. For Old Norse there is not only a lack of written evidence from the critical period, but also a lack of scholarly consensus as to the influence on Old English.

2. The phonological approach aims to compare the phonological structure of the inseparable prefixes and offers phonotactic strength (Lutz 1997) as an explanation for different life spans of inseparable prefixes.

3. The lexicographical approach lists the properties of prefixes and is first applied in unsystematic attempts by Lenze (1909) and Bechler (1909), who tried to illuminate the internal structure of prefixes.

4. The interchangeability approach attributes the loss of prefixes to their increasing interchangeability in the Old English period. Studies such as Horgan 1980, Hiltunen 1983, Ogura 1994 and Ogura 1995 examine the weakened semantics of prefixes which results in the capacity of verbs to occur with two or more different prefixes in the same context. They ascribe their interchangeability to their breakdown.

5. The functional approach tries to expose the ultimate functions of prefixes that could have different effects on the life spans of the prefixes that perform these functions. Recent studies distinguish different functions of prefixes by applying the criterion of predicativity and non-predicativity. This distinction is important

for aspectuality, as both predicative prefixes and non-predicative route path prefixes add a telic aspect to verbs derived by prefixation, while a non-predicative destination path prefix maintains the atelic aspect of the verb to which it is attached. Petré stresses that one and the same prefix in principle takes different functions.

Petré gives two examples with the prefix *for-* where it adds perfective aspect (from Petré 2005: 16, his example 10):

(117)*Hæfde ða **forsiðod** sunu Ecgþeowes under gynne grund (Beo: 1550ff)*
   had   then ***for*-travelled** son of Ecgtheow under spacious ground
   'Then the son of Ecgtheow traveled amiss [i.e. perished] under spacious ground'

(118)*hi   heom sylfe ælc oðerne **forfore**. (ChronC [Rositzke]: 1052.34)*
   they themselves each other ***for*-fare** [destroy]
   'they destroyed each other.' (cf. De la Cruz 1975: 52-53)

By the Old English period, the prefix *for-* no longer seems to add the literal spatial meaning to verbs (function a), but performs the other three different functions proposed by De la Cruz (1975):
   (function b) adding perfective adding perfective / intensive aspect,
   (function c) transitivization or another change in valence structure,
   (function d) specialization as markers of past participles, mainly *ge-, for-* and *of-*.

Petré goes on to explain that the examples (a) and (b) seem to confirm De la Cruz's function categories. Neither example exhibits spatial meaning in the prefix. In both examples perfective aspect is added, while in (b) the prefix transitivized the verb. The simplex verb *siðan* 'travel' and its prefixed derivation *forsiðan* morphologically and aspectually correspond to the Croatian verb *putovati* whose prefixed derivation is *otputovati*. The prefix *for-* in Old English seems to have the same semantic function as the Croatian prefix *od-* 'away', whose allomorph is *ot-* in the case of the verb *putovati*.

Even though he finds the last two approaches useful, Petré thinks they still leave many things unexplained. He considers that a general account of the prefixes' functions offered by those two approaches is not sufficient in order to find out what caused such differences in the life spans of prefixes. The interchangeability approach, on the one hand, observed that some usages of spatial prefixes were replaced by phrasal particles way before other prefixes, but it does not explain why. The functional approach, on the other hand, fails to give an account for semantic extensions that were based on originally predicatively or non-predicatively structured prefixes. For these reasons, Petré sets out to analyse all possible differences between the functions of prefixes, both on the structural and the semantic level, proposing an approach that is encyclopaedic and systematic at the same time (2005: 26).

In the chapter that deals with the constructional properties of inseparable prefixes, Petré (2005: 27-56) explains how the meaning of constructions is independent of lexical items, giving as an example the aspectual meaning of particles in phrasal verbs as in *look up the information*. The prepositional or adverbial counterpart of *up* has a different meaning, as we can see in *the *information is up*. When grammatical templates such as **[verb]** *up* are filled with different lexical items such as the simplex verb *look*, new constructions can be formed. Petré assumes that this is what happened to inseparable prefixes. They lost their links with their independent counterparts (e.g. Old English *be-* vs. *be*) and sometimes they even died out (e.g. *to-* 'asunder'). He observes that non-predicative prefixes are productive longer than abstract predicative ones, since they were more salient during an early stage of their grammaticalization. Petré points out that a prefix can contain more than one construction, structured in a constructional network.

Petré develops a good model for studying other prefixes. He dedicates special attention to semantics and it is a constructionally oriented approach which views prefixes as constructions.

Constructions are form-meaning correspondences which also apply to morphemes, being the smallest units of meaning. Verbal prefixes should be looked upon as constructions, as they show a remarkable degree of regularity. Petré's thesis was written within the framework of construction grammar, dealing with the prefixes *be-* and *to-*. Petré's example of how prefixed verbs show some regularity can be seen in these two *be-*prefixed verbs:

(119) *benight* 'cover with night'
bespatter 'cover with spatters'

The preverbs from inseparable prefixed verbs, or let us call them inseparable prefix constructions, are commonly assumed to have had spatial meanings which gradually developed more abstract meanings that were related to the original spatial meaning. Petré also starts from this assumption in his thesis that happens to work for the prefix *be-*. However, if we go back to De la Cruz's article from 1975, "Old English Pure Prefixes: Structure and Function", which was the first systematic analysis of the functions that inseparable verbal prefixes perform, we will see one problem.

De la Cruz calls the seven prefixes *a-, be-, ge-, for-, of-, on-* and *to-* "Old English pure prefixes" as they are "without an etymological prepositional counterpart or with an etymological prepositional counterpart which, however, differs widely in function" (1975: 47). The group without an etymological prepositional counterpart includes the prefixes *a-, ge-, on-* and *to-*, whereas the group with an etymological prepositional counterpart includes the prefixes *be-, for-* and *of-*. De la Cruz claims that *on-* corresponds to Gothic *and-* (Modern German *ent-*), while *to-* corresponds to Gothic *dis-* (Modern German *zer-*), and not to the etymological counterparts of the homonymous *on* and *to*, which would be the prepositional adverbs *ana* and *du* in Gothic (Modern German *an* and *zu*) respectively. Thus, if the prefixes *a-, ge-* and *on-* and *to-* do not have a prepositional counterpart, what would be their original spatial meaning? This problem deserves careful consideration.

When construction grammar is used in diachronic research, then we speak of *diachronic construction grammar* which is currently being developed. Some of the works that deal with this new emerging theory of construction grammar include Noël 2007, Petré & Cuyckens 2008, Traugott 2008 and Trousdale 2008. However, the fact that not all meanings of prefixes can be regarded as constructions makes a thorough application of construction grammar questionable.

3.5 Elenbaas (2007)

Elenbaas's doctoral dissertation entitled *The Synchronic and Diachronic Syntax of the English Verb-Particle Combination* is divided into three parts. The first offers a detailed description of the verb-particle combination in Present-Day English, including a critical review of existing analyses. Her focus is on syntax, although semantic and morphological characteristics of the verb-particle combinations have also been touched upon in her overview.

The final chapter of the first part proposes a lexical decomposition analysis of the syntax of Present-Day English verb-particle combinations, arguing that they are ambiguous between head and phrase. Elenbaas suggests that particles are hybrid between head and phrase, supplying evidence from the syntactic, morphological and semantic features of verb-particle combinations. The separability of the verb and the particle as shown in the example below is for Elenbaas a conclusive proof that English verb particle combinations are phrases exhibiting a paradox between word-like behaviour and phrase-like behaviour:

(120)a. That hilarious anecdote **spiced up** his speech.
    b. That hilarious anecdote **spiced** his speech **up**.
(Elenbaas 2007: 81)

The two different word orders do not have a different meaning, which point to a mismatch between syntax and semantics. Elenbaas (2007: 84) generalizes that English verb-particle combinations have "a uniform event semantics" (with the exception of non-resultative VPCs containing the particles *on, along, away, around/about*, as she notes in a footnote.), expressing "a complex event which consists of an activity or process, denoted by the verb, and an endstate or –point, denoted by the particle", illustrating this with the following example:

(121)*The forester* **chopped** *the diseased trees* **down**.
        (activity) (affected object) (end result)
(from Elenbaas 2007: 84)

She also generalizes that "VPCs are typically change-of-state verbs, which are often resultative. Particles function as secondary predicates, and predicate over the object, which is understood as their (semantic) subject" (ibid.).

In her lexical decomposition approach (originally proposed in the work of Hale and Keyser 1993), semantic decomposition is directly reflected in syntactic structure. Her analysis takes into account the dual nature of verb-particle combination, which show both unit-like and phrasal behaviour, so she combines "the intuitions of complex predicate analysis (VPCs are units) and those of small clause analyses (VPCs are separable, particles are predicates)." (2007: 99)

The second and the third part of her dissertation are diachronic, focusing on the syntax of particles and prefixes in late Old English. Elenbaas discusses the prefix and the particle system and its position within the overall syntax of Old

English. She examines the inseparable and separable complex verbs and proposes their structural and semantic analysis.

In her discussion of Old English prefixes, Elenbaas (2007: 115) divides prefixes roughly into two groups based on rather dubious semantic criteria:

> "The group of Old English prefixes includes aspectual (or temporal) such as *be-* and *ge-* and spatial prefixes, such as *a-, ut-, for-, of-, to-, on-, þurh-/ðurh-, ymb-, wið-/wiþ-*."

Such a rough division into aspectual and spatial prefixes, with *be-* and *ge-* as the only aspectual prefixes simply does not do them justice. Most of these prefixes can take aspectual functions, and only one of four meanings of *be-* is aspectual, as the analysis in Petré (2005) shows.

She then treats the prefixes in alphabetical order, giving for each an average of two example sentences with glosses from her corpus that contain a prefixed verb. In this brief description, she often relies on the findings by Hiltunen (1983) or other authors.

Her analysis of Old English separable complex verbs is much more informative and illuminating. Elenbaas manages to prove that Old English particles are phrases which act as secondary predicates, backed up by Van Kemenade and Los (2003), who argue that inseparable and separable complex verbs share a common historical origin as predicates. They claim that their semantics typically encodes a change of state, adding "telic aktionsart, resulting in an accomplishment or an achievement" (Van Kemenade & Los 2003: 79).

Elenbaas's dissertation is syntactically oriented, which is perhaps the reason why her bibliography does not include Brinton's study (1988) or the articles by Juan de la Cruz (1975), which address similar questions from a semantic rather than a syntactic point of view.

Let me take one example how Elenbaas cautiously analyses the meaning of the prefix *a-*. She quotes Hiltunen's example of *aberan* 'carry, bear' who claims that the prefix *a-* adds no meaning at all to the verb *beran*, in other words that they are interchangeable. Elenbaas picks an example with *asendan* to make the same point, claiming that it is not clear what meaning, if any, *a-* in *asende* 'sent' adds to the verb:

(122) Þa **asende** he þone ylcan sunu to ðisum life to ure alysednysse
    then sent he the same son to this life to our redemption
"Then he sent the same son to this life to reedem us"

(from Elenbaas 2007: 116)

She also compares it with some Present-Day English VPCs in which the particle does not appear to add any semantic content to that of the verb and merely gives expressive force to the verb's meaning, e.g. *open up*.

The hedge phrase 'does not appear to add / alter' was certainly well used here, allowing for a possibility that there could be difference in meaning, but the author is uncertain. These are the kinds of uncertainties that this study further investigates.

In my opinion, the difference in meaning both with *open up* vs. *open* and *asendan* vs. *sendan* is that of a subtle aspectual nuance. The prefix *a-* is a perfectivizer of *sendan* which is an imperfective verb, as opposed to *asendan*, which would be its perfective opposite, if we force the Slavic aspectual dichotomy to the English verbal system. As for *open* vs. *open up,* the particle 'up' does add the notion of an instantaneous action to the verb

3.6 Synchronic research of verb-particles

Verb-particles have only relatively recently attracted much attention in linguistics. So much has been written in the past few decades that it is impossible to give a complete overview of synchronic research, so it will not be presented in such detail as the overview of diachronic research. In fact, only the works that shaped the ideas of the present discussion are mentioned.

Verb-particles form lexical units with verbs known as particle verbs or phrasal verbs[32]. Early grammarians reluctantly dealt with phrasal verbs, as they did not fit traditional description models that had been taken over from Latin and Greek where no such verb construction existed (Hiltunen 1994: 130). Phrasal verbs have also often been left out from lexical studies, as they "do not always have the grammatical and semantic integrity of a single word" (Nevalainen 1999: 423).

There have been many discussions about the status of the verb-particle and the part of speech that it belongs to. In addition to prepositions and adverbs, Bolinger (1971: 23-44) proposed *adprep* as another category for the particle, which he coined based on clipping *adverb* and *preposition* and then blending them into one word. Other exponents of Bolinger's proposal for an additional part of speech include Sroka (1972) and O'Dowd (1998) as they also observed the particle's dual nature, behaving both as an adverb and as a preposition. Chomsky does not see the importance of this word's part-of-speech status, so he simply uses the term *particle* (1957: 75-76). Traditional grammarians regard it as an adverb, such as Kennedy (1920) or Baugh (1957:401). Gerhard Dietrich (1960) wrote a 173-page book on this subject (*Adverb oder Präposition?*) and concluded (1960: 165) that it is difficult to make a distinction.

Previous attempts to apply traditional methods in semantic analysis of phrasal verbs did not yield the best results (Morgan 1997: 327). For this reason, many linguists rather focused on their syntax. Some scholars, such as Dixon (1991) gave up looking for systematicity in the semantics of phrasal verbs, regarding them as arbitrary and idiosyncratic (Bolinger 1971). However, there are authors like Susan Lindner (1983), Pamela Morgan (1997) and Brygida Rudzka-Ostyn (2003) who managed to contribute significantly to the account of the semantic systematicity of particle verbs.

Traditional approaches to teaching English as a foreign language typically labelled phrasal verbs as 'idiomatic' or that it is not possible to understand them on the basis of their constituent elements, so they had "to be learned one by one,

---

[32] The term *phrasal verb* was first used in 1925 by L.P. Smith in the essay *English Idioms* (Sroka 1972:17). Other terms include *verb-adverb combination* (Kennedy 1920), *compound verbs* (Kruisinga 1931), *discontinuous verbs* (Live 1965), *verb-particle construction* (Lipka 1972), *verb-particle combination* (Fraser 1976), *particle verbs* (McIntyre 2001, Dehé et al. 2002, Cappelle 2005).

an arduous, time-consuming and not very rational task" (Rudzka-Ostyn 2003: 3). Particle verbs have always been considered the most difficult part of English lexicon. According to Rudzka-Ostyn, a cognitive analysis of particle verbs can make their learning process much easier. This avenue of research was taken up by Geld (2009) who examined Croatian and Mexican learners' strategic construals[33] of particle verbs whose function ranges from expressing topology to verbal aspect.

One of the most important recent studies of verb-particles is Cappelle (2005), whose last but lengthiest chapter deals with aspectual impact of particles on event structure. The first part of the chapter addresses some common misconceptions of particles' aspectual properties, whether particles can express perfective aspect or if they are markers of telicity, or that only directional particles are resultative. Further, he divides particles into relatively pure aspectual particles and semi-aspectual particles. The relatively pure aspectual particles include examples such as *on* as in *chatter on* (continuative) or *up* as in *touch up your look* (resultative). The semi-aspectual particles include *back* as in *talk back* (reciprocal), *down* as in *calm down* (decrimental), *off* as in *be pissed off* (exasperation), *out* as in *pass out* (unusual mental state), *away* as in *dance the night away* (the "time" - *away* construction).

Cappelle challenges the views that particles express telicity and proposes that *up* is a resultative particle (2005: 423), although it does act as a telicizer of consumption verbs such as *eat up, drink up, munch up* etc.

Another important discussion of the verb-particle construction can be found in a recent study by Thim (2012), whose main concern is to "examine the actual degree of Englishness of the phrasal verb" (2012: 247), taking into account comparative and cross-linguistic perspectives. Thim's study is also valuable for its historical overview of the syntactic, semantic and word-formational properties of the phrasal verb, as well as a discussion of preverbs (2012: 75-89).

To round off the overview of previous research, let me just say that I think it is no coincidence that a synchronic discussion of English verb-particle construction is the last topic in the seminal books of two of the most prominent linguists of the 20th century: Chomsky (1965) and Langacker (1987).

As well known, Chomsky tried to divorce the lexicon from grammar, but at the end of *Aspects of the Theory of Syntax* (1965) he acknowledged that his vision of grammar runs into problems when the verb-particle construction in question.

> is possible that we are approaching here the fringe of marginal cases, to be expected in a system as complex as a natural language, where significant schematization is just not possible."
>
> (Chomsky 1965: 192)

Langacker also deals with the verb-particle construction at the end of his book, almost as if to show to Chomsky that verb-particles are no fringe of marginal cases but a case in point which proves that

> there is no meaningful distinction between grammar and lexicon. Lexicon, morphology, and syntax form a continuum of symbolic structures, which

---

construals are meaning construals in a foreign language.

> differ along various parameters but can be divided into separate components only arbitrarily."
>
> (Langacker 1987: 3)

The collapse of the strict boundary between grammar and lexicon has already been discussed in the distinction between grammatical and lexical aspect. However, it needs to be stressed that this does not mean that there are no strictly grammatical phenomena or strictly lexical phenomena, or that grammar or lexicon as such do not exist. The point is that grammar and lexicon *form a continuum* of linguistic knowledge.

Chapter 4
Theoretical Foundations and Methodology

In this chapter I will discuss the theoretical assumptions that underlie the analysis presented in this book. A great deal of aspect-related theoretical frameworks and problems have already been discussed in chapter 2, so this chapter will deal with those theoretical foundations that have not previously been discussed. These are grammaticalization theory and lexicalization theory.

4.1 Grammaticalization (and Lexicalization) Theory

The grammaticalization theory as expounded in the textbooks such as Lehmann (2002 [1982, 1995]) and Hopper & Traugott 2003 [1993] seems to offer a good descriptive framework for accounting for changes in grammar. This theory has its origins in the 18th century (Heine et al. 1991: 5ff and Lindström 2004: 39ff).

It has to be stressed that grammaticalization is a theory only in the sense that it helps to explain "how and why grammatical categories arise and develop" (Heine 2003: 578), but much like cognitive linguistics is not a theory but rather an approach to language, in a similar vein

> "Grammaticalization theory is neither a theory of language nor of language change; its goal is to describe grammaticalization, that is, the way grammatical forms develop through space and time, and to explain why they are structured the way they are"
>
> (Heine 2003: 575)

In other words, it is a research framework with a tradition that has been culminating in the past three decades, parallel to and often in conjunction with cognitive linguistics. In fact, grammaticalization theory can be situated within the framework of cognitive linguistics, as the process of grammaticalization is considered to be cognitively motivated.

According to Lehmann (1982: 8), the theory of grammaticalization evolved from Indo-European historical linguistics and language typology, but the term *grammaticalization* was coined by Meillet in 1912. The most widely accepted definition is that by Kuryłowicz:

> "Grammaticalization consists in the increase of the range of a morpheme advancing from a lexical to a grammatical or from a less grammatical to a more grammatical status, e.g. from a derivative formant to an inflectional one."
>
> (Kuryłowicz, 1965: 69)

In the next paragraph, Kuryłowicz goes on to define lexicalization, "A reverse process is the *lexicalization* of a morpheme" (ibid.), but the reverse process today is better captured by the term *degrammaticalization* (Norde 2009: 8-9, 106ff), as lexicalization can also be used synchronically for any process of word formation and diachronically to five different types of phenomena (Brinton &

Traugott 2005: 20-21). When the term *lexicalization* is used in this study, what is assumed follows the definition proposed by Brinton and Traugott:

> "Lexicalization is the change whereby in certain contexts speakers use a syntactic construction or word formation as a new contentful form with formal and semantic properties that are not completely derivable or predictable from the constituents of the construction or the word formation pattern. Over time there may be further loss of internal constituency and the item may become more lexical."
>
> (Brinton and Traugott 2005: 96)

The standard or prototypical example of grammaticalization in English is the construction *be going to,* a motion verb which developed into a future auxiliary. This example exhibits all characteristics which are typical of grammaticalization, such as phonological reduction (*going to* > *gonna*), syntactic reduction (from a full verb to a kind of auxiliary) and semantic change (from a verb with lexical content to a grammatical marker), while at the same time the directional meaning of *be going to* has not died out, i.e. it still co-exists today. Furthermore, its cross-linguistic co-occurrence has been noted in a number of languages (e.g. French *aller* or Dutch *gaan*).

Typical examples of lexicalization include the processes of univerbation (combining several words into one word) such as *garlic* (OE *gar* 'spear' + *leac* 'leek') or *handicap* (*hand in the cap*) and fusion (loss of original morphological boundaries) such as *goodbye* (*God be with you*) or *lord* (< OE *hlaf* 'loaf' + *weard* 'guardian'). Two processes that typically accompany lexicalization are demotivation (the loss of identifiable compositional form) and idiomaticization (the loss of identifiable compositional meaning) (Brinton & Traugott 2005: 69).

Grammaticalization and lexicalization share a number of features, which is why it is sometimes difficult to distinguish them (much like the difference between metaphor and metonymy in cognitive linguistics). Both processes involve some kind of reduction, fusion, coalescence, gradualness, demotivation, metaphorization and metonymization (Traugott and Brinton 2005: 105-106).

Some of the examples include *today* (< OE *to* + *dæge*) or *maybe* (*may* + *be*), or the adverbializer *–ly* (< OE *lic* 'body'). There are many instances of derivational morphology that different researchers conceptualize differently. However, there is a list of features that are characteristic only of grammaticalization, such as decategorialization, bleaching, subjectification, productivity, frequency and typological generality (Traugott and Brinton 2005: 107-109).

Grammaticalization theory proves to be a suitable framework for the study of verbal prefixes, as they are, like verbs of motion, likely to undergo grammaticalization because of their high frequency, wide range of meanings, conceptual saliency and propensity to take on metaphorical meanings, particularly the all-pervasive time-as-space metaphor. Verbal prefixes grammaticalize as aspectual markers along similar or even same paths independently not only in Slavic and Germanic languages, but also in genetically unrelated and geographically separated languages.

Some studies of verbal within this framework in Dutch include Van der Auwera 1999 and Blom 2005, where Givón's slogan "Today's morphology is yesterday's syntax" (1971: 413) generally applies.

Van der Auwera (1999) examined grammaticalized and lexicalized meanings of verbal prefixes in Dutch, such as the prefix *ver-* as in the following examples (1999: 128-130):

(123) *ver-'branden*
    PRE-burn
    "burn down"

(124) *ver-'jagen*
    PRE-hunt
    "chase away"

(125) *ver-'dwijnen*
    PRE-?
    "disappear"

One and the same prefix may be productive in one meaning but non-productive in another. In the first example (123), the prefix *ver-* exhibits a meaning that is productive in Dutch, and therefore we can say that this meaning of *ver-* is grammaticalized. The second example (124) contains the prefix *ver-* in a less transparent meaning, so it is not productive. Therefore, we can say this meaning of *ver-* is lexicalized, as it falls outside the predictable patterns or rules of grammar. The third example (125) illustrates a situation where the semantic contribution of the prefix to the verb as a whole is not compositional at all and the resulting combination of the prefix and the verb is idiosyncratic (van der Auwera 1999: 130), even though the prefix in (125) is more transparent than the prefix in (124).

We see that productivity coincides with grammaticalization and semantic transparency, whereas non-productivity overlaps with lexicalization and lack of semantic transparency.

Van der Auwera observed that productivity and transparency also correlate with separability of prefixes to a large extent[34]. This points to an analytic tendency of Dutch in terms of typological development, as semantically analysable prefixes gain more syntactic freedom, whereas the inseparable ones remain fused or univerbized with the root, often fading into petrification or fossilization. This is comparable to what happened to the prefixes such as *a-* and *ge-* in earlier stages of the English language.

Van der Auwera (1999) and Blom (2005)'s insights from their study of Dutch prefixes are quite heuristic and can easily be transferred to the study of prefixes in Old English.

---

[34] Blom, however, does not think that the loss of spatial meaning is a necessary or sufficient condition for a prefix to become inseparable (2005: 72). Nevertheless, semantic transparency does not need to correspond to absence or presence of spatial meaning.

4.2 Methodological Tools

Little needs to be said about corpus linguistics as an indispensable tool in present-day research in historical linguistics. "Empirically based textual research is a *sine qua non* of historical linguistics", to use a frequently quoted opening sentence by McEnery and Wilson (2001: 123). They say that historical linguistics can also be seen more specifically as a species of corpus linguistics, which is, of course, a hyperbole used to emphasize the importance of using corpora in diachronic linguistics.

For the purpose of this research I have used two basic corpora. For Old English, it was *The York-Toronto-Helsinki Parsed Corpus of Old English Prose* (YCOE). For Middle English, the *Penn-Helsinki Parsed Corpus of Middle English, 2nd edition* (PPCME2)[35]. The concordancing programme used to search the corpora was *Abundantia Verborum* (AV). The two corpora used are tagged for parts of speech, which enables a more efficient query. However, this still does not imply that the prefixed verbs in this research were easy to obtain. When one runs a query for all verbs starting with *a-*, for example, there are initially some 5,175 observations in Old English and 4,198 observations in Middle English. For *ge-* verbs, there were more than 19,000 observations. There are far too many instances of verbs which are not the desired combination, particularly for the prefix *a-*, as the programme cannot know if the initial letter *a* is the prefix or an indivisible part of the verbal stem.

All verbs which are not prefixed verbs had to be manually discarded, which is a painstaking and laborious process. This search method is known as sifting. Once the files (called workshops in AV) were cleaned from all instances of verbs that were not the prefixed combination investigated, a real figure was reached showing the number of occurrences of the construction under investigation. Table 20 shows the number of observations and the number of tokens after the files were cleaned of all spurious hits:

	Prefix	Period	Initial hits	Tokens
1	*ge-*	OE	19,652	16,878
		ME	5,434	4,332
2	*a-*	OE	5,175	4,091
		ME	4,198	1,201
3	*for-*	OE	2,812	2,071
		ME	1,712	1,575
4	*on-*	OE	2,560	2,212
		ME	225	94
5	*of-*	OE	823	407
		ME	341	114

Table 20
**Corpus results for early English prefixes:
initial hits vs. tokens**

---

[35] See Appendix for a complete list of Old English and Middle English texts in YCOE and PPCME2 with abbreviated filenames used in this book, including text names and references to text editions.

For the prefix *ge-*, which was reduced to *y-* or *i-* in Middle English, the string search had to be specially adjusted. The most drastic difference between the number of initial hits and the actual prefixed verbs are the results for the prefix *a-* in Middle English. Some of these problems will be discussed later in this chapter.

However, the two basic corpora were not sufficient in order to perform a comprehensive investigation of the phenomenon of aspectuality as expressed by preverbs and particle verbs. All the instances of prefixed verbs had to be checked against their simplexes, for which all other available sources were used. They include the Toronto Dictionary of Old English (DOE), which was unfortunately still at the time of writing this book only available up to the letter G, and the online edition of Bosworth-Toller Anglo-Saxon Dictionary which was digitized at the Charles University in Prague. For Middle English, the electronic version of the Middle English Dictionary digitized at the University of Michigan was used.

On the other hand, for a more thorough and consistent examination of semantics and syntax of prefixed verbs it was necessary to reduce the number of tokens that the corpus results yielded. This was achieved by means of the method known as randomization. In order to obtain a controlled random sample of prefixed verbs whose diversity of meanings and functions would proportionately correspond to the overall data, the number of tokens was reduced (i.e. randomized) to 200. These 200 prefixed verbs were then studied closely within their contexts and then their simplex counterparts had to be investigated elsewhere in any available resources in order to determine how the prefix from a certain token affects the semantics and syntax of the verb as a whole.

This chart (Figure 4) shows prefix occurrences per 1,000 lexical verbs for five prefixes.

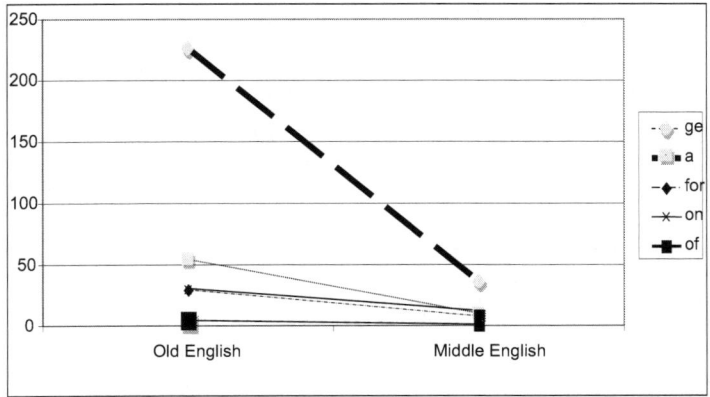

Figure 4
Prefix occurrences per 1,000 lexical verbs

4.3 Problems in identifying preverbs

In this process of studying each observation and deleting those verbs that do not meet the criteria, there were a number of problems. These problems can be categorized into the following groups:

1) Many verbs begin with *a-* but they are not *a-*prefixed verbs, such as *acsian*. There are also many verbs beginning with the prefix *and-* or *an-* such as *andswarian*. This problem was present with other prefixes too. The search programme also lists prefixed verbs that begin with the same string of letters, such as the following:

    of - ofer   *on - onder*   *for – forð*

2) Dealing with homonymy is very time consuming. Many verbs share a certain form or several forms (but not, for example in in the infinitive), so their contexts had to be studied in order to be able to distinguish them, as the following examples show:

    acwellan 'kill' vs. *acwelan* 'perish'
    adrygan 'dry' vs. *adreogan* 'do, perform, carry out' (27 and 16 tokens respectively)
    agytan 'understand' vs. *ageotan* 'pour' (6 and 19 tokens respectively)
    adon 'take away, remove' vs. *adyden* 'kill, put to death' (59 and 2 tokens respectively) (forms such as *adydde, adyddest, adyddon*)
    afyllan 'fill' vs. *afylan* 'defile, polute'
    The form *alede* is shared by *alædan* 'lead away' and *alecgan* 'lay down'
    The form *alefede* is shared by *alyfan* 'cripple' and *alyfan* 'permit'
    The form *alese* is shared by *alysan* 'deliver' and *alesan* 'choose'

3) The diversity of spellings in Middle English makes it really difficult to recognize a verb form, as the following examples illustrate:

    afendyt → MF *offendre*
    ascapen → ONF *escaper* OF *eschaper*
    astonyed → OF *estoner* 'stun, daze'
    acomered → *encumbered* 'oppressed' (OF *encombrer*)

4) In Middle English, many English verbs were respelt according to French patterns and the other way round, making it difficult to tell apart Old English *a-*prefixed verbs from French *a-*prefixed verbs. Old French also had the prefix *a-* but with somewhat different meanings and functions. The following selection of examples illustrates this problem. Only the underlined verbs count as *a-*prefixed.

    acwiten (OF *acquitter* 'settle a claim', from *à* 'to' + *quite* 'free, clear')
    but <u>*aquenched*</u> (OE *acwencan* 'quench')
    <u>*amased*</u> (OE *amasian* 'stupefy, make crazy')
    allegen (OF *alegier*) vs. OE <u>*aleian*</u> 'lay, be situated'
    amunted (OF *amonter*) 'climb'
    as(s)ent (OF *ascender*) 'rise' vs. OE <u>*asendan*</u> 'send (away)'
    awaitan (ONF *awaitier*, corresp. to CF *agaitier*)
    <u>*astruen*</u> 'destroy' replacing the French prefix *de-* with the native *a-* even if the verb stem is a borrowing from French (thus creating hybrids)

Chapter 5
An Analysis of the Preverb *a-*

5.1 Introduction

This chapter will discuss the Old English verbal prefix *a-*, which is no longer productive in Modern English, but survives in a number of lexical relics such as the univerbated forms *arise, awake* or *ashame*. For present-day speakers of English the meaning of this fossilized morpheme is not transparent.

After a brief overview of how the meaning of the prefix *a-* is explained in the literature, this chapter investigates the etymology of *a-*, followed by a subchapter that illustrates the most frequent function of *a-*, which is that of a perfectivizer. This subchapter also compares *a*-prefixed verbs with their prefixless counterparts in context. The next subchapter examines completive and resultative meanings of *a-*, followed by two subchapters that explore inchoative and instantaneous meanings of *a-* respectively. Then there is a subchapter that shows the results of a contrastive analysis of *a*-prefixed verbs: Old English is contrasted with Modern English and with Croatian, presenting the correspondences of the prefix *a-* to Modern English post-verbal particles in a map. The following subchapter is dedicated to a brief analysis of the prefix *a-* co-occurring with particles. The next two subchapters briefly show the use of the prefix *a-* in Middle English. Finally, some conclusions are reached and discussed in the last section of this chapter.

One of the main objectives of this chapter is to investigate a range of meanings and functions that the verbal prefix *a-* had in early English. As presented in section 4.3 (Table 20), the prefix *a-* is the second most frequent preverb in Old English with more than 4,000 occurrences identified in the corpus. It needs to be stressed that virtually all *a*-prefixed verbs also exist in their prefixless variant, i.e. in their simplex form. Therefore, one of the methods used to account for the meaning of *a-* is comparing *a*-verbs with their simplexes. Another method is contrastive analysis with Modern English and with Croatian. A comparison with Modern English can show if the preverb *a-* is or can be translated with a post-verbal particle, whereas a comparison with Croatian can show how the corresponding verb is marked for aspect and if a prefix is used.

Table 21 shows the corpus results in terms of frequency for types and tokens of *a*-prefixed verbs.

	Old English	Middle English
Tokens	4,091	1,201
Types	326	124
Type/Token ratio	0.08	0.10
Number of *a-* per 1,000 lexical verbs	55	10

Table 21
Corpus results: types and tokens for *a-*

We see that in Old English 55 verbs out of 1,000 are *a*-prefixed verbs, and this number drops sharply to only 10 verbs in Middle English, clearly pointing to a loss in productivity. Table 22 shows the most frequent types of *a*-prefixed verbs.

	Type	Token frequency	Meaning
1	āwrītan	239	to write (out / down)
2	ārisan	226	to rise, get up
3	ācennan	162	to generate, to give birth, to bear
4	āstigan	133	to go up/down, ascend, descend
5	āhebban	121	to lift
6	āweorpan	100	to throw, cast
7	āgyfan	95	to give, grant, bestow
8	āhōn	94	to hang, fasten, suspend
9	ālysan	94	to deliver, release, rescue, free
10	āsettan	69	to set, put, place

Table 22
The most frequent *a*- types in Old English

The only verb from this list that survived into Modern English with this prefix is the verb *arisan*. Verbs like *acennan, astigan, aweorpan* and *alysan* have died out together with the prefix, whereas the simplex versions of *awritan, ahebban, agyfan, ahon* and *asettan* have been preserved as Modern English *write, heave, give, hang* and *set*.

In the literature the meaning of the Old English prefix *a*- has always been considered as vague and elusive. Therefore, it comes as a surprise that it has been so under-researched, compared with the prefix *ge*-, which has received a great deal of attention from both students and scholars. Quirk and Wrenn (1957: 109) say that *a*- is

> "used to modify verbs; in many cases it changes the aspect from durative to perfective, in many it is a mere intensifier and in many others it appears to have no semantic function."

Hogg also finds the prefix *a*- problematic:

> "It is not always possible to give a clear indication of meaning to some of the prefixes. Thus *a*-, a verbal prefix found in verbs such as *acalan* 'become frozen', is clearly an intensifier of *calan* 'become cold', but *afysan* and *fysan* can both mean 'drive away'."

(Hogg 2002: 106)

The view that in many cases it does not seem to add to or alter the meaning of the verb is also present in the works of Hiltunen (1983), Brinton (1988) and Elenbaas (2007), as well as Kastovsky who also notes that it is "difficult to give precise semantic patterns" to this prefix, arguing that it is "questionable whether it was still productive in Old English in view of its many shades of meaning reflecting its different origins", namely as a reduced form of *of-*, *on-* or *un-* (Kastovsky 1992: 378).

In the first systematic analysis of the functions of verbal prefixes, De la Cruz (1975: 47) labels the prefixes *a-*, *ge-*, *on-* and *to-* as pure prefixes without an etymological prepositional counterpart. The prefix *a-*'s Gothic cognates are *uz-* and *ur-*, whereas its Modern German cognate is the inseparable prefix *er-*. However, an important difference between the German *er-* and the Old English *a-* is that the German prefix *er-* is still productive today and has preserved some of the idea of 'forth', 'from within', or 'up' as in the German verbs *ersteigen* 'climb, rise up' (OE *astigan*) or *erhitzen* 'to heat' (OE *ahatian*).

5.2 The Etymology of *a-*

In order to examine the semantic categories expressed by the Old English prefix *a-*, we should try to trace back its etymology to its original spatial senses. However, before we do so, it is worthwhile to describe three types of scenario of evolution from prepositions or adverbials to preverbs. The third scenario is that of the preverb *a-*.

All preverbs are assumed to have developed from prepositions or adverbials with a spatial (locational/directional) and/or temporal meaning. More often than not, verbal prefixes thus evolved remain in co-existence alongside the prepositions or adverbials, such as the present-day English *over*, *under* or even *out* and *up*, as in the verbs *to overhear*, *to underestimate*, *to outnumber* and *to upgrade*. The meanings of these prefixes will remain conceptually related with those of the prepositions, although their semantic structures are usually not as complex as those we find in prepositions due to a number of different factors that play a role in their word-formational restrictions.

The co-existence of such linguistic items actually goes hand in hand with economy, one of the principles of cognitive linguistics that accounts for polysemy. The fact that one and the same morpheme exists both as a word and as a prefix contributes to its productivity and conservation, re-inforces its use in terms of frequency and thus resists dying out.

Sometimes the prefix and its counterpart preposition may evolve into different directions as a result of orthographic, phonological and semantic changes. This was the case with the prefix *be-*, whose counterpart preposition *be* underwent respelling, vowel lengthening and diphthongization in the course of history only to emerge as the present-day preposition *by*. This is the second type of historical development scenario.

In Present-Day English this prefix is not really productive, yet it has not become extinct either. This prefix was very productive in Old English (cf. Petré 2005) – and it also happened to have a spatial prepositional counterpart, used four times with the same meaning in the following sentence:

(126)*Burgendan habbað þone sæs earm **be** westan him & Sweon **be** norþan,*
      Burgundians have   the sea.GEN arm **by** west   them and Swedes **by** north
  *& **be** eastan him sint Sermende, & **be** suþan him Surfe.*
      and **by** east   them are Sermende and **by** south them Surfe

'The Burgundians have the arm of the sea **to** the west of them, and the Swedes **to** the north: **to** the east of them are the Sermende, and **to** the south the Surfe'.

*c*925. coorosiu,Or_1:1.13.22.218

In (126) it is used in the meaning of direction or vague localization. This function in Present-Day English has been taken over by the preposition *to,* but there are still many examples where English would use the same preposition, as in:

(127)*æt fruman   he hine clypode **be** his naman. Benedicte. þæt is gebletsod.*
    at beginning   he   him   called   **by** his   name   Benedict   that   is   blessed
'At first he called him **by** his name, Benedict, that is blessed.'

*c*995 ÆCHom II, 11 97.182

The same preposition is still used in a number of other contexts such as '*by* a certain point in time' or in fixed expressions such as *be nihte* 'by night' or *word be worde* 'word by word'. However, the etymological link between the prefix *be-* and the preposition *by* is not easily established in the minds of present-day speakers of English.

The third historical development scenario is what happened to the prefix *a-*. It lost its prepositional counterpart before the written documents of Old English, but it can be traced back in Gothic. The Gothic cognate of *a-* is the preverb *us,* which can be attested by comparing the translations of gospels in the examples such as

(128) Gothic *us-wairpan*   OE *aweorpan*   'throw away'

(129) Gothic *us-dreiban*   OE *adrifan*   'drive out'.

It was phonologically unstable even in Gothic, as can be seen in its allomorph *ur* in the examples such as

(130) Gothic *ur-rinnan*   OE *arinnan, ayrnan* 'go out' and

(131) Gothic *ur-reisan*   OE *arisan*   'go up, arise'.

In Gothic, the allomorph *ur* was used if the verbal stem began with an 'r'. This phonological change is known as rhotacism. Once the *s* changes into *r,* it is a small step to lose the *r* in a subsequent stage of Germanic. Phonological reduction occurs commonly in grammaticalization processes.

The Gothic prepositional counterpart of this prefix is *us,* which meant 'out of' or 'away from'. Lehmann (1986: 380) says its Proto-Germanic reconstruction is **uz,* but he goes on to list several possible PIE origins, such as Uhlenbeck (1906 TNTL 25:302) who notes that the etymology is uncertain, possible from PIE **aw-* **wē-* 'away from, down' (Skt *avás, áva* 'downward', Lat *au* 'away' in *au-ferō, au-fugiō*), but Brugmann (1904: 463), 468, Schmidt (1889: 219) and Jacobsohn (1920 ZVS 49:195) consider that the possible origin is PIE **ud-s.*

Blažek (2001: 24-25) elaborates this possible origin, offering attestations from a handful of languages, but also brings it into connection with Gothic *ut* 'out' and *uta* 'outside' and OE, OFris, OSax *ūt* (cf. Lehmann 1986: 384). He notes that the reflex of PIE **uds* is Germanic **uz,* which he thinks are both the origins of Gothic *us* and *uz-*, ON *ór* as well as OE *or-* as a privative prefix that denotes origin or antiquity as in *oreald* (Modern German *uralt*). In the Slavic branch he identifies it as OCS *vъz / vъs* 'for; up', whose Modern Russian reflex is *vy-* 'out', a frequent perfectivizing prefix, or Croatian *uz-* as in *uzeti* 'to take', rather than OCS *iz* 'from, out of' reconstructed as ProtoSlavic **jьz*, going back to PIE **eg'hs*, the reflexes of which are Latin *ex* and Greek *éx* (Blažek 2001: 18), but with no reflexes in Germanic.

It is really interesting that Germanic would not have a cognate with Latin *ex* or Croatian *iz* and that Gothic *us, ut, ur* and *uz-* would all be reflexes of a single Proto-Germanic or PIE preposition. Investigating more on this issue would take us well beyond the scope of this study, but I am not convinced that the proposed etymologies are true. To sum up this short discussion, the etymology of the Old English prefix *a-* is rather dubious or shrouded in mystery. The transition from **uz* to *a-* shows a drastic reduction in the phonological structure, but its original sense was established as a source prefix (='out, out of') whose inherently source oriented meaning had already been bleached by the time of the first Old English written data.

5.3 *A-* as a perfectivizer

The main function of the Old English prefix *a-* is aspectual, as this analysis aims to show. This subchapter will examine how this preverb expresses perfectivity.

Very often in the literature, Old English prefixes such as *a-, for-* or *be-* are said to add telicity to verbs (e.g. Brinton 1988: 202-204, Dehé 2002: 6, Kemenade and Los 2003: 79, Petré and Cuyckens 2008: 144), rather than perfectivity. If they add telicity, it means we regard aspectual meaning arising from the unit of the verb and the prefix as lexical, rather than grammatical. However, if we regard prefixes as constructions which exhibit a predictable meaning, then we could argue that at the sentence level they express perfective aspect, rather than telic aktionsart. Furthermore, if we claim that prefixes have grammaticalized, then we speak of grammatical aspect rather than lexical aspect, so the term *perfective* is more appropriate in most of these cases.

Telicity, as discussed in section 2.10.3, refers to the inherent meaning of the verb, i.e. telic verbs have an endpoint. Table 14 featured one telic verb (*arrive*) and one atelic verb (*play*). The inherent meaning of the verb can be modified by grammatical means, so if we use a telic verb such as *arrive* in a continuous tense, we can change the inherent temporal property of the verb on the sentence level:

(132)*Peter was arriving.*

As we can see, the situation no longer has an endpoint or culmination. The verb's inherently telic value has been dissociated by means of syntax. It is argued here that preverbs act like function words (grammatical words), a closed set of words with little lexical meaning which serve to express grammatical relationship with other words in a sentence. However, verbal prefixes such as *a-, ge-* and *for-* are not words but morphemes, so they affect the meaning of the verb by means of morphology. We can regard them as inflections rather than derivations, as they express grammatical and not lexical meaning.

Let us consider some corpus examples of the most frequent type – the verb *awritan* 'to write' – and see what kind of aspectuality the prefix *a-* expresses there.

(133) *Esdras se writere **awrat** ane boc, hu þæt folc com ongean*
      Ezra the scribe ***a*-wrote** a book, how that people came back
fram Chaldea lande to Iudea lande
     from Chaldea land.DAT to Judea land.DAT'
'Ezra the scribe **wrote** a book, how that people returned from Chaldea to Judea'

                                                    ÆLet 4: 726.292

(134) *Þara abbuda stær & spel þisses mynstres [...]*
    the.GEN.PL abbot.GEN.PL histories and stories this.GEN.SG monastery.GEN.SG
*on twam bocum ic **awrat**.*
    in two.DAT.PL books.DAT.PL I ***a*-wrote**.
'The history and account of the abbots of this monastery [...], I wrote in two books.'

                                        c897. cobede,Bede_5:22.484.15.4856

(135) *Paulus se apostol **awrat** manega pistolas, for þan þe Crist hine*
     Paul the apostle ***a*-wrote** many epistles,   for   Christ him
gesette eallum þeodum to lareowe.
    appointed all.DAT.PL people.DAT.PL to teacher.DAT
'The apostle Paul **wrote** many epistles, for Christ appointed him to be a teacher of all peoples.'

                                                    ÆLet 4: 938.392

In the examples (133) - (135), the prefix *a-* expresses perfectivity when attached to the verb *writan*. Perfectivity includes several subtypes, two of which can be identified in the above examples: completive and resultative. The context shows us that the endpoint is reached – the book, two books or the many epistles have all been finished, completed, or there is a result of the action of writing. The preterite tense signals that the action took place in the past and the prefix *a-* is an aspect marker that additionally shows that the event of writing in all three sentences was carried out until its culminating point or end point. We have to bear in mind that progressive tenses as well as the present perfect were not developed at the time, so the system of verbal prefixes performed many of the aspectual functions. We can see that from the contrast with the prefixless version of the verb *writan* in example number (136):

(136) *He **wrat** mid his fingre on ðære eorþan.*
    he **wrote** with his finger.DAT on the earth. DAT
'He **wrote/was writing** with his finger on the earth.'

                                                            Jn. Skt. 8, 6, 8

The verb *writan* is an atelic verb. However, its inherent semantic aspect is affected if it is used in a sentence with a direct object. In example (136) there is no direct object that is normally required in the predication of this verb acting as an endpoint. The absence of the prefix *a-* could signify that the action is not finished or complete, and can have a progressive reading, as suggested with alternate translations.

Another instance where the simplex verb is used giving an imperfective reading on the sentence level is evident in example number (137):

(137) *Se halga godspellere swa be   him **wrat** & cwæþ*
     the holy   evangelist   thus about them **wrote** and spoke
'The holy evangelist thus **wrote** and spoke about them'
                          *c*971. coblick,LS_12_[NatJnBapt[B1Hom_14]] : 161.26.2055

Even though the action of writing was most likely in reality completed in the past, this did not need to reflect in using the prefix. The context enables either form, the perfective or the imperfective, but the latter was chosen most likely for stylistic reasons. This sentence was basically a summary of what the holy evangelist did, so more context in case of this example would not help us to reduce the aspectual ambiguity of the verb in question.

The following example also shows the imperfective form of the preterite in a context where the perfective meaning does not fit.

(138) *Witodlice gif ge gelyfdon on moyse. ge gelyfdon eac me; Soðlice he **wrat** be me. gif ge his stafum ne gelyfað. hu gelyfe ge minum wordum;*
     indeed   if you believed in Moses you believe also me   truly   he **wrote**
     of me   if you his letters.DAT not believe how believe you my.DAT.PL words.DAT
'Indeed if you believed Moses, you would believe me. Truly, he **wrote** of me. But if you do not believe his writings, how will you believe my words?'
                                  *c*990 John V.47

If we contrast the examples (133) to (138) with their Croatian translations, we will see that *writan* consistently corresponds to *pisati* and *awritan* to *napisati*. Even the problematic example number (137) is likely to be translated with *pisao* rather than *napisao*.

As discussed in section 2.8, the Croatian examples (71) and (71) or the Spanish example (77) illustrate what Jakobson termed as "semantic unmarkedness". This is another point of similarity of aspect between Old English and Slavic. Prefixed verbs are perfective, so they are semantically marked, whereas simplexes are not marked, which means that normally they denote imperfective actions but they can also take on perfective meanings.

For this reason, in many example sentences with a prefixless verb that are here described as imperfective, a perfective reading is possible as well.

Let us consider other sets of examples where the prefix *a-* marks perfectivity and contrast them with their 'imperfective pairs'. The following two examples feature the verb *afyllan* 'to fill (up); make full; supply' exhibiting perfective senses.

(139) *Eac ðis land wæs swiðe **afylled** mid munecan*
     also this land was   much ***a*-filled** with   monks
'Also this land was abundantly **supplied** with monks'
                                            A.S. 1086

(140) *on þisum geare wæs þis land swiðe <u>astirad</u> & mid mycele swicdome*
     in   this   year   was this land much <u>up-stirred</u> and with great   treachery

***afylled**, swa þet þa riceste frencisce men ... wolden swican heora hlaforde*
 a-**filled**   so   that the mightiest   French   men   wanted betray.INF their   lord
þam cynge.
         the king.DAT
'In this year the land was stirred up and **filled** with great treachery, so that the most powerful French men ... wanted to betray their lord the king.'
A.S. 1087.1

Example (140) also features another *a*-prefixed verb: *astyrian* 'stir up' which has been underlined. In Modern English translation we have the post-verbal particle *up* that shows the same function that the prefix *a*- had. Such Old English – Modern English correspondences will be discussed in section 5.8.

The prefixless counterpart to the verb from (139) and (140) is the verb *fyllan* 'fill', as the following pair of examples illustrate.

(141)*þa   yða   weollon & ymbsweopon & æghwonan   þæt scip **fyldon**,*
         the waves seethed and round-swept and on all sides that ship **filled**
þæt heo him nænigra gesynta wendon
that they them none   safety.GEN.PL turned
'The waves seethed and swept round them, and **filled** the ship on every side, so that they utterly despaired of safety.'
c897. Bede 3.13.200.14

It is also possible to translate *fyldon* with the progressive "were filling the ship", but it is not necessary, as even the simple form in Modern English in the right context can convey the imperfective meaning.

As late as the Peterborough Chronicle (mid-12th century), prefixed verbs were still used to express perfective meaning and prefixless increasingly for both perfective and imperfective, as the prefixes were dying out. The following example contains the verb *fyllan,* whose meaning can be both perfective and imperfective:

(142)*hi suencten suyðe þe uurecce men of þe land mid castelweorces;*
       they oppressed much   the wretched men of the land with   castle works
*þa   þe castles uuaren maked, þa **fylden** hi mid deoules & yuele men.*
when the castles   were   made   then **filled** they with   devils   and evil   men
'They greatly oppressed the poor men of the land with castle building work; when the castles were made, then they **filled** the land with devils and evil men.'
ChronE 1137.14

The verb *fedan* 'to feed' behaves as an imperfective verb when without a prefix, as we see in example (143):

(143)*Se goda mete ægðer deð, ge þone lichoman **fedeð** ge þæt mod gladað to*
       the good food either does both the   body   **feeds** and that mind gladdens for
ælcere hælo,
each   health
'Good food does two things: it **feeds** the body and it gladdens the mind, for the health of each.'
HomU 11 (Verc 7) 95

If a prefix is attached to this verb, it is perfectivized, as example (144) demonstrates. In fact, we have a situation with two different prefixes attached to the same verb stem, both acting as perfectivizers.

(144)*þær [on ðam toweardan life]   we beoð **gefedde**. and we ðær nænne ne*
    there in the future.DAT life.DAT we are   **ge-fed**   and we there no one not
afedað (BG fedæð).
***a*-feed**
'There [in the future life] we shall be **fed**, and we shall **feed** no one'.
c995. ÆCHom II, 34 258.88

Another situation where the prefixless verb signifies an imperfective action is exemplified in numbers (145) and (146).

(145)*Hwæt getacnað ðonne se wind buton ða costunga   ðæs   <u>awirgdan</u>*
    what   signifies that the wind but the temptations the.GEN cursed
gæstes, & hwæt ðæt wolc ðe bið astyred from ðæm winde buton ða
spirit.GEN and what that cloud that is *a*-stirred from the wind but the
*wiðerweardnesse unryhtwisra monna? Se wind **drifeð** ðæt wolcn. Sua deð*
    opposition   wicked   men.GEN the wind **drives** that cloud so does
se unclæna gæst mid his winde; He onstyreð unryhtwise men.
the unclean spirit with his wind   he stirs up   wicked   men
'What does the wind signify but the temptations of the <u>accursed</u> spirit, and what does the cloud which is stirred by the wind but the opposition of wicked men? The wind **drives** the cloud. So does the unclean spirit with his wind; he stirs up wicked men.'
c894. cocura,CP:39.285.18.1867-1870

(146)*se muð   **drifð** ut ða clypunge, and seo lyft byð geslagen*
    the mouth **drives** out the sound   and the air is struck
'The mouth **drives** out the sound and the air is struck'
Ægram 4.9

In example (146) we also have the particle *ut* 'out' which does not have an aspectual function but clearly a spatial (directional) one. The prefixed counterpart of the verb *drifan* appears in the next example, but the prefix *a-* does not perfectivize. In this case it re-inforces the spatial adverb *aweg* 'away'.

(147)*ðæt gode mod ðe sio hælo ful oft aweg **adriefð** ðæt gemynd*
    the good spirit that the health very often away ***a*-drives** that memory
ðære medtrymnesse geedniewað
that.DAT illness.DAT   restores
'The good spirit which the health very often **drives** away that the memory of illness restores.'
c894. cocura,CP:36.255.13.1672

Number (147) is one of the few examples where the preverb *a-* has a spatial rather than an aspectual meaning. Moreover, it is also a very rare example where an *a*-prefixed verb is used in a sentence whose reading can be imperfective.

Numbers (148) and (149) are prefixed and simplex instantiations of *wyrgan* 'curse, damn'.

(148) *hi synd **awyrgede** swa swa hi wiscton him sylfum.*
    they are ***a*-cursed** so so they wished them selves
    'they are **damned**, as they wished upon themselves.'

ÆLS B1.3.2

(149) *Ond þeah þe wærgcweodole Godes rice gesittan ne mægen, hwæðre*
    and though those curse-speaking God's kingdom inherit not may whether
*is gelyfed, þætte þa be gewyrhte **wyrgde** wæron for heora arleasnesse,*
    is believed that those be justly **cursed** were for their wickedness
þæt heo hræðe þurh Drihtnes wrace heora scylda wite þrowedon.
    that they quickly through Lord's penalty their guilt punishment suffered
'And although those who curse cannot inherit the kingdom of God, yet one may believe that those who were justly **cursed** for their wickedness quickly suffered the penalty of their guilt at the avenging hand of God.'

c897. cobede,Bede_4:27.356.26.3595

    The prefixed form of this verb is also featured in the first lines of examples (145) and later in (181). It has a perfective reading in all four examples, so why is the prefixless form used in (149)? Again, we have a case where a simplex can convey a perfective meaning. Being a semantically unmarked form (Jakobson's concept), the simplex in context such as we see in (149) can express both aspects. However, both forms are possible in a Croatian translation of this example (*koji su bili prokleti* [perfective] or *koji su bili proklinjani* [imperfective] 'who were cursed'), even though there is a sequence of actions (i.e. "those who were cursed quickly suffered a penalty").

5.4 Resultative and completive

As mentioned in the first examples of this chapter, an aspectual subcategory of perfectivity where the verb *awritan* 'to write' also belongs is *resultativeness* or *resultativity*. According to Marina Gorlach (2000), in Modern English the category of resultativeness is represented by a system of lexical-grammatical oppositions, among them

(150) *break the vase* vs. *break up the vase* vs. *break the vase up*
    simple verb + NP - [V Prt NP] construction – [V NP Prt] construction

(from Gorlach 2000: 256)

She suggests that these oppositions are different degrees of resultativeness in their meaning, its intensity increasing from the left to the right. In all three Modern English examples the aspectuality of the verb is perfective, but the resultativeness is the one that is gradable.

    As has been suggested many times, Old English prefixes are ancestors of Modern English post-verbal particles in terms of their function, so if we transfer this idea of the resultative *up* from the phrasal verb *break up* onto the prefix *a-* in *abrecan*, whose root verb was telic in the first place, we see that perhaps the gradable property of resultativeness could have been expressed with the particle reinforcement back in the Old English period.

(151) *break the vase*   *break up the vase*   *break the vase up*
      crocca brecan[36]   *crocca abrecan*   *crocca up abrecan*

    As English has drifted towards the analytical side in the meantime, the position of the particle in the sentence can slightly alter the meaning. Placing the particle after the object was a means to show a higher degree of resultativity. As the word order in Old English was less fixed, the means to show a higher degree of resultativeness was to reinforce the prefix *a-* with the particle *up*. I am going to return to the phenomenon of particle re-inforcement in section 5.8.

    Lexicographic treatments of the prefix *a-* often pointed to its property of adding intensity to the verb. The literature on aspect tends to dispute the category of intensity as an aspectual category (Binnick 1991: 145), but based on the previous examples of degrees of resultativity I am likely to conclude that the lexicographers' choice of the word *intensity* to describe the meaning of the particle actually referred to the category of resultativity.

    The nature of the verb *awritan* is such that once the action has reached its natural endpoint, with a strong emphasis on the final stage because only then we see the result of it as a concrete object – something that is written, whether it be a book or a psalm. We also have the metonymy PRODUCT FOR PROCESS involved in which the book is the product of the activity of writing and comes to stand for the activity itself.

    Another perfective verb – *asingan* 'to sing (a song) through to its end' - seems to show less a resultative property but more a completive one in example (152):

(152) *siððan he on siðe wæs, he **asong** ælce dæge tuwa his saltere ond his*
      when he on journey was he ***a*-sang** each day twice his psalms and his
mæssan
mass
'When he was on a trip, every day he **sang** twice his psalms and his mass.'
                                                    *c*1000. Mart 5 Se 25, A.8

    The essential property of the completive aspectual category is the emphasis on the totality of the situation, rather then on its final stage which is the distinguishing property of the resultative category. But again, the prefix functions as an aspectual marker, that of a completeness that the psalms were sung in their entirety, from the beginning to the end. Numbers (153) and (154) also show that.

(153) *Leoð wæs **asungen**, gleomannes gyd.*
      song was ***a*-sung** minstrel.GEN lay
'The song was **sung**, the minstrel's lay.'
                                                            c1015. Beo 1159

(154) *ða se Wisdom ða ðis leoð swiðe lustbærlice & gesceadwislice **asungen***
      when the wisdom then this song very   pleasantly and   wisely   ***a*-sung**
hæfde, ða hæfde ic ða giet hwylchwugu <gemynd> on minum mode ðære

---

[36] These particular Old English examples have not been attested, but are reconstructed here for the purpose of contrasting them with the Modern English examples originally appearing in the paper by Gorlach.

> had then had I then yet some memory on my mood the
> <*unrotnesse*> *þe ic <ær> hæfde*
> sadness that I before had
> 'When wisdom had **sung** the song so pleasantly and wisely, I still remembered some of the sadness that I had felt previously.'
> c950. Bo 36.103.23

The prefix *a*- marks the completeness of the action: the song was sung through to its end. The next two examples show the verb *singan* without the prefix, i.e. in the imperfective meaning.

> (155) *ða mid ðam þe he his gebedu* **sang**. *ða tær þæt hors þæt ðæc of ðære*
> then with that he his prayers **sang** then tore the horse the thatch from the
> *cytan hrofe. and þær feoll adune swilce of ðam hrofe wearm hlaf mid his*
> cottage roof and there fell down such from the roof warm loaf with his
> *syflinge.*
> food
> 'Then while he **was singing** his prayers, the horse tore the thatch from the roof of the cottage, and there fell down, as from the roof, a warm loaf with some food.'
> c995. ÆCHom II,10 82.54

Example (155) features the verb *singan* in the preterite tense without the prefix because it signifies an action that is ongoing or in progress. The act of singing prayers was not completed, but was interrupted by another action, that of the horse tearing the thatch from the roof of the cottage. The verb *tær* 'tore' is prefixless but its meaning is perfective. Its perfectivity is signalled by the adverbial conjunction *ða* 'then'.

Example (156) shows that the simplex verb *singan* in the present tense cannot have the prefix *a*- because it would interfere with the progressive aspect of the situation:

> (156) *Hwæt is ðis folc ðe ðus hlude* **singeþ**?
> what is this people that thus loudly sing.3.SG.PRES
> 'Who are these people who **are singing** so loudly?'
> c971. Blickl. Homl. 149, 30

In a similar vein, example (157) features the verb *singan* 'to sing' in the past participle form without any prefix, as part of a passive construction. The meaning of the verb could be interpreted as imperfective:

> (157) *On hwylcum tidum alleluia sceole beon* **sungen**
> in which times hallelujah shall be **sung**
> 'In which hours will Hallelujah be **sung**?'
> c1025. Cobenrul, BenR:16.6.21.85

The reason why an imperfective is used here is because the information whether the Hallelujah will be sung in its entirety is not in focus or is irrelevant. Moreover, there is more stress on the adverbial *on hwylcum tidum* 'in which hours', which suggests that the action will take place on several occasions or could function as a time adverbial that marks perfectivity. Given that it is a monastic rule, it is crucial that the Hallelujah is sung in its entirety on these occasions.

Furthermore, the distinction between completive and resultative (both subtypes of perfectivity) will depend on the inherent semantics of the verb. The action of writing will eventually produce the result of something written that is visible, whereas the action of singing does not produce a visible result. The event of singing can only be described in terms of completeness – whether it was performed in its entirety or not.

5.5 Ingressive / inchoative / inceptive

Another observed aspectual property of the prefix *a-* is to indicate the beginning of a situation, which has variously been called *ingressive* or *inchoative* or *inceptive* aspect. There is a group of Old English *a-* prefixed verbs which are derived from adjectives and can only be translated analytically into modern English with the verbs such as *become* or *grow*. These verbs express ingressive aspect as their meaning refers to the moment of entering into a state of whichever adjective from they were derived. The following examples have been taken from the corpus:

(158) *ageolwian* 'become yellow'
asweartian 'to become black'
ablindian 'to become blind'
adeafian 'to become deaf'
adumbian 'to become dumb, silent'
acealdian 'to grow cold'
ahatian 'to become hot'
adeorcian 'to become dark'

Some of them can also be rendered into Modern English by adding the verbalizing suffix *–en,* which is considered to be an ingressive marker in Present-Day English (cf. example number (40)):
ahyrdan 'harden'
afyrhtan 'frighten'

Numbers (159) and (160) are contextualized examples of ingressive verbs.

(159) *seo sunne **asweartade**, ond se dæg wæs on þeostre niht gecierred fram*
    the sun   **blackened**   and the day was in dark night turned from
midne dæg oð non
middle day until noon
'the sun **turned black** and the day turned into the dark night from midday to the ninth hour'

c1000. Mart 5 Ma 25, A.13

(160) *þa hit æfen wæs, ða **acwicode** ic hwon & mine geferan mec ham bæran*
    when it evening was then **livened up** I little and my companions me home carried
'when evening came, then I **revived** a little and my companions carried me home'

c897. Bede 5 6.402.3:

Although ingressive verbs refer to the moment of the beginning of the action, they are considered to be a subcategory of perfective, just like resultative. In order to determine the aspectual meaning of this group of verbs, I tried translating them into Croatian because of its typological similarity to Old English.

Aspectual nuances are very difficult to explain in one's mother tongue, let alone in a foreign or even a dead language. When I tried to pinpoint what kind of aspectuality I sensed in the Croatian translation equivalents to the examples in (158), I could not make up my mind whether they referred to the beginning of the action, as in entering a state of being whatever the adjective means, or if they referred to the result of the action, in which case they would belong to the category of resultativity.

5.6 Instantaneous / Momentous / Punctual

Let us move away now from the group of aspectual categories with fuzzy borders to another group whose borders are more clear-cut. These would be the categories of durative vs. instantaneous, which represent a clearly marked opposition, as they refer to situations which either endure through time or take place instantly and have no duration. The instantaneous is also called momentaneous or punctual.

When prefixed with *a-*, the verb *feallan* denotes an instantaneous action, a short-lasting punctual single event.

(161) *þa his here geseah þæt he mid þy horse **afeoll***
when his army saw that he with the horse ***a*-fell**
'when his army saw that he fell down together with his horse'
c925. Or 3 7.64.30:

When the subject is in plural, such as the noun *tearas* in number (162) the action is no longer instantaneous, as the tears did not fall simultaneously at once but one after another and can be viewed as a series of events of falling. For this reason, the Modern English translation of the simplex verb could also have the verb in the progressive tense:

(162) *& he [Joseph] wearð swa swiðe astyred, þæt him **feollon** tearas of his*
and he [Jospeh] was so very *a*-stirred that him **fell.**3.PL tears of his
eagan for broþor þingon
own for brother things
'And he was so strongly stirred that his *tears* **fell** for his brother's sake'
c1000. cogenesiC,Gen_[Ker]:43.30.333

Alternatively, the simplex verb, being semantically unmarked, can also have a perfective reading. In Croatian, both perfective and imperfective is possible (*suze su mu pale* [perfective] and *suze su mu padale* [imperfective] 'his tears fell').

Number (163) is another example of the prefix *a-* signifying an instantaneous action:

(163) ***ahleopon*** *þa ealle & hiene mid heora metseacsum ofsticedon inne on*
    ***a*-jumped** then all   and him with their   daggers   stabbed inside in
heora gemotærne.
their meeting-place
'then [the consuls and the senate] all **jumped up**, and stabbed him [Julius Cæsar] with their daggers in their senate-house'
c925. Or 5 12.129.2

Even though the subject is in plural, the prefix *a-* modified the meaning of the simplex verb adding the notion of an instantaneous action – all the consuls jumped up at the same time and this happened very quickly. In a translation of this sentence into Croatian, the perfective verb *skočiti* 'jump' can be further modified with the prefix *po-*, in which case its meaning denotes a very short action. In this case the prefix *po-* is not a perfectivizer since the verb is already perfective, but as a derivational prefix modifying what is traditionally called the aktionsart. A similar function of *a-* can be observed in the following example:

(164) *Ða **ahleop** se lichoma sona up of ðam wætere, ond þæt heafod on oðre*
    then ***a*-leapt** the body   soon up from that water and the   head   on other
stowe.
place
'Then the body immediately **leapt up** from that water and the head on that place.'
c1000. Mart_5_[Kotzor]:Oc31,A.13.208

Example (165) features the same verb without the prefix:

(165) *Þa sealde se cyning him sweord, þæt he hine mid gyrde; & nom his spere*
    then gave the king   him sword   that he him with gird   and took his spear
*on hond & **hleop** on þæs cyninges stedan & to þæm deofulgeldum   ferde.*
in hand and **jumped** on the king's   stallion and to the devilish idols.DAT fared
'Then the king gave him a sword to gird on and took his spear in his hand and **jumped** on the king's stallion and set out to the devilish idols.'
c897. cobede,Bede_2:10.138.4.1327-30

The adverbial conjunction *þa* sets the frame of the narrative in example (165), making it optional for verbs to take prefixes. The verbs in this sentence signify a sequence of actions in perfective reading.

The simplex verb *hleapan* apart from 'jumping' also means 'dancing', which shows that the prefixless version of the verb has a durative quality, as dancing can be perceived as a series of events of jumping:

(166) *Ðonne beoð geopenode blindra manna eagan, and deaffra manna earan*
    then   are   opened   blind   men's eyes and deaf   men's ears
*gehyrað;   þonne **hleapð**   se healta swa swa heort,*
hear.3.PL.PRES then **leap**.3PL.PRES the halt   as   hart
'Then shall be opened the eyes of blind men, and the ears of deaf men shall hear; then shall the lame **leap** as a hart
c995. Homl. Th. ii. 16, 18.

(167) *lætan scralletan sceacol se þe **hleapeð** nægl   neome   cende*
    let   shrill   schackle which **leaps**   nail harmonious sounds generate

> *biþ him neod micel*
> be him eagerness great
> 'let the shackle which **leaps**/dances be shrill, the nail produce harmonious sounds, great is his eagerness'
>
> *c*970. coexeter R 83-85

It is very interesting that *a*-prefixed verbs also appear in contexts where the sentence-level aspect is in fact durative, a kind of imperfective aspect (see section 2.10.2). Numbers (168) and (169) exemplify such situations.

> (168)*þas ðry dagas wæron buton sunnan & monan, & steorran & eallum*
> those three days were without sun and moon and stars and all
> *tidum,gelicere wægan mid leohte & þeostrum* **aðenede**
> hours equal balance with light and dark **stretched out**
> 'those three days were without the sun, the moon, the stars and all the hours, **stretched out** with light and darkness in equal balance'
>
> ÆTemp 1.11

> (169)*gif ge swelce þegnas sint, swelce ge wenað <þæt> ge sien, þonne*
> if you such heroes are such you think that you are, then
> *sceoldon ge swa lustlice eowre agnu brocu* **aræfnan**, *þeh hie læssan sien,*
> should you as willingly your own sorrows **bear**.INF since they less are
> *swa ge heora sint to gehieranne*
> as you theirs are to hear
> 'if you be such heroes, as you think you are, then should you as willingly **bear** your own sorrows, since they are less, than what you hear of theirs'
>
> *c*925. Or 3 7.65.30:

However, the durative aspect is conditioned by the inherent lexical meaning of the simplex verbs themselves, much like the durativity of the Modern English verb *stretch* is further enhanced by adding the particle *out*.

The verb *aþenian* 'stretch out' can also used in a more literal, i.e. spatial sense, as the following example vividly illustrates:

> (170)*Þa yrsode he ond gebealh hyne ond het hig* **aðenian** *on yren bed*
> then raged he and angered him and commanded them **stretch out** on iron bed
> *ond hig begeotan myd weallende leade.*
> and them cover with boiling lead
> 'Then he raged and became angry and commanded to **stretch them out** on the iron bed and to cover them with boiling lead.'
>
> *c*1060. Mart 2.1 [Herzfeld-Kotzor]: De10, A.10.280

One could argue that the prefix *a*- is used in a non-aspectual sense, but in the end both the literal spatial and the metaphorical aspectual meanings can be detected in this verb form at the sentence level. The situation can in fact be interpreted as imperfective. The corresponding verb in Croatian is *rastezati* with its perfective pair *rastegnuti*, in both cases prefixed. The imperfective form is more likely to be used in the Croatian translation of example (170), as it would intensify the meaning (i.e. the suffering of the victims) and place focus on the duration of the situation. In this way we have two different examples of the same verb where the prefix *a*- exhibits different degrees of aspectual roles, and in both cases an interesting interplay of the semantics of time and space. Bollinger's observation makes a good point:

> "There is a deep-seated relationship between notions of action, state, progression, inception, completion and the like, on the one hand and notions of direction and position on the other – a kind of geometry of semantics."
>
> (Bollinger 1971: 110)

5.7 Contrastive analysis

In order to gain a better understanding of the function of the Old English prefix *a-*, one of the methods was translating a randomized sample of 200 tokens into Modern English and Croatian. Both comparisons yielded interesting results.

As the aspect of Croatian verbs is morphologically marked, translations into Croatian can immediately confirm if the aspectual meaning in Old English is perfective or not. There is no point in presenting these translations, but a sample of 30 verbs has been extracted from the token translations and listed here in the infinitive form:

aþwean	**o**prati 'wash'	*agymeleasian*	**za**nemariti 'neglect'
acennan	**za**četi 'conceive'	*alyfan*	**do**pustiti 'permit'
aclænsian	**o**čistiti 'clean up'	*alysan*	**iz**baviti 'deliver'
acigan	**sa**zvati 'summon'	*arisan*	**po**dignuti 'arise, get up'
acwellan	**u**biti 'kill'	*arasian*	**ot**kriti 'discover'
acwican	**o**živjeti 'revive'	*arœran*	**iz**graditi 'erect, raise up'
adelfan	**is**kopati 'dig (up)'	*ascufan*	**iz**baciti 'expel, push away'
adilegian	**iz**brisati 'destroy'	*asecgan*	**iz**govoriti 'say, speak out'
adrifan	**od**vesti 'drive away'	*asendan*	**po**slati 'send (out)'
afedan	**na**hraniti 'feed'	*asettan*	**po**staviti 'set, put'
aflowan	**is**teći 'flow away'	*asiftan*	**pro**sijati 'sift'
afindan	**sa**znati 'find out'	*asmorian*	**u**gušiti 'suffocate'
afyllan	**is**puniti 'fill up'	*aswellan*	**na**teći 'swell up'
agyfan	**od**ustati 'give up'	*aweorpan*	**od**baciti 'throw away'
agyltan	**z**griješiti 'sin, transgress'	*awritan*	**na**pisati 'write (down)'

Table 23
Old English – Croatian verb correspondences

As many as 98% of Old English tokens are translated with a perfective verb in Croatian. Moreover, all of them are prefixed, as can be seen in the table.

Translating the tokens into Modern English has showed that in as many as 74% of cases, the meaning of the prefix *a-* can be conveyed with a post-verbal particle. In a randomized sample of 200 tokens, the following distribution has been identified:

away / off	22%
up	34%
down	2%

apart	2%
out	14%
become/grow	4%
other	22%

Table 24
The distribution of post-verbal particle correspondences
to the prefix *a-*

The meanings "become/grow" refer to ingressive meanings, whereas "other" refers to verbs that typically correspond to Latinate verbs which incidentally contain a prefix such as *suffocate, degrade* or *ascend*.

The following page presents a map of the prefix *a-*'s correspondences to Modern English post-verbal particles, as well as prefixes in Old High German, Latin and Croatian. It also serves as an overview of the meanings that the prefix *a-* can take, though it needs to be stressed these are not distinct meanings of *a-*. 'Apart' and 'asunder' meanings occur only with verbs that already mean breaking. Therefore, the prefix *a-* signals completion or results of the process in this case.

The following page:
Figure 5
A map of Old English *a*-V correspondences to Modern English post-verbal particles

An Analysis of the Preverb A-

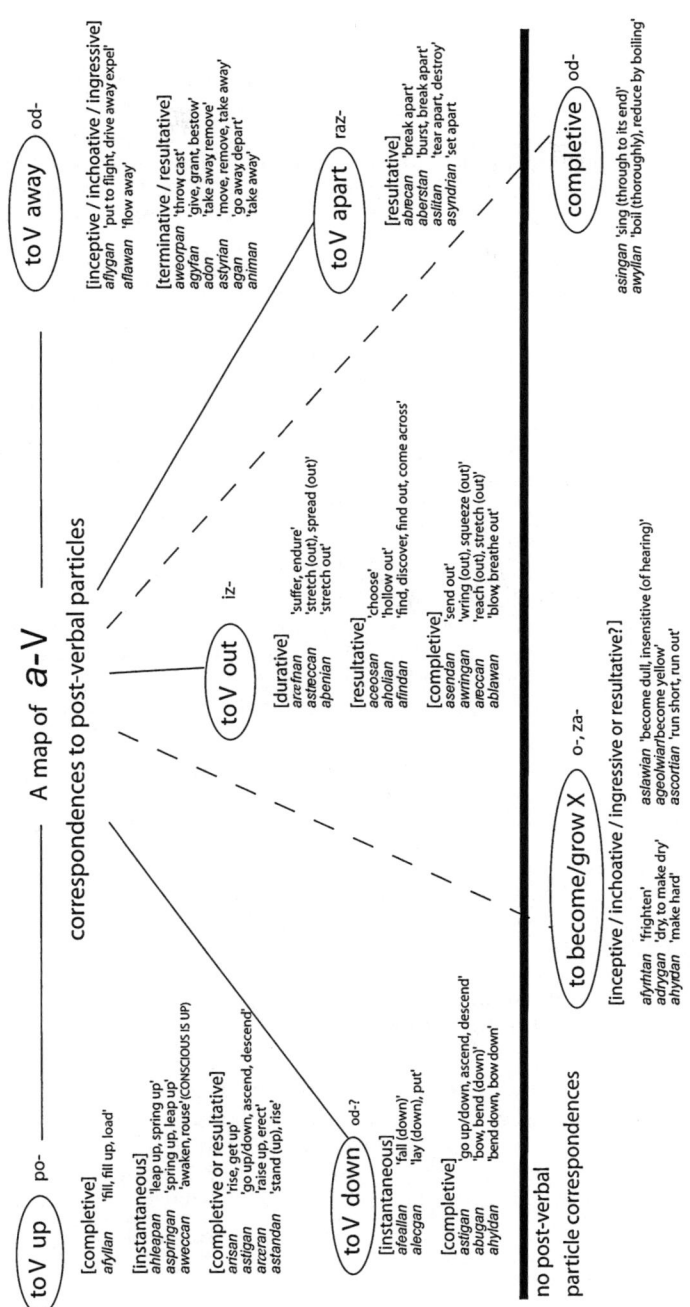

5.8 Co-Existing Systems of Prefixes and Particles

The meanings of prefixes in Old English sometimes overlap and there are numerous examples where prefixes are interchangeable (Ogura 1995). Other times when a prefixed verb's meaning is compared to its simplex version's meaning, the meaning of the prefix is not immediately identifiable. As the meanings are sometimes indistinct, prefixes are often found co-occurring with particles which have a similar meaning. The prefix *a-* in particular is frequently re-inforced by an adverbial particle.

In a random sample of 200 tokens, it has been calculated that in 17% of cases *a-* prefixed verbs are backed up with a particle. This number is too small to make any conclusive claims that there was a change underway, but it *can* serve as a piece of evidence regarding the ongoing change. 17% is not a neglectable number and in combination with other evidence, it does contribute to the overall picture of prefixes losing their semantic and phonological structure.

Let us take a look at some sets of examples where prefixed verbs are used with and without particle.

a) **aceorfan of** 'cut off'

(171)*Gif mon folcleasunge gewyrce, & hio on hine geresp weorðe,*
    if man public slander makes and it on him proved becomes
*mid nanum leohtran ðinge gebete þonne him mon **aceorfe** þa tungon **of**...*
    with no lighter things amends than him man ***a*-cuts** the tongue **off**
'If anyone utters a public slander, and it is proved against him, he shall make amends on no easier terms than that his tongue be **cut off**...'
LawAf_1:32.103

(172)*He **cearf of** heora handa and heora nosa.*
    he **cut off** their hands and their noses
'He **cut off** their hands and noses'
O.E. Chron. an. 1014

(173)*Gif þu scyle **aceorfan** oððe asniþan unhal lim of halum lice þonne*
    if you should ***a*-cut** or *a*-sever unhealthy limb from healthy body then
*****ceorf** þu þæt on þam gemære þæs halan lices*
    cut you that on the side the.GEN healthy body.
'If you should **cut off** or remove an unhealthy limb from a healthy body, **cut** it on the side of the healthy body.'
c1025. Lch_II_[1]:35.4.1.1060

In the above set of examples we see the verb *ceorfan*[37] 'cut' in all four possible combinations: prefixed in the first part of example (173), prefixless in the second part of example (173), with a particle only (172) and prefixed with particle (171). Incidentally, in all the three examples the objects are body parts, but this only makes it easier to compare them, make generalizations and conclusions.

---

[37] The verb *ceorfan* is the ancestor of Modern English *carve*.

In all three examples the meaning of the verb is perfective (a body part is "successfully" amputated in all cases), except for the second instance of (173) where *ceorf* is very likely imperfective, as the focus is on the action and not on its entirety. In the first of these three examples (171), the prefix – or the particle – one of these two seems to be redundant. Or perhaps the action only intensified by the particle, as the prefix on its own was too weak. This intensification can also be interpreted as a higher degree of resultativity, as was discussed in examples (150) and (151).

b) **adrifan ut / onweg** 'drive out'

(174)*Adam, wearð of his gecyndan are þurh Euan his wif* **ut adræfed**.
   Adam   was of the lawful   property through Eve his woman **out** *a*-**driven**
   'Adam was **driven out** of the property of his kind because of Eve.'

   c1075. ChrodR_1:54.24.732

(175)*Cwædon him to: Gif þu ne wilt us geðafian in swa æðelicum þinge,*
   said.3.PL him to if you not want us assent   in so   easy   thing
   þe we biddað, ne meaht þu in usse mægðe ne ussum gemanan wunian.
   which we   ask,   not may you in our province not our   society live
   & **dreofon** *hine* **onweg***,*
   and **drove** him **away**,
   'They said to him: if you will not assent to us in a matter so easy, which we request, you may not remain in our province or in our society. And they **drove him away**,'

   c900. cobede,Bede_2:5.112.24.1060-1061

(176)*ða ne mihte Iosep hine leng dyrnan, ac he* **draf** *ealle þa Egyptiscan* **ut**
   then not could Joseph them long hide   but he **drove** all the Egyptians **out**
   'when Joseph could not hide them any longer, so he **drove** all the Egyptians **out**'

   Gen 45.1:

(177)*Se broðor, þe for his agenum lehtre oðþe unðeawe of mynstre   færð*
   the brother who for his own   sin   or vice from monastery goes away
   oðþe **adræfed** *bið, gif he eft gecyrran wile, behate ærest bote*
   or **a-driven** is if he back turn   wants promise first amendment
   and geswicenesse ealra þæra unþeawa, þe he fore **adræfed** *wæs*.
   and cleaning   all.GEN the vices   that he before *a*-**driven** was
   'The brother, who because of his own sin or vice goes away from the monastery or is **expelled** and if he wants to turn back, he should first promise to amendment and cleaning of all the vices for which he was expelled before.'

   c1025. cobenrul,BenR:29.53.8.653

As with the previous set of examples, we see the verb *drifan* 'drive' in the sense of 'drive out, expel' in all different combinations: simply prefixed (177), prefixless but with two different particles (175) and (176) and prefixed with particle in (174).

c) **up aþenian** 'stretch out, elevate'

(178) *sie he for ealle **up aðened** mid ðære godcundan foresceawunge his*
    be he for all **up a-stretched** with the divine contemplation his
inngeðances
inner thought
'Be he above all **elevated** with the divine contemplation of his inner thought'

c894 CP:16.97.22.642

Number (178) features the verb *aþenian* 'stretch out', which was already dealt with in (168) and (170), but in this sentence it co-occurs with the particle *up*. However, I would argue that the particle *up* in this case appears in its spatial meaning, contributing to the entire phrasal verb the meaning of elevation, rather than stretching, while the prefix *a-* contributes to its aspectual meaning, possibly resultative. A similar morphological distribution of meaning can be found in the Croatian translation equivalent *uzdignut*, where the prefix *uz-* corresponds to the meaning of OE up, while the perfective non-terminal suffix *-nu-* corresponds to the prefix *a-*. If we interpret the functions of the prefix and the particle in this way, then their co-occurrence is not redundant.

The following two examples feature two different verbs co-occurring with the prefix *a-* and the particle *ut*. In both examples the particle seems to be reinforcing the meaning of the prefix:

d) **ut aþringan fram** 'to force (someone) out (of a group)'

(179) *me witodlice þæt godcunda mægen þæs ganges bewerede,*
    me certainly that divine might the.GEN going.GEN prevented
*and ic sona wæs **ut aþrungen** fram eallum þam folce*
    and I soon was **out a-forced** from all the people
'The divine might have prevented me from going in, and I was soon thrust out from all the people.'

c1010. comary, LS_23_[MaryofEgypt]:406.264

e) **ut aberstan** 'to burst out'

(180) *þunor cymð of hætan & of wætan ... ðonne hi gegaderode beoð ...*
    thunder comes from heat and from water ... when they together are
binnon þære lyfte, þonne winnað hi him betwynan mid egeslicum swege,
    inside the air then win they them between with terrifying noise
*& þæt fyr **aberst ut** ðurh ligette*
and the fire **a-bursts out** through lightning
'Thunder comes from heat and from moisture... when they are together... in the air, they contend between themselves with terrifying noise, and the fire **bursts out** in lightning'

ÆTemp 14.1

Both *aþringan* and *aberstan* appear in other contexts without the particle. They also appear prefixless, as *þringan* 'press, crowd, throng' and *berstan* 'burst'.

f) **afeallan of / nyðer / adune** 'fall off/down'

(181) *ða wæs þam deofle waa on his awyrgedum mode þæt se mann sceolde*
then was the.DAT devil woe in his accursed mind that the man should
*ða myrhðe geearnian þe he **of afeoll** for his upphefednysse.*
then pleasures deserve which he **off** *a*-**fell** for his pride
'Then was there sorrow to the devil in his accursed mind, that man should deserve the pleasures from which he **fell** on account of his pride'

ÆHex 449

(182) *And Tyrus þa **nyðer afeoll** on eorðan astreht*
and Tyrus then down *a*-**fell** on earth *a*-stretched
'And then Tyrus **fell down** prostrate on earth'

c1085.covinsal,VSal_1_[Cross]:9.7.70

(183) *ða mid ðam þe he his gebedu sang. ða tær þæt hors þæt ðæc of ðære*
then with that he his prayers sang then tore the horse the thatch from the
*cytan hrofe. and þær **feoll adune** swilce of ðam hrofe wearm hlaf mid his*
cottage roof and there **fell down** such from the roof warm loaf with his
syflinge.
food
'Then while he was singing his prayers, the horse tore the thatch from the roof of the cottage, and there **fell down**, as from the roof, a warm loaf with some food.'

c995. ÆCHom II,10 82.54

The last set of examples show the verb *feallan* 'fall' in different combinations of prefixes and particles. In (181) the perfective verb *afeallan* is accompanied by the (preverbal) particle *of,* where both *of* and *a-* seem to have a similar meaning. Example (182) is particularly interesting because it contains the adverbial particle *nyðer* 'down', also in preverbal position, co-inciding with the prefix *a-*. The redundancy is further complemented by another adverbial which could also perform an aspectual function: the meaning of the phrase *on eorðan* 'on earth' is actually already conveyed with the adverbial *nyðer* 'down'. *Astreht* 'prostrate' is etymologically a past participle of the *a-*prefixed verb *astreccan* 'stretched out', but it is lexicalized in the phrase *astreht feallan* 'fall prostrate' where it could perform an aspectual function. In other words, it could be argued that in this example there is triple redundancy in terms of aspect.

Finally, example (183) features the verb *feallan* without the prefix but with the post-verbal particle *adune,* the ancestor of modern English *down*[38]. The verb *feoll* 'fell' has a perfective meaning in the sentence exemplified even though it is without a prefix. Its perfectivity is signalled by the particle *adune,* but it is also contextually clear it comes as a sequence from the previous clause which starts with *ða*.

To summarize this section, the question that arises is as follows: Are the particles featured in the examples (171) to (183) redundant in cases where they

---

[38] The particle *adune* 'down' is an interesting example of grammaticalization. The origin of this adverb, preposition and particle can be traced back to OE *dun* 'hill, mountain'. Its grammaticalization is described in Sadej (2009).

co-occur with the prefix *a-*? One of the conclusions that we can make is that sometimes the meaning of the prefix was not enough and that it was losing its meaning, so a particle was added as re-inforcement. Other times the co-occurring prefix and the particle actually perform different functions and are therefore not redundant.

5.9 Prefix *a-* in Middle English

Many Old English *a*-prefixed verbs can still be encountered in the Middle English period, but the ratio of tokens and types points to a drop in productivity. Table 25 shows the most frequent types in Middle English.

	Type	Token frequency	Meaning
1	*abiden*	226	to wait, be patient, delay, hesitate
2	*arisan*	215	to stand up, move upwards, appear
3	*arēren*	54	to raise, erect, set up
4	*alēsen*	38	to deliver, redeem, release
5	*agilten*	36	to be guilty of sin, transgression or offense
6	*alighten*	36	to descend from a position, to lighten
7	*acursen*	31	to excommunicate, curse
8	*alighten*	27	to light, set on fire
9	*ashāmen*	25	to feel shame or embarrassment
10	*abīen*	24	to buy or pay for, obtain at the cost of labour or suffering

Table 25
The most frequent *a-* types in Middle English

When we compare this frequency list with the one for Old English (Table 22), we can see that the only verb that stayed in the top 10 is the verb *arisan*, which is ranked as the second most frequent verb in both periods. Incidentally, it has survived with this prefix until present day, as have the verbs *abide*, *alight* and *ashame*.

The verb *abidan*, which was the most frequent *a*-prefixed verb in Middle English, appears twice in the following short extract:

(184) *and þo **abode** þe Danois neuer , til þai hade conquerede al*
    and then **stopped** the Danes never till they had conquered all
    Northumberland and in þat contre þai made Werdeynes , & went ferþer

Northumberland and in that country they made wardens and went further
*into þe lande , and token Notyngham . and þere þai **abiden** al þe wynter ,*
into the land and took Nottingham and there they **waited** all the winter
and deden al þe sorwe þat þai myght .
and did all the sorrow that they might
'Then the Danes never **stopped** until they had killed and conquered the whole of Northumberland and in that country they installed their wardens and moved on into the land. And they took Nottingham, and there they **remained** the whole winter and did all the harm they could.'
c1400. CMBRUT3,106.3196-3201

According to the MED, the verb *abidan* had twelve different meanings, two of which are featured in example (184). Even though both verbs give a perfective reading in this example, we cannot say that the function of the prefix *a-* in them is to mark perfectivity. In both examples the prefix *a-* is already lexicalized, as it is in the Modern English verb *abide.* The following example shows the verb *abidan* in an imperfective reading:

(185)*Lord , ne ben hij nouʒt <u>aschamed</u> in me þat **abiden** þe , Lord of vertuʒ .*
Lord not be they nought <u>ashamed</u> in me that **abide** you Lord of virtue
'Lord, let not those who **wait** for you be <u>ashamed</u> of me, Lord of virtue'
c1350. CMEARLPS,80.3521

By this point in Middle English, all instances of grammaticalization of the preverb *a-* have been lost, so any remaining verbs with this prefix tend to represent instances of lexicalization. Example (185) also contains another frequent *a*-prefixed verb which has been underlined. As it appears in the past participle form, it might be argued that the function of the prefix *a-* in this case was to mark a past participle in the same way the prefix *ge-* did in Middle English (see section 6.11), though it is more likely that it was also already lexicalized.

Another very interesting development is *awritan* 'write', the most frequent type in Old English. Not only is the prefixed verb *awritan* no longer among the top 10 most frequent verb types, but it has disappeared from English altogether. There are only sporadic occurrences of *awritan* in Middle English, the last attested use dated to 1225, according to ME:

(186)*hit is **awriten** on boken . þet þe bið al swa sculdig þe þet uuel iþeuað ;*
it is **a-written** in books that which is all so guilty which that evil serves
swa þe þe hit deð . ʒif he hit betan mei ; and umbe þe bota ne hoʒað .
so which it does if he it mend may and about the amendment not heeds
'It is **written** in books that he who allows evil is as guilty as he who commits it, if he may amend it and takes no heed of the amendment.'
c1225 CMLAMBX1,113.1070

In the corpus of Middle English texts used in this research, there are only four occurrences of *awriten,* all appearing solely in the Lambeth Homilies from 1225.

Another verb that faced a similar destiny is the verb *acennan* 'generate, give birth', which was the third most frequent type in Old English. Its last attested usage was in 1250:

(187) *He was **akenned** þurh þe mihte of þan halge gast, Geboren of þa maden Marie.*
'He was **born** through the power of the holy spirit, born from the maiden Mary'

c1250. Creed (Blick 6864) p.138

All the instances of Middle English *awriten* and *akennen* are past participles, which suggests that the preverb *a-* followed a similar grammaticalization path like the preverb *ge-*, from a marker of aspectuality to a marker of past participles, whose inherent grammatical semantics contains a notion of resultativity.

However, there are still some cases where other *a*-prefixed verbs appear in non-past-participle forms, such as the ingressive verb *ablindian* 'to become blind':

(188) *Gif þet eȝe **ablindað**; ne bið naut þe hond wel lokinde.*
    if that eye ***a*-blinds**, not is naught the hand well looking
'If the eye **becomes blind**, the hand will not be well-seeing.'

?c1200. CMLAMBX1,109.1008

5.10 Middle English Additions

When a large influx of French words entered English at the beginning of the Middle English period, many French words also contained a prefix *a-*, whose original spatial meaning was 'to', coming from Latin *ad* 'to'.

(189) *ap(p)roven* O.Fr. *aprover from* L. *approbare* 'to assent to as good, regard as good' from *ad-* 'to' + *probare* 'to try, test something (to find if it is good)'

(190) *ap(p)eren* O.Fr. *aparoir* (12c.) *'appear, come to light, come forth'* from L. *apparere* 'to appear' from *ad-* 'to' + *perere* 'to come forth, be visible'

However, such vocabulary came sealed as a package and native speakers of English most likely could not morphologically analyse verbs such as *approve* and *prove*. Incidentally, the prefix *a-* also performed a number of aspectual roles in Old French, as for example an inchoative reading in the verbs (Dufresne et al. 2003: 34):

(191) *penser* 'to think' → *apenser* 'to begin to think'

(192) *parler* 'to talk' (durative activity) → *aparler* 'to address someone' (inchoative)

or boundedness as in

(193) *river* 'to sail along the shore' (durative activity) → *ariver* 'to reach the shore' (accomplishment)

The two homonymous prefixes, the Old English *a-* and the Old French *a-* originated from two different spatial prefixes, but by an accidental historical process both were bleached by the beginning of the Middle English period, and evolved into prefixes that mark aspectuality. It is interesting that the bleaching process can make two spatial prefixes of opposite directional meanings overlap in their function of markers of inchoativity.

After the Old English period as the whole prefixal system was gradually waning and English was undergoing major sound reductions, the prefixes *on-*, *of-* and *ge-* reduced to *a-*, as for example *alive* (on life) *ablaze* (on blaze, on fire), *anew* (of new) or *aware* (*gewær*). However, it must be noted that these are not verbs. Furthermore, English borrowed the homophonic *a-* as a negative prefix imported from Greek as in *atypical* or *amoral*.

Once all these morpho-phonological changes and borrowings were added to the English language, the Old English prefix *a-* burst under the functional load and eventually disappeared. These Middle English factors quite possibly merely speeded up the process.

It is also worth mentioning that for present-day speakers of English, the prefix *a-* is more likely to be associated with another verbal prefix *a-* as in the following examples:

(194) *I went a-hunting.*

(195) *He came a-running.*

(196) *I've been a-courting Mary Jane.* (from Lyons 1977: 719)

Such constructions are still used in some dialects like Appalachian English. One of the most famous example is a song by Bob Dylan – *The times they are a-changin'*. The use of *a-* before participles is recorded from the 16th century. This *a-* prefix is a reduction of the preposition *on* whose function was to express durative or progressive aspect, but has nothing to do with the prefix *a-* from the Old English period. This prefix *a-* in fact shows how the progressive construction developed in the first place – it is locative in origin (cf. Comrie 1976: 99). Close relatives of English, i.e. Dutch and German, make use of similar locative constructions to express progressive meaning, as was noted in example (4) in the beginning of the book. Perhaps the German and the Dutch progressive constructions will grammaticalize further in the future and evolve into tenses like in English.

5.11 Conclusion

The aim of this chapter was to describe the numerous meanings of the prefix *a-* in Old English. By contrasting *a*-prefixed verbs to their simplex verbs in context, we have seen how the prefix *a-* adds perfective meanings to the verb. These perfective meanings include resultativity, completiveness and even inchoativity. In fact, the range of aspectual meanings is so wide the prefix comes to present a number of highly divergent and even directly opposite aspectual senses, such as durative and instantaneous.

However, it is a very unlikely situation that the prefix itself represented so many distinct aspectual meanings. The different categories that have been discussed here are a result of the combination of the verb's inherent semantics and the prefix. A more likely scenario is that the prefix *a-* originally had one or perhaps two spatial senses and then it bleached to become a *préverbe vide*. The proof for this is to be found in the etymology of this prefix, which was originally a source prefix meaning 'out' or 'out of'. Cross-linguistic evidence, something that grammaticalization theory acknowledges as proof, also shows that source prefixes were the initially most productive prefixes in Slavic expressing resultativity.

When re-inforced with the particle, the prefix shows a seeming redundancy or points to the fact that its meaning was already bleached in the Old English period and needed a particle back-up.

Based on cross-linguistic evidence, source prefixes such as 'out' have been very productive as resultative prefixes in Slavic, Germanic and Baltic languages where they also graduate to perfectivization of inchoative verbs. The productivity of the prefix a- as a perfectivizer is yet another confirmation of the productivity of source prefixes as perfectivizers, which is not really predictable, as the space-for-time metaphor might lead us to think that goal prefixes would be most productive as perfectivizers rather than source prefixes.

The analysis of verbs has shown that a-prefixed verbs are perfective, whereas their simplex counterparts can express both perfective and imperfective meaning. This biaspectual property of simplexes is explained by means of Jakobson's concept of semantic unmarkedness. Perfective forms, in this case a-prefixed verbs, are semantically marked so they will denote perfective meaning, whereas imperfective forms, in this case prefixless verbs, are semantically unmarked. This means that they are imperfective by default, but they also have an ability to convey a perfective meaning.

The functions of the prefix a- were gradually replaced by two analytical systems, one of post-verbal particles and the other of progressive tenses.

The multifunctionality of this prefix led to semantic opaqueness, which was later further aggravated by other uses and new roles that certainly contributed to its demise. The prefix a- could not bear the brunt of the semantic load that it still carried from the Old English period, so the Middle English sound changes and borrowings probably put the last nail in its coffin.

Chapter 6
An Analysis of the Preverb *ge-*

6.1 Introduction

This chapter will investigate what kind of meanings are expressed by the verbal prefix *ge-*. Unlike Chapters 5 and 7, this chapter includes a section on previous studies (in particular re-visiting Lindemann 1970) which discusses a number of previous attempts to explain the meaning and function of this preverb. Chapters 5 and 7 do not include such a section because there are no previous corpus-based studies of the preverbs *a-* and *for-*. The present analysis of the prefix *ge-* takes the categories of meaning proposed by previous researchers and examines them in the present corpus.

This analysis will show that the meanings of *ge-* can be aspectual (i.e. grammatical), but also entirely bleached (showing no difference between the prefixed and the simplex pair), as well as lexicalized. For this reason, this chapter also includes a section on lexicalized cases, which does not exist for the prefix *a-*, as hardly any such cases were identified in the Old English period.

The meaning and function of the preverb *ge-* is one of the most puzzling questions in the study of Old English grammar. This preverb is the most frequent morpheme in Old English. It is four times more frequent than the preverb *a-*. Therefore, it is little wonder that it has generated significant interest amongst scholars and students, borne out by the fact that even by 1965, according to Lindemann's count, as many as 35 dissertations, monographs and articles were written on this ubiquitous and multi-faceted prefix.

The following table shows the most frequent types of *ge-*prefixed verbs in a randomized sample of 1,655 tokens.

	Type	Token frequency	Meaning
1	*geniman*	~1140	take, take up, take away, assume
2	*geseon*	~790	see
3	*gehyran*	~550	hear
4	*gecweþan*	~350	speak, say
5	*gesettan*	~340	set, put, fix, confirm, compose
6	*gelyfan*	~310	believe, confide, trust, hope
7	*gedon*	~30	do, perform, act, achieve, make
8	*gefyllan*	~290	fill (up), load, make full
9	*gehælan*	~270	heal, cure, save
10	*gebetan*	~250	make good, mend, repair

Table 26
The most frequent *ge-* types in Old English

There were 16,557 *ge-*verbs in the entire corpus, so their number was reduced by ten to make the research more manageable. For this reason, token frequencies have been multiplied by ten to get approximate values in the above table so that they can be compared to type frequencies of other prefixes.

A closer look at the table will show that all the verbs survived into Modern English in their prefixless form except for the first one and the last one. The verb *niman* has been replaced by the Old Norse borrowing *take* and *betan* has been replace by other verbs. The verb *cweþan* now survives as an archaic form *quoth*.

6.2 Previous studies

The most authoritative and comprehensive account of this prefix's meaning and function is Lindemann (1970) consisting of two parts, the first of which is a reprint of his paper from 1965. Lindemann reviewed all the previous studies on this prefix that were permeated by the assumption that *ge-* is a marker of perfective aspect, which he put down to

> "an inordinate, romantic preoccupation on the part of some scholars of the Germanic dialects with the Slavic dialects and a generous amount of what Hjelmslev was wont to refer to as "transcendental linguistics" – the substitution of pure speculation for the laborious, objective examination of a prefix per se."
>
> (Lindemann 1970: 19).

The first evidence against *ge-* as a marker of perfectivity that Lindemann presents is a study by the Russian scholar L. S. Limar who investigated the prefixes' potential to express aspect in Beowulf. Limar (1963: 159-161) remarks that there are no purely aspectual prefixes even in Slavic languages and that perfectivization is a phenomenon of a semantic nature.

> "In Old English essentially there was no form for the imperfective aspect, and since there was no imperfective aspect, that is, one of a correlative pair was absent, there obviously could be no system of aspects, since the system is built on correlatives" (1963: 160).

Limar's Slavic-centered view of aspect is grist to Lindemann's mill – since Limar was a scholar whose native language is supposed to make him "especially sensitive to aspectual distinctions" (Lindemann 1970: 19).

What also adds weight to the discussion is the fact that there are many aspectual categories which are unpaired (such as iteration) in many different languages, which does not pose a threat to the existence of an aspectual system.

Limar claims to have found numerous examples of simplex verbs in contexts with perfective meaning and *ge*-prefixed verbs in contexts with imperfective meaning – in other words, completely contrary to what Streitberg's theory proposes (as discussed in sections 2.4 and 2.8). However, it is somewhat surprising that Limar did not think of modifying Streitberg's theory and find a different way of interpreting the prefix *ge*- in his data. Additionally, as we have seen in the chapter on aspect in Slavic (examples listed in (47), section 2.8) – there are many instances of prefixed verbs with imperfective meaning and simplex verbs with perfective meaning. The results of this research also show numerous instances like those of Limar, but this still does not mean that *ga*- does not have aspectual properties, as Lindemann and Limar are quick to judge. Lindeman singles out the following conclusion by Limar as the most important observation:

> "Old English verbs, alone, taken out of context and not connected to any particular adverbs, can *not* be recognized as particular aspectual forms... Neither can the verbal prefixes be in any way considered aspectual determinants."
>
> (Limar 1963: 166)

This is to a certain extent true and the present study also confirms this statement for the majority of *ge*-prefixed verbs. However, neither Limar nor Lindemann offer a solution as to what is the meaning and the function of this prefix. They prefer to talk about what it is not.

Lindemann's study is at times very convincing (e.g. the discussion why *ge*- is not a cognate of Latin *con*-), at times contradictory (e.g. that *ge*- is monosemous, i.e. had only one abstract meaning) and at times mystifying (e.g. that he examined 45,000 simplex and compound verbs in their contexts). The number 45,000 certainly seems quite exaggerated, as it takes about a week to study 100 Old English verbs in their contexts with the use of electronic corpora, so studying that many verbs (in their contexts!) back in the 1960's would require a several-year project with more than one researcher. This is quite dubious if the result is a book of only 70 pages.

Furthermore, Lindemann says that his corpus was Skeat's edition of Old English dialect translations (West-Saxon, Mercian and Northumbrian) of the

Gospel of St. Matthew and Sweet's edition of Alfred's *Orosius*[39]. These two texts do not contain 45,000 verbs.

A further problem could be that these two texts were not originally composed in English but were translations from Latin, so the authenticity of the Old English idiomatic use is questionable. For this reason, it is always good to include a text that was originally written in Old English.

After Lindemann's milestone work in a rather long tradition of studies on *ge-*, there were only a few studies worth mentioning here. Innovative approaches were taken in Zbierska-Sawala (1997), Dollinger (2001) and Martín Arista (2008).

Zbierska-Sawala (1997) analyses the axiological functions of Old English prefixes, believing that prefixes should be analysed as modifying texts in addition to modifying just words. She claims that *ge-* acts as a paragraph organizer. In this light, she thinks that the prefix *ge-* adds positive evaluation to the meaning of the verb. Dollinger (2001) analysed the prefix *ge-* as a linguistic replicator in the light of the Darwinian theory, applying the neo-Darwinian framework to the field of diachronic morphology. Finally, Martín Arista's (2008) quantitative rather than qualitative analysis looks at *ge-* as the most widespread affix in Old English, distributed over four lexical categories (verbs, nouns, adjectives and adverbs). This is something that previous authors typically brushed aside and instead merely focused on *ge-* as a verbal prefix.

Trobevšek-Drobnak (1994) and Maylor (2002) also deal with the Old English prefix *ge-*, although their results do not show anything of significance.

Unlike *a-*, which could in Old English be attached as a prefix only to verbs, the prefix *ge-* was also an adjectival and a nominal prefix and it was the most common of all affixes.

> "The system of the OE verbal prefixes was in a state of advanced decay, both semantically and formally, and many prefix combinations had lost their transparency: it was no longer possible to associate a consistent meaning with a given prefix."
>
> (Kastovsky 2006: 236)

> "Verbal ge-, when it can still be attributed a recognizable meaning, denotes 'perfectivity, result', often also transitivising an intransitive verb, e.g. *ge-ærnan* 'gain by running', *ge-āscian* 'learn by asking'. But many instances do not seem to exhibit a semantic difference between the simplex and the prefixation, e.g. *(ge)-ādlian* 'be, become ill', *(ge-)æmtigian* 'to empty', or the meaning difference between the simplex and the prefixation is idiosyncratic, e.g. *standan* 'to stand': *ge-standan* 'endure, last', *weorþan* 'be worthy': *ge-weorþan* 'agree'."
>
> (Kastovsky 2006: 237)

The prefix *ge-* is often said to be semantically empty, which is not possible from the point of view of cognitive linguistics. This problem will be discussed further later on.

Hogg (2002: 105) says that the prefix ge- "can come close to being an

---

[39] Wischer and Habermann (2005) also use *Orosius,* but as the only text for their exploration of aspect and aktionsart in Old English.

inflectional marker rather than a prefix". This is in line with one of the hypothesis of this study – that prefixes were grammaticalized and that even though they occurred before the stem or root, they exhibited inflectional properties rather than derivational.

In spite of all the academic research that *ge-* accumulated over the years, it is interesting that many textbooks on the history of the English language still give a largely inaccurate description of this prefix, such as Strang (1970: 335): "completive (perfective)"or Singh (2005: 87) "all past participle forms also carried the prefix *ge-* (sometimes known as the *completive prefix*)". It is interesting that Pyles & Algeo (1993) and Baugh & Cable (2002) make no mention of this prefix. However, Pyles & Algeo (1993) consistently attach the prefix *ge-* to all past participles in all their conjugation tables, thus suggesting that this prefix was a regular past participle marker.

In the chapter on Old English affixing, Millward (1996: 123) discusses the most common prefix *ge-*, saying that it was

> "so widely used and in so many different ways that it came to be virtually meaningless and was ultimately lost from the language. It was a marker of the past participle of verbs, but it was also used throughout the entire conjugation of many verbs, usually to indicate perfective aspect (completion of an action). Sometimes it distinguished a special meaning of the verb. For example, *gān* meant "to go", while *gegān* meant "to conquer". Often *ge-* was attached to a verb with no discernible change in meaning at all: both *mænan* and *gemænan* meant "to mean"."

Millward quite rightly points to no discernible change in meaning between the simplex and prefixed versions of the same verb, but the example such as *gan* vs. *gegan* is somewhat problematic. It is true that *gegan* can mean conquer, but it is only one of the meanings that the prefixed verb has (in which case it also changes transitivity). Its primary meaning remains 'to go' in the very basic sense of movement just like with its simplex counterpart *gan*, but it has also developed a number meanings of going with an idea of attainment which DOE subsumes under the heading 'to get by going'.

(197) *hie heora here on tu todældon; oþer æt ham beon heora lond to*
   they their army in two divided   other at home are   their land to
*healdanne, oþer ut faran to winnanne; hie siþþan **geeodon** Europe &*
      hold   other out go   to   win   they after   ***ge*-went** Europe and
Asiam þone mæstan dæl.
       Asia   the   most   part
'They divided their army into two parts; one to be at home to hold their land, the other to go out to war; they afterwards **conquered** the greatest part of Europe and Asia.'

Or 1 10.30.2

Example (197) is the kind of instance that Millward had in mind when she suggested that *gegan* meant 'to conquer'. However, in a very large number of contexts, *gegan* has all the meanings that *gan* has:

(198) *Eall þas **geeodon** in ussera tida timan.*
       all   that ***ge*-went** in   our   tide time

'All of that **passed** in the span of our era"

GuthA 753

And a number of other idiomatic meanings can be observed in the examples such as the following:

(199) *Þa þæt **geeode** þy sylfan dæge þe gyrsandæg was.*
    then that ***ge*-went** the self day that yesterday was
    'Then it **happened** on the very day that was yesterday.'

HomU 10 (Verc 6)

This idiomatic meaning can also be expressed with the unprefixed verb in combination with the particle *forþ* 'forth', which not only tells us of the semantic relationship between *gan* and *gegan* but also of the prefix *ge-* and the particle *forþ* in a case like this:

(200) *þe sceal wintrum frod on woruld bringan Sarra sunu, soð **forð gan** wyrd*
    that shall winters old in world bring Sarah son, true **forth go** fate
    æfter þissum wordgemearcum.
    after these word-marks
    'Sarah shall bear a son though old in years, true fate shall **happen** according to these terms.'

GenA 2355

It is interesting to note that in standard Old English textbook anthologies such as Mitchell and Robinson (2007) and Marsden (2004), the prefix *ge-* is ignored in alphabetical ordering, so *gehelpan* should be looked for under *h* and *gemunan* under *m*. Such lexicographic practice clearly points to the fact that by and large the meaning of *ge-* is empty or has no explicit function.

The other frequently quoted example of difference between a simplex and a *ge*-prefixed verb is *acsian* vs. *geacsian*. The former corresponds to 'ask', whereas the latter is said to mean 'learn by asking' or 'find out'. The following example shows this particular meaning:

(201) *sende þa his cwelleras. & ofsloh ealle þa hysecild þe wæron on þære*
    sent then his killers and killed all the male-children that were in the
    byrig Bethleem ... fram twywintrum cilde to anre nihte: be þære tide
    town Bethlehem from two-winters child to one night about the time
    *þe he **geaxode** æt ðam tungelwitegum.*
    that he ***ge*-asked** at the star-prophets
    'Then he sent his killers and murdered all the male children who were in the town of Bethlehem... from two years old to one night: around the time when he **learned from** the astrologers **by asking** (sought information from astrologers).'

*c*995. ÆCHom I, 5 218.48

However, as with *gan* and its prefixed counterpart *gegan*, the verb *geacsian* is synonymous with *acsian* in certain contexts like the following:

(202) *He **geascode** hia, Huu feolo lafo habbað gie?*
    he ***ge*-asked** them how many remnant have you
    'He **asked** them: "How many relics do you have?"'

MkGl (Li) 8.5

The inadequacy of Streitberg's doctrine when applied to Old English data has been observed in a number of dissertations from the beginning of the 20th century, such as Hesse (1906) and Weick (1911). Friedrich Weick analysed the prefix *ge-* in the Lindisfarne Gospels, which he thought would show to be a perfectivizing morpheme, but realized that it does not behave at all in accordance with Streitberg's hypothesis. Weick commented different verb forms, as if suggesting textual emendations in order to comply with the hypothesis, "Das Simplex sollte stehen an Stelle des fälschlich gesetzten Kompos" ('There should be a simplex verb instead of this wrongly used compound verb') (1906: 3). Frustrated, he comments on one verb that "Das Simplex ist einige Male belegt, aber sonderbarerweise immer an unrechter Stelle" ('The Simplex is attested, but strangely enough always in the wrong place') (1906: 5). Finally, rather than concluding that Streitberg's theory does not work with Old English, all the 'wrong uses' make Weick believe that the Old English scribes did not know how to use their language correctly:

> "Noch deutlicher führen uns die zahlreichen Beispiele, wo geschrieben werden mußte: 'das Simplex oder das Kompositum sollte stehen' vor Augen, wie sehr groß schon die Verwirrung in bezug auf die Anwendung von Simplex und Kompositum war"[40]

(Weick 1906: 49)

6.3 The etymology of *ge-*

There is no doubt that the cognate of the Old English prefix *ge-* is the preverb *ga-* in Gothic. Numerous examples of comparing Old English and Gothic texts confirm that. According to Streitberg's hypothesis, the Gothic preverb *ga-* corresponds to "Indo-European *co-*" and meant 'together'. Its function was to perfectivize, as its meaning had been completely reduced, suggesting that the reflexes of Proto-Germanic **ga-* had been entirely bleached of its lexical meaning and became fully grammaticalized. This is, in fact, still widely believed, even though research in the twentieth century proved otherwise.

Streitberg was not the first to propose that this prefix was devoid of lexical meaning. In 1580 Johannes van Gorp from Antwerp published that *ge-* corresponds to Latin *ad-*, but also suggested that *ge-* prefixed to a verb indicates that the action expressed by that verb is more "carried out", making it the earliest documented statement that asserts the perfectivizing property of the prefix *ge-* (Lindemann 1970: 30-31). Almost a century later it was documented in Somner's Old English – Latin dictionary (1659) and later repeated in Benson's (1701) abridged version of that dictionary:

> "ge- apud Saxones semper fere superfluum".

Lindemann (1970: 22-23) discusses the matter saying that it is not possible for **ga-* being without a concrete meaning in Proto-Germanic because it was a

---

[40] 'Numerous instances where it says 'a simplex or a compound should be used' make it even clearer that there was a big confusion with respect to the usage of simplex and compound verbs' (the translation is mine).

member of a system of preverbs, whose every other member had lexical meaning. According to Dorfeld (1885), Gothic *ga-* is not a reflex of the Proto-Indo-European **ko* but is a cognate of Latin *com-,* which is one of the morphemes that the reflexes of *ga-* correspond to. Lindemann (1970: 24) claims that *ge-* being equivalent to Latin *cum* 'with' constitutes "the very nucleus of our problem and obstructs our understanding the morpheme, both as to meaning and as to function". He elaborates five different points why it is impossible that *ge-* means 'with, together' or is a cognate of Latin *com-* or *cum* (Lindemann 1970: 24-26) and claims that no one in the past 300 years has ever been able to prove it. Even Lehman's *Gothic Etymological Dictionary* notes that "some, however, doubt this origin" (1986: 133). The only evidence that it could ever have been based on is that *ge-*compounds translate Latin compounds with *com-* in a substantial number of instances, but according to Lindemann's statistics, the Latin prefix *ad-* could also be the semantic equivalent of *ge-*, as it appears in an equal number of instances of translations of Latin compounds.

The Latin prefix *com-* may have originated from the preposition *cum* (even though Lindemann also doubts that), and the whole analogy of Latin was transferred onto Old English. Lindemann warns of making such analogies, particularly when they spread over several part-of-speech classes. Lindemann thinks that *ge-* may be compared to Latin *com-* because both are preverbs, but not with Latin *cum* since the latter is a preposition, insisting that *com-* and *cum* have nothing to do with each other. The two grammatical categories are parts of two different systems (preverbs and prepositions) and they have different functions and meanings:

> "Defining one of these grammatical categories in terms of several other ones constitutes a kind of morphemic miscegenation conducive to results that one would expect to produce semantic chaos. [...] The meanings may remotely resemble one another, but they rarely or never precisely co-incide"
> (Lindemann 1970: 26).

Lindemann discusses the marked differences between preverbs and prepositions and takes great efforts in refuting the dominating

> "Streitbergian hypothesis that the reflexes of Proto-Germanic **ga-* became "empty" grammatical morphemes indicating aspect or that they could have meant the same as the Latin preposition *cum.*"
> (Lindemann 1970:28).

Interestingly, Lindemann believes that the most respectable suggestion that explains the meaning of this morpheme is the one offered by Jacob Grimm, which had never been mentioned in the vast literature on this preverb produced in the course of over a hundred years. Grimm explains the meaning of the prefix by means of an opposite to the German prefix *ab-* (English 'off'). In other words, *ge-* means something like 'on' or 'to' as in *ge-hâr* (Lat. *compilis*) vs. *ab-hâr* (Lat. *depilis*).

Even though Lindemann praises Grimm's unostentatious discussion of *ge-* in his *Deutsche Grammatik,* saying that "very sensibly he avoids entangling it in anything approximating aspect or Aktionsart" (1970: 28), Lindemann lists as the second obstruction that "frequently it adds to the action expressed by such a compound the idea of duration and continuity" (ibid.). Streitberg rejected this idea since it disproves his own hypothesis that *ge-* expresses perfectivity.

Nevertheless, Lindemann overlooks two important facts in his discussion. Firstly, Grimm actually carries on the tradition of co-relating the semantics of Germanic *ge-* to Latin *con-*. Secondly, the ideas of duration and continuity are *essentially* aspectual, which is in clear contradiction with Lindemann's claim that Grimm sensibly avoided "entangling it in anything approximating aspect or Aktionsart".

Lindemann wrote his work before the major advances in the theory of grammaticalization, which today can account for recruiting adverbs or prepositions and converting them into preverbs or prefixes, adapting their meaning if needed. In fact, it is a perfectly normal phenomenon that a full word evolves into an affix without producing "semantic chaos", as Lindemann dramatically suggests.

In his chapter-length discussion of the etymology of *ge-*, Lindemann perhaps did not stress enough an important piece of evidence from diachronic phonology – the fact that Old English *ge-* cannot be a cognate of Latin *con-*, as there is no sound law that would account for that. According to Grimm's law or First Germanic sound shift, Proto-Indo-European *k can only give Germanic *h (e.g. English *hound* and Latin *canis*), never Germanic *g. Lindmann (1970: 34) does, however, mention, an attempt by the Norwegian linguist Bugge (1889: 313-314) who thought it was possible to find a common source of Germanic *g and Latin *k by "subtle applications of Verner's Law" (Lindemann 1970: 34).

The only likely candidate for the ancestor of *ge-* on phonological grounds is the Indo-European demonstrative pronominal stem *$ghō$. Its reflex in Croatian is, for example, the 3rd person genitive and accusative masculine and neuter personal pronoun *ga*[41], as well as the Latin pronouns *hic, haec, hoc*. Based on Brugmann's discussion of Indo-European demonstrative pronouns (1904b: 53-60), Lindemann proposes that the origin of *ge-* should be sought in this

> "highly deictic morpheme stressing the progression of an action from one point forward toward another and, as a verbal prefix, capable of expressing such ideas a those inherent in *von, zu, zu-, ver-,* ideas which of course did not correspond to the static, reciprocal relationship expressed by *with, together*".
> (Lindemann 1970: 25)

Lindemann believes that the equivalent Modern English translations of the prefix *ge-* are morphemes such as *at, on, to, toward, out, forth* or *away* (1970: 63). Even though he lists so many Modern English translational equivalents for a single prefix, he suggests that *ge-* was not polysemous but that "it is the exigencies of translation that make it seem so" (Lindemann 1970: 64). Suggesting that this prefix is monosemous seems to be rather far-fetched, given the widely varying uses the prefix is put to.

---

[41] Croatian *ga* is considered to be a contraction of *$jega$ from *njega* 'him'. It also appears in genitive singular endings *-oga, -ega* as in *toga* 'of that', *ovoga* 'of that', *mojega* 'of mine'.

6.4 The meanings of *ge-*

Lindemann (1965: 67-71) discusses the meanings and functions of the prefix *ge-* on the basis of what previous scholarship had accumulated. He claims that none of them are acceptable and therefore names them *doctrines*. There are five of these "doctrines":

1. *ge-* is without meaning
2. *ge-* stresses or intensifies the action of the verb
3. *ge-* converts an intransitive verb into a resultative verb that is transitive
4. *ge-* indicates completion
5. *ge-* expresses perfective aspect

According to Lindemmann, these are only subjective impressions that all previous scholars based on a limited number of examples. He dismisses all five of these prevailing theories, even as partial solutions. Due to the apodictic tone of his style and the suggestion that all previous theories were wrong, Lindemann's conclusions simply invited re-examination.

This analysis of meanings started from the assumption that the prefix *ge-* possibly exhibits the meanings Lindemann refuted. In a controlled randomized sample of 200 tokens, the prefix *ge-* showed the following meanings:

1.	Empty	45%
2.	Intensifying	6%
3.	Transitivizing	0%
4.	Completive	0%
5.	Perfective	26%
6.	Resultative	17%
7.	Change of meaning	2%
8.	No corresponding simplex	4%

Table 27
The meanings and functions of the prefix *ge-*

Numbers 1 to 5 in the table correspond to the meanings Lindemann dismissed. We see that transitivizing and completive meanings have not been identified in the randomized sample, but this does not mean that these two meanings of *ge-* do not exist. This analysis only suggests that they are rare, possibly only a few examples that are unfortunately often quoted as paradigmatic.

Meanings 6-8 are new additions that have not been discussed by Lindemann.

Once we clear the meanings that have not been found and reduce them to six possible combinations, the following pie chart gives a good illustration of ratios of meanings and functions present in this analysis of the prefix *ge-*:

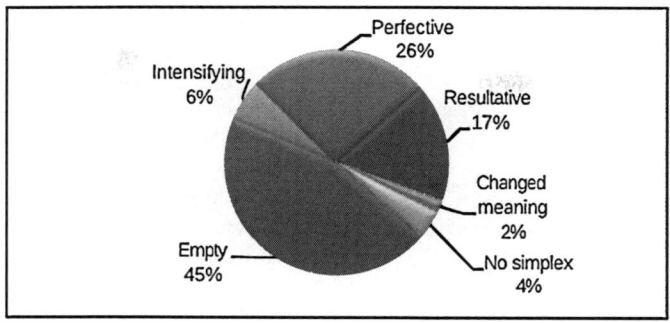

Figure 6
The meanings of *ge-*

6.5 "Empty" *ge-*

Since all morphemes have to be meaningful as meaning is an essential part of each linguistic sign, how is it possible that in as many as 45% of examples the meaning of the prefix is empty? This goes against the basic postulates of cognitive linguistics. However, in almost half of the *ge*-prefixed verbs, their semantic effect is not immediately identifiable. In those cases the addition of the prefix *ge-* leaves both the lexical and the grammatical meaning of the prefix untouched.

Perhaps their function is stylistic or they act as discourse markers, as Zbierska-Sawala (1997) suggests, but then we could conclude that they are meaningful after all. What is relevant for this study is that the prefix *ga-* did not change the grammatical or lexical meaning of verbs in such a high number of tokens.

A good example of "meaningless" *ge-* is the verb *gebiddan* 'pray':

(203) *in þære cirican seo cwen gewunade hire **gebiddan**, þe we ær cwædon*
    in that church the queen accustomed her **pray**.INF who we before said
þæt heo Cristen wære.
    that she Christian were
'The queen usually **prayed** in the church, who, we have already said, was a Christian.'
c897. cobede,Bede_1:15.62.2.576

Its simplex counterpart *biddan* means exactly the same thing:

(204) *Crist cwæð þæt mon sceal to Gode almihtig ane **biddan***
    Christ said that man shall to God almighty only **pray**.INF
'Christ said that one shall **pray** to God Almighty alone'
HomU 1 143

According to the corpus of the DOE; there are 3,200 occurrences of *biddan*, 1,250 occurrences of *gebiddan* and 130 occurrences of *abiddan*. The semantic structure of this verb is so complex that it is difficult to determine its meanings even without the involvement of prefixes. For *biddan*, the following explanation is given:

> "The semantic gradation 'ask, pray, exhort, urge, direct, enjoin, command' is such that the exact meaning at each occurrence cannot usually be established; but in late Old English the sense 'command' appears, perhaps by contact with bēodan."

One would be inclined to conclude that the prefix adds towards a higher degree in this semantic gradation, so that *biddan* means more like 'ask' and 'pray' and *gebiddan* more like 'command', but this is not true. Both *biddan* and *gebiddan* can have any of the above listed meanings, thus making the effect of the prefix non-identifiable in the case of this verb.

Another example of meaningless *ge-* can be identified in the verb *geniman* 'take', whose occurrences considerably contributed to the overall picture of *ge-* as an empty morpheme. In a random sample of 1,665 *ge-* tokens, 75 occurrences were the second person imperative of this verb (*genim*) appearing in Bald's Leechbook (colaece.o2), an Old English collection of medical texts that reflects medical practice of the Anglo-Saxons. Many of the recipes begin with the instruction *genim* or *nim* 'take', as the following examples illustrate.

(205) *Wið   heafodece **genim**   sealh & ele, do ahsan, gewyrc þonne to*
against headache ***ge*-take**.IMP willow and oil do ashes   work   then to
slypan...
viscous substance
'For headache, **take** willow and oil, reduce to ashes, work to a viscid substance...'

c950. colaece,Lch_II_[1]:1.6.1.37-39

(206) *Wið   sare   &   unluste   þæs magan se þe ne mæg ne mid mete*
against soreness and appetite-loss that may the who not may not with meat
*ne mid drincan beon gelacnod, & bitere hræcetunge **nim** centaurian,*
not with drink   be   cured   and bitter hreaking   **take**.IMP centaury
þæt is felterre, sume hatað hyrdewyrt, sume eorðgeallan...
that is fel terrae some call herdsmans-wort some earth-gall
'For soreness and loss of appetite in that maw, which may not be cured neither with meat nor with drink, and for the bitter retching; **take** centaury, that is fel terrae, some call it herdsmans wort, some earth gall...'

c950. colaece,Lch_II_[2]:8.1.1.2241

(207) *Leoht drenc wiþ weden heorte, elehtre, bisceopwyrt,   ælfþone,*
light drink against wood heart lupine   bishop-wort enchanters nightshade
*elene, cropleac, hind hiolopþe, ontre, clate, **nim**   þas wyrta þonne dæg*
helenium cropleek hindheal   ontre clote take.IMP these herbs when day
& niht scade.
and night divide
'A light drink for the wood heart, lupine, bishop's wort, enchanter's nightshade, helenium, cropleek, hindheal, ontre, clote; **take** these herbs when day and night divide'.

c950. colaece,Lch_II_[3]:68.1.1.4098

Bald's Leechbook contains 226 instances of *genim* and 93 instances of *nim,* but their use seems to be interchangeable. The writer of these recipes uses them at whim, as there is no reason why this verb is prefixed in one sentence and prefixless in another. As far as aspect is concerned, it is more likely to be perfective than imperfective based on the comparison with Croatian *uzmi* ('take', perfective) as opposed to *uzimaj* ('take', imperfective). And indeed, all the actions expressed refer to a sequence of events, each of which is finished in order to follow a procedure of making a remedy. The imperfective would suggest that the action is repeated several times, which accidentally works for example (207) but not for (206). Therefore, how can one account for the fact that in the very same text they are used interchangeably?

A similar situation can be found in laws where the verbs *betan* and *gebetan* 'make good, improve, compensate, pay' are also used interchangeably, as the following two examples show.

(208) *Gif ðeowmon þeowne to nedhæmde genede,* **bete**
if slave slavewoman to violation-chastity compels **compensate.3SG.SUBJ**
mid his eowende.
with his genitals
'If a slave rapes a slavewoman, he is to **pay compensation** with his genitals.'
*c*900. colawaf,LawAf_1:25.1.92

(209) *Oðres biscepes oððe ealdormonnes borges bryce oððe mundbyrd*
other.GEN bishop.GEN or ealdorman.GEN surety breaking or protection
gebete *mid twam pundum.*
*ge-*compensate.3SG.SUBJ with two pounds
'For violation of the protection or the guardianship of any other bishop or of an ealdorman, two pounds must be **paid as compensation**.'
*c*900. colawaf,LawAf_1:3.2.20

In Laws of Alfre (colawaf), there are 7 occurrences of *bete* and 33 occurrences of *gebete*. There is absolutely no reason to believe that there is any difference in meaning between the two forms (the prefixed and the prefixless) of that verb, as illustrated in examples (208) and (209).

Examples like these are numerous, so we should not entirely believe Lindemann when he says

> "Far from being an "empty morpheme", *ge-* was replete with shades of meaning roughly equivalent to the NE morphemes *to* and *out,* and we can no longer rest upon the idle assumption that, because they appear to make no distinctive sense to us, such pairs as *seon – geseon* or *sittan – gesittan* appear in our texts as pseudosynonyms produced by indifference or sheer caprice. Not at all; each word is a separate and distinct lexical unit."
>
> Lindemann (1970: 65)

The functions of *ge-* in cases like (203) to (207) are far from being equivalent to Modern English morphemes *to* and *out*.

6.6 *Ge-* as a past participle marker

There is a common misconception that the Old English *ge-* is a past participle marker in the same way as it is in present-day German or Dutch, but it also appears in other inflected forms, as the following statistics show.

past participle	22%
3. p. sg. preterite subjunctive	21%
infinitive	15%
3. p. sg. present indicative	12%
3. p. sg. present subjunctive	10%
2. p. sg. imperative	10%
3. p. pl. preterite indicative	3%
2. p. sg. present indicative	2%
3. p. sg. preterite subjunctive	2%
1. p. sg. present indicative	1%
2. p. sg. present subjunctive	1%
2. p. sg. preterite indicative	1%

Table 28
Inflectional distribution of *ge*-verbs in Old English

The prefix *ge-* grammaticalized as a marker of past participle in the Middle English period, as will be discussed in section 6.11.

6.7 *Ge-* as a perfectivizer

In a number of cases the prefix *ge-* has a perfective meaning, but in proportionately fewer cases than the prefix *a-* which did not exhibit any 'empty' meanings. If we go back to Table 27 and add the resultative meanings to the perfective meanings (since we have defined resultativeness as a type of perfectivity), we will see that there is a similar ratio of perfective and "empty" meanings. Let us consider some examples.

(210) *ða sende God slæp on Adam, & ða ða he slep, ða **genam** he an rib of his*
then sent God sleep on Adam and when he slept then ***ge*-took** he one rib from his
*sidan, & **gefylde** mid flæsce ðær ðæt rib wæs*
side and ***ge*-filled** with flesh where that rib was
'Then God sent Adam to sleep and when he was asleep, he **took out** one of his ribs and **filled up** with flesh where the rib was.'
Gen 2.21

In the above example we see two *ge*-prefixed verbs in context which clearly have perfective meanings. The verb *gefyllan* 'fill up' could specifically be categorized as resultative. However, this sentence also features the verb *sende* 'sent', whose meaning is also clearly perfective but the verb is simplex. As earlier discussed, the imperfective form is semantically unmarked, so with sufficient context, which example (210) definitively has, the simplex can take on perfective meanings as well.

Example (211) contains two verbs, *geseon* 'to see' and *gefyllan* 'to fill', which refer to actions in the past (signified by the past tense) and that took place in their entirety, so we may assume that the prefix *ge-* adds the notion of perfectivity in this case.

(211)*þa **geseah** heo openum eagum, þæs þe hire þuhte, of þæs huses*
    then ***ge*-saw** she open.DAT eyes.DAT that.GEN which her thought from the house's
*hrofe ufan micel leoht cuman; & eal þæt hus **gefylde***
    roof above great light come and all that house ***ge*-filled**
'Then she **saw** with open eyes, as it seemed to her, a great light coming from the roof above and it **filled** all that house.'

c897. Bede 4, 24.340.7

It is interesting to note that in example (211) there are two simplex verbs which have imperfective meaning – *þuhte* 'seemed' and *cuman* 'coming'.

Another parameter that was investigated in this research was the appearance of *ge*-prefixes in the sentence final position. It has been calculated that in 21% of tokens the *ge*-prefixed verb was in the last position in the sentence. This number did not seem sufficient to corroborate a hypothesis that the preferred slot of *ge*-prefixed verbs in the sentence was the final slot. However, it might be interesting to check the ratio between *ge*-prefixed and simplex verbs in the sentence-final position.

6.8 Co-occurrence with *ða*

One assumption that has been tested is the co-occurrence of the time adverbial *ða* 'then, when' with the *ge*-prefixed verbs. The conjunction *ða* is often used to separate parts of a story, as we can see in the following example:

(212)*Þa **gewilnode** he his wambe **gefyllan** of þam beancoddum þe ða swin*
    then ***ge*-wanted** he his stomach ***ge*-fill**.INF from the beanpod that that pigs
æton, and him mon ne sealde.
    ate.3.PL and him man not gave
'Then he **longed** to **fill** his stomach with the pods that the pigs were eating, but no one gave him anything.'

Luke XV

But assumption of the existence of such constructions were abandoned because *ða* did not seem to collocate consistently with *ge*-prefixed verbs, as the simplex version of *wilnian* shows in the following example:

(213)*Þa **wilnode** ic Indeum innanwearde to geseonne.*
    then wanted I India inward to *ge*-see.INF
'Then I **longed** to see India [the Indians] on the inside'.

5, 17. On Indea, Chr. 883; P. 79, 7

Moreover, even if it was part of a structure *ða* + *ge-*, this would not be an aspectual function of this prefix, but rather a stylistic one. We cannot say that the adverbial *ða* 'then' can exclude imperfective meanings even though it refers to a particular point in the past. This can be backed up by evidence from Modern English or Croatian:

(214) *Then he was eating cheese.   Tada je jeo sir.* (imperfective)
Then he ate cheese.   Tada je pojeo sir. (perfective)

Example (212) is also interesting because of the underlined verb *æton* 'ate', which is a simplex with a clearly imperfective meaning in this particular context. The verb *sealde* 'gave' is also a simplex, but could have both a perfective and an imperfective meaning.

The following set of examples is another case where we see the unpredictability of the adverbial *ða* co-occurring with *ge*-prefixed verbs:

(215) *ða **genom** se engel sona þone mon; <u>wearp</u> eft   in þæt fyr*
 then **ge-took** the angel soon   the   man   threw again in   the fire
'Then at once the angel **took** the man and threw him into the fire.'
                              *c*897. cobede,Bede_3:14.216.1.2197-8

(216) *ða **nom** heo arest þeo rode ðe þe sceaðe on hongode & hire uppon ðene*
 then **took** she first the cross the which robber on hung   and it   upon   the
deaden <u>alægde</u>
 dead   *a*-laid
'then she first **took** the cross on which the robber had hung, and laid it upon the dead man.'
                              *c*1150. corood,LS_5_[InventCrossNap]:521.545-6

The aspectual meaning of both (215) and (216) is perfective. Furthermore, the underlined verb *wearp* is a simplex with a perfective meaning, though in other contexts that verb frequently comes with the prefix *a*- or *for*-. Only the form *alægde* is predictably perfective being an *a*-prefixed verb.

6.9 Stylistic functions of *ge*-

Co-ordinating verbs of different stems with the same prefix is a stylistic feature of Old English. Ogura also observes "a stylistic necessity for the use of the same prefix in coordinate pairs" (1995: 92). Here are a few corpus examples that show how the preverb *ge*- may be used to co-ordinate verbs:

(217) *Ða eodan hie eft to ðæm tune, ond þæt gild **gebræcan ond gefyldan***
 then went they after to the   town and that idol **ge-broke** and ***ge*-(cause to) fall**
eal oþ grund.
 all to ground
'They went afterwards to the town, **broke down** the idol and **cast** it all to the ground.'
                              *c*971. coblick,LS_17.1_

(218) *Forðæm him ætwat   Petrus ða dæde ðe he walde, siððan hi ongeaten*
 therefore them reproached Peter the deed that he wished after   he perceived
*hiora wælhreownesse, ðæt hi wæren **gedrefde** & **geeaðmedde**, & ðæs*
 their   cruelty   that they were ***ge*-disturbed** and ***ge*-humbled**   and that
ðe nytweorðlicor gehierden ða halgan lare, ðe hi   ær wilnodon ðæt hi

the more useful   hear   the holy doctrine that they before wished   that they
gehiran mosten.
    hear   might
'Peter reproached them with the deed, because he wished them, after perceiving their cruelty, to **become contrite and humble**, that they might hear the holy doctrine with more advantage, after previously desiring to hear it.
c894. cocura,CP:58.443.10.3163

(219) *Manslagan & manswaran, hadbrecan &   æwbrecan*
       killers   and perjurers   clergy-breaker and marriage-breaker
   gebugan & gebetan*, oððe of cyððe mid synnan gewitan.*
   ge-submit and **ge-mend**   or   from home with sins   depart
'Killers and perjurers, violators of the clergy and adulterers shall **submit** and **make amends**, or leave their native land with their sins.'
c1050. colaw2cn,LawIICn:6.19-20

Co-ordinating two verbs with the same prefix could also be a device to achieve special rhythm or cursus, as well as alliteration.

These coordinate pairs are reminiscent of double constructions that were also a feature of high style in Later Middle and Early Modern English, as can be seen in Caxton's *Prologue to Eneydos:*

(220) *For we Englysshe men ben borne under the domynacyon of the mone, whiche is never stedfaste but ever **waverynge, wexynge** one season and **waneth and dyscreaseth** another season.*
'For we Englishmen are born under the domination of the moon, which is never steadfast but ever wavering, waxing one season and waning and decreasing another season'
c1490

Juxtaposing a Germanic and a synonymous Latinate word was a feature of high style in Late Middle and Early Modern English, such as exemplified by *waneth and dyscreaseth*. The extinction of aspectual preverbs took place at the same time when English received a strong injection of Romance (i.e. Latin and French) vocabulary (roughly the 13th to 15th century), so it could be argued that a feaure of high style such as co-ordinating pairs of prefixed verbs was gradually replaced by a new one, in which Germanic and Latinate synonyms are juxtaposed as we can see in (220).

6.10 Lexicalization Cases

In a few cases the *ge-*prefixed verb does not have a predictable meaning when contrasted with its simplex counterpart. For example, *cyþan* 'say' and *gecyþan* 'show', as can be observed in the following two examples:

(221) *Ac ðonne he gemette   ða scylde ðe   he stieran scolde, hrædlice he*
     but then   he discovered then sin which he punish   should immediately he
   ***gecyðde** ðæt he wæs magister & ealdormonn.*
   ge-showed that he was   master   and alderman

'But when he discovered the sin which he had to punish he soon **showed** that he was master and lord'

c894 cocura,CP:17.117.5.783

(222)*eft ða comon fleogende of ðære heofenlican digelnysse englas.*
    again then came   flying from the   heavenly   secrecy   angels
*and **cyddon** þæt he sceolde eft to worulde gecyrran.*
  and   **said**   that he should again to   world   return
'Again there came angels flying from the heavenly secrecy, and **said** that he should again return to the world.'

c995. ÆCHom II, 22 195.172

A strikingly similar lexicalization process took place in Croatian. When the most frequent aspectual prefix (*po-*) is attached to the verb *kazati* 'say', the newly derived verb is *pokazati* 'show', exactly like in Old English. Is this a mere coincidence? To what degree is the prefixed verb *ge+cyþan* predictable from the sum of its parts, or the Croatian prefixed verb *po+kazati* for that matter? One could argue that there is some kind of resultative property in the prefixed verb and that it is not an entirely arbitrary combination, but rather motivated by the meanings of the components. However, the semantics of this prefixed verb remains a somewhat puzzling question, as the resultative property is not the only meaning that has been added to the root when the prefix *ge-* was attached.

A case where the resultative property is more easily identifiable is the "aspectual pair" *cnawan* 'know' and *gecnawan* 'recognize'. The way the prefix *ge-* modifies the verb *cnawan* is still not entirely predictable, but it is more motivated than the case of *cyþan* 'say' and *gecyþan* 'show'. Cross-linguistically, the same lexicalization like the one in *cnawan* and *gecnawan* can be seen in a number of modern languages, such as German (*kennen* 'know' and *erkennen* 'recognize'), Spanish (*conocer* 'know' and *reconocer* 'recognize') or Croatian (*znati* 'know' *prepoznati* 'recognize').

(223)*Se druncena ne **gecnæwð** naðer ne fæder ne modor, ne freond ne feond,*
    the   drunk   not **ge-knows** neither not father not mother not friend not fiend
'The drunk does not **recognize** neither father nor mother, neither friend nor enemy.'

c1075. cochdrul,ChrodR_1:60.41.824

The following example features the simplex verb *cnawan*:

(224)*se hælend cwæð to him. Philippus swa lange tid ic wæs mid eow & ge*
    the saviour said to him   Phillip so long time I was with you and you
*ne **cneowan** me*
not **know** me
'The saviour said to him: "Phillip, I have been with you for such a long time and you do not **know** me"'.

Jn (WSH) 14.9

However, the DOE lists versions found in other manuscripts (Cp *gecneowun*, A *gecneowon*, Li *ongetto*, Ru *ongetun*), which can be interpreted in several ways. First of all, the verb might just as well be translated with 'recognize' in Modern English ("and you do not recognize me"), which would in this context be only a slight difference in meaning. In other words, Modern

English *know* and *recognize* overlap in meaning in certain contexts, and so did *cnawan* and *gecnawan* in Old English.

Very often *ge*-verbs are part of idiomatic expressions where their simplex counterparts have not been attested, as for example *bringan* and *gebringan:*

(225) *on fleame gebringan* 'to put (someone) to flight'

(226) *gebringan on beteran/wyrsan* 'to improve (something) / to make (something) worse'

The latter appears in the following corpus example:

(227) *Styr   þeah   ælces yfles swa þu swiðost mæge, swa ðeah þæt þu hit to*
correct however each   evil   so you most   may   so yet that you it to
*wyrsan ne **gebringe**: ne bið þæt yfel to nohte gebet,   ðe bið to wyrsan*
worse not **ge-bring**   not is that evil to nothing improved that is to worse
gebroht.
ge-brought

'Correct each wrong as best you may, however, so that you don't **bring** it to a worse pass; that wrong is in no way improved which is brought to a worse pass.'

c1100. codicts,Prov_1_[Cox]:1.79.149-150

In these expressions it is the resultative property of the prefix's meaning that seems to contribute to the meaning of the fixed expression as a whole, as the following set phrases show:

(228) *gebringan on þeowote* 'to enslave (someone)'

(229) *gebringan on orwennesse / ormodnesse* 'to bring (someone/something) to despair'

(230) *gebringan to deaþe* 'to put (someone) to death'

6.11 *Ge-* in Middle English

After the Old English period, the prefix *ge-* grammaticalized into a marker of the past participle, the same grammaticalization path that this prefix followed in German and Dutch. However, Modern German and Dutch have preserved it (Dutch to an even higher degree) until the present-day, whereas English lost it altogether before the beginning of the Early Modern English period.

The prefix *ge-* disappears gradually during the Middle English period, going from *ge-* to *i-/y-* to nothing. In terms of grammaticalization theory, the prefix *ge-* is a paradigmatic example of a language unit that went all the way down the cline, as follows:

Content item > grammatical word > inflectional affix > Ø

The zero, nothing or loss is thought to be the end product of grammaticalization (Hopper and Traugott 2003: 172-175). Heine (2003: 165) also discusses loss of grammatical meaning as "the final stage of grammaticalization: As a result of desemanticization, grammatical forms (G1, G2) increasingly lose in semantic content, and in the end there is no more content to lose, that is, all semantic properties are bleached out (=G0)"

The prefix *ge-* is one of the best examples of this process, and in the analysis conducted here it was identified that this prefix behaved according to Heine's formula G2 > G0, which "describes the stage of grammaticalization where once meaningful forms end up as meaningless 'empty morphs'".

According to van Gelderen (2007: 93), "*ge-* virtually disappears after 1130", i.e. we do not see it in that form any longer, which "symbolizes the true start of Middle English" (ibid.).

There is a problem with a gap in attestation of the English language after the Battle of Hastings, after which English was changing very rapidly. The only 12th century text that we have available is the Peterborough Chronicle dated from 1154/5 consisting of 7,348 words.

According to the corpus results, the prefix *ge-* in this particular form appears solely in the Peterborough Chronicle with only 25 occurrences. Only one of these occurrences is not a past participle. That is the verb *gelimpan* in the following sentence:

(231) *þa **gelamp** hit on dæges Annuntiatio Sancte Marie þet se eorl Waleram of*
    then **happened** it on day Annunciation Saint Mary that the earl Waleran of
Mellant ferde fram his an castel, Belmunt het, to his an oðer castel
    Meulan fared from his one castle Belmunt called to his one other castle
Watteuile.
    Vatteville
'then it **happened** on the feast of the Annunciation of St. Mary that Waleran, the earl of Meulan, went from one of his castles, called Beaumont-le-Roger, to another of his castles, called Vatteville.'
*c*1150. CMPETERB,45.109

The other 24 remaining verb forms are all past participles, 13 of which are *gehaten* 'be called'. All past participles have a resultative quality, as the following example illustrates:

(232) *Oc se eorl weard **gewunded** at an gefiht fram anne swein*
    and the earl became ***ge*-wounded** at one fight from a commoner
'And the earl got hurt at a fight by a commoner.'
*c*1150. CMPETERB,50.252

After the Peterborough Chronicle, the prefix *ge-* does not appear in this particular form ever again, but only reduced to *i-* or *y-*. In fact, the corpus results give the combinations presented in table 29.

Prefix version	Number of occurrences
i*verb*	2,436
i-*verb*	961
I*verb*	19
y*verb*	635
y-*verb*	256
Total	4,307

Table 29
Versions of the prefix *ge-* in Middle English

Table 30 shows the most frequent *ge*-types in Middle English, spelled in their most frequent past participle form:

	Type	Token frequency	Meaning
1	*icleped*	183	called
2	*isaied*	161	said
3	*imade*	155	made
4	*iherd*	135	heard
5	*islawe*	72	slain
6	*iboren*	61	born
7	*iwriten*	58	written
8	*iwurðen*	50	become
9	*itake*	47	taken
10	*iset*	42	set

Table 30
The most frequent *ge-* types in Middle English

The following three examples show the past participle forms formed with the prefix *i-* in the most frequently spelled form.

(233)*An oðer half nan mon ne mei wel iuge blod ear hit beo **icolet** .*
   one other half no   man not may wel judge blood before it   is   ***i*-cooled**

'On the other hand, no one can examine blood well before it is **cooled**.
*c*1225 CMANCRIW-1,II.95.1134

(234) *al þis lif   þe   we on liuen is to nihte **iefned**   for þat it is swa þester of*
      all this life which we in   live   is to night ***i*-compared** for that it is so   dark   of
ure ateliche synnes
our horrible sins
'All this life in which we live is **compared** to night because it is so dark through our horrible sins.'
*a*1225. CMTRINIT,39.543

(235) *Marie haueð **icore** þat beste del þat is heuenliche wunienge, þe hie habbe*
      Mary   has ***i*-chosen** the best part that is   heavenly   abode   that she have
shal abuten ende.
shall without end
'Mary has **chosen** the best part, that is the heavenly abode that she shall have without end.'
*a*1225. CMTRINIT,143.1932

In the first example we see the past participle of the verb *colen* 'to cool' in a passive construction with the prefix *i*-. The second example is also an example of the past participle in a passive construction. The verb *evenen* (Old English *efnan*) did not survive in Modern English in this sense, but specialized in the meaning of 'to make level'. The third example features the past participle of the verb *ichesen* 'choose' in the present perfect, a tense/aspect construction that was being grammaticalized in the Middle English period.

The following examples contain two *i*-prefixed verbs, the first spelled with a hyphen (*i-escad* 'asked') and the other without (*ifunden* 'found')

(236) *oðer he heo wat   ðurh . þet he heo dude him seolf oðer he heo hafð*
      either he it knows through that he it   did   him self   or   he it   has
***i-escad** oðer hafð **ifunden** on boke.*
***i*-asked**   or   has ***i*-found** in books
'Either he knows it through having done himself, or he has heard of it, or has found it in books'
*c*1225 CMLAMBX1,35.457

When the verb *acsian* 'ask' was prefixed with *ge*- in Old English, its meaning was resultative - 'to find out, learn, hear', and we see the same meaning present in Middle English, notwithstanding of the verb's reduced phonological form and distorted spelling[42].

The following example features three *y*- prefixed verbs with a hyphen, even newly borrowed French verbs like *confermen* 'to confirm' have succumbed to *y*-prefixation, proving a high degree of grammaticalization.

(237) *But þat þou vnderstonde betere what is to seye ' þi name be halewed in*
      but that you   understand   better what is to say your name is hallowed in

---

[42] Other attested Middle English spellings of the verb *asken* 'to ask' include *aski, hasken; as(s; axen, axi(en, aksen, aixe, auxen, haxen; asshen, aishen, aissen; esken, easki, exen, esshhen, hesshen, essen; isk, ix; ōsken, ōxi(en* with the past forms as *asked(e, axed(e, axte, aste; eschte, echste, esste; ōxed* (from MED)

> *vs , ' þou schalt vnderstonde þat þilke name ' holy ' is as moche as cler and*
> us   you   shall   understand   that same name   holy   is as   much as clear and
> *wiþ-out erþe and **y-halewed** to þe seruice of God , as **y-died**   in blod*
> without earth and   **y-hallowed** to the   service of God   as **y-coloured** in blood
> *and as **y-confermede**.*
> and as   **y-confirmed**
> 'But that you understand better what is to say your name is hallowed in us, you shall understand that the same name holy is as clear and without earth and **hallowed** to the service of God, as **coloured** in blood and as **confirmed**.'
>
> a1225. CMVICES4,105.166

Just a few lines before the previous example we see the verb *confermen* in the past participle form occurring without the prefix, which shows that the prefix was optional.

> (238)*þat is to seye , þat is oure souereyn desire, and þat bidde we ouer alle*
>   that is to say   that is our   sovereign   desire and that ask   we over all
> *þing , þat þin holy name, þat is þin good renomee , þi knowleche , þi fey ,*
> things that your holy name   that is your good reputation your knowledge your faith
> *be **confermed** in vs.*
> be **confirmed**   in us
> 'That is to say, that is to our sovereign desire, and that we ask over all things, that your holy name, that is your good reputation, your knowledge, your faith be **confirmed** in us.'
>
> a1225 CMVICES4,104.161

According to Mustanoja (1960: 447), the loss of the prefix *ge- (i- or y-)* starts in the north due to the influence of Old Norse which did not have this prefix. In London it becomes archaic by the end of the 14th century. Chaucer uses it in poetry only for metrical purposes; he never used it in his prose. In Kent it remains in use until the 15th century.

6.12 Conclusion

The prefix *ge-* is the most frequent prefix in Old English, whose etymology and semantics are difficult to understand. In almost half of the cases in Old English this preverb does not exhibit any grammatical or lexical meaning at all, which indicates a very high degree of bleaching. However, an aspectual sense can be identified in about 40% of the cases. This aspectual meaning is perfective – and depending on the inherent semantics of the verb, it is resultative. In some cases the meaning is stylistic.

Many *ge*-prefixed verbs became conventionalized with time, showing a number of cases of lexicalization. The aspectual meanings could be regarded as cases of grammaticalization. The Middle English evidence shows that this preverb is a prototypical example of grammaticalization. In Old English, however, the function of *ge-* exhibits more lexical properties, rather than syntactic.

It is difficult to determine precisely in which situations the preverb *ge-* is used, so perhaps we should believe Lindemann when he says that

> "...the prefix was never mandatory; it could be used in general at the discretion of the writer, depending upon whether he wanted to make a general statement or a specific descriptive one."
>
> (Lindemann 1970: 42)

Chapter 7
An Analysis of the Preverb *for-*

7.1 Introduction

This chapter presents an analysis of the verbal prefix *for-*. Hardly any previous research has been carried out on this preverb, except for a rather obsolete monograph on Germanic *for/ver* by Leopold (1907) and a very short article by Fraser (1975). *For-* is usually mentioned as one of the seven inseparable prefixes by De la Cruz (1975), Hiltunen (1983) and Brinton (1988), having received considerably less elaboration than the other prefixes such as *ge-*.

Its meanings and etymology are examined first, followed by a discussion of corpus examples which mostly show the prefix *for-* grammaticalized as a perfectivizer. There are also many cases of lexicalization in which the lexical meaning of the root is modified once the prefix *for-* is attached.

Table 31 shows the most frequent types of *a*-prefixed verbs.

	Type	Token frequency	Meaning
1	*forlætan*	526	to let, permit, allow; leave
2	*forgyfan*	250	to give, grant, allow; forgive
3	*forleosan*	87	to lose, be deprived of
4	*forseon*	71	to despise
5	*forbeodan*	67	to forbid
6	*forberan*	62	to bear, endure, suffer
7	*forbærnan*	55	to burn up, consume by fire
8	*forweorðan*	50	to perish
9	*forgyldan*	48	to pay, repay
10	*forniman*	46	to seize, grasp

Table 31
The most frequent *for-* types in Old English

The only verbs that survived into Modern English with this prefix are the verbs *forgyfan* and *forbeodan*. The verb *forleosan* survived in the past participle form *forlorn*, now used as an adjective. Verbs like *forweorðan*, *forgyldan* and *forniman* have died out together with the prefix, whereas the simplex version of *forlætan*, *forseon*, *forberan* and *forbærnan* have been preserved as Modern English *let*, *see*, *bear* and *burn*.

7.2 The meanings and etymology of *for-*

According to Quirk and Wrenn (1957: 110), the prefix *for-* is used for actions "which it usually intensifies (especially in a destructive sense), often with a shift to perfective aspect". The prefix can also be attached to adjectives and adverbs, modifying their meaning in terms of intensity and are usually translated into Modern English with 'very', 'too' or 'completely'. This usage can still be found in Modern Scandinavian languages (Norwegian and Danish *for,* Swedish *för*) but as an independent word rather than a prefix. Besides being related to Old Norse *for-,* this prefix is a cognate of Old High German *fir-* and Modern Dutch and German *ver-,* with very complex sense developments.

The original spatial meaning of this prefix is 'away, opposite, off', which could in Old English still be felt in verbs such as *forbugan* 'turn away, avoid' or *forweorpan* 'throw away, reject'. However, even in those two examples the resulting combination of the verb and the prefix is not solely spatial but also exhibits some properties of lexicalization (the meaning is no longer the sum of its parts) and grammaticalization (both become perfective).

The meaning of the Old English or Modern English preposition *for* has nothing to do with the prefix *for-.* The prefixal counterpart to the preposition *for* is actually the prefix *fore-* 'in front'. It has also been preserved in Modern English, as can be seen in examples such as OE *foreseon* → ModE *foresee* or OE *forebodian* → ModE *forebode.* Even though these two examples show a shift from spatial to temporal meanings, the prefix *fore-* has not acquired any aspectual meanings.

Even though the prefixes *for-* and *fore-* had different meanings already in Old English, they are thought to derive ultimately from the same root. Fraser (1975: 21) explains that the preverb *for-* had three counterparts in Gothic (*faúr-, fair-* and *fra-*) which in turn correspond to Greek παρά, περί and πρό. Fraser (1975: 22) suggests that all three Gothic or Greek preverbs stem from a single Indo-European root (**per*).

The DOE has a somewhat more elaborate description of the meanings of *for-*. According to the DOE, *for-* is an intensive prefix attached to adjectives/adverbs, verbs and nouns (which are usually deverbal nominalizations). The prefix gives verbs "a sense of intensive or completive action or process". The DOE further breaks down the verbal meanings of *for-* into the following five subsenses:

a. with sense of 'away, off'
b. with sense of prohibition, exclusion or warding off
c. with sense of abstaining from or neglecting
d. with sense of 'wrongly'
e. with sense of destructive, painful or prejudicial effect

In other words, in addition to perfectivizing, which is a grammatical property, this prefix also adds something negative or pejorative to the meaning of the verb such as destruction or loss. The above listed meanings have been checked in a controlled randomized sample of 200 tokens, yielding the following results:

1.	Completive	16%
2.	Intensive	19%
3.	Literal spatial	0%
4.	Prohibition	5%
5.	Abstaining from / Neglecting	42%
6.	Wrongly	0%
7.	Destructive	18%

Table 32
The meanings and functions of the prefix *for-*

All *for*-prefixed verbs also exist in their simplex (prefixless) forms. It needs to be stressed that it is very difficult to single out one meaning in the prefix and its way of affecting the resultant combination with the verb. In most tokens the presence of the prefix points to a perfective reading, which is not necessarily completive. However, if the prefix indicates both neglecting and perfective meanings, it has not been classified under completive but neglecting.

In other words, the table shows that the meanings identified by the DOE should be revised, as the senses of (d) 'wrongly' and (e) destructive, painful or prejudicial effect are difficult to tell apart, whereas the sense of (c) abstaining from and neglecting yielded has been identified in the highest number of tokens. In fact, the senses of 'abstaining from' and 'neglecting' can more easily be differentiated than the senses (d) and (e) so they merit independent categorization. Nonetheless, the meanings 4-7 in table 30 could be grouped or labelled as "negative" in the sense of the action acquiring a negative, pejorative or undesired meaning. Sometimes the prefix only enhances the effect of a verb that is negatively connoted to begin with, in which case we could also say that it acts as an intensifier. It goes without saying that all the meanings are conceptually related.

The original spatial meaning that is supposed to be easily noticed in verbs of movement has not been identified in any of the tokens in the randomized sample.

7.3 Perfectivizing *for-*

The meanings discussed in the first subsection can be amply illustrated by corpus examples. The first example features the verb *formeltan* 'melt away'. The prefix *for-* perfectivizes the meaning of the verb.

(239) & hi gaderodon on morgen þæt hi genoh hæfdon, & þa seo sunne
and they gathered in morning that they enough have and when the sun
scean ða **formeolt** hit
shone then ***for*-melted** it
'and they gathered [manna] in the morning so that they have enough, and when the sun grew hot, it **melted** away.'
*c*1000. coexodusP,Exod_[Ker]:16.20.12-13

The object of melting, manna[43], is mentioned earlier in the text. It could also be argued that apart from perfectivizing, this prefix is attached to a verb which is used in a destructive context, as it refers to food that is destroyed by melting or decays.

The next example is the verb *forswelgan* 'swallow (up), swallow something whole' used for actions performed in their entirety, i.e. indicating a completed action.

(240) *ond þa sædeor hine sona forswulgon, þæt his ne com þy furðor an*
and the sea-beasts him soon *for*-**swallowed** that his not came the furher one
ban to eorðan.
bone to earth

'and the sea-beasts immediately **swallowed** him, so that not even one bone of his came to the land again.'

*c*1000. comart3,Mart_5_[Kotzor]:Ja19,A.21.177

Much like in the first example, the prefix indicates perfectivity or completiveness and is used in a context which is also destructive. The sea-beast swallows up the person in question (a reeve), which is a rather violent and painful way to die.

All the examples of *forswelgan* translate into Croatian with the perfective verb *progutati,* whose imperfective pair is *gutati.* There is no negative (destructive or pejorative) connotation whatsoever in the prefixed form of this verb in Croatian. The prefix merely denotes perfectivity. It is interesting that in most corpus examples *forswelgan* appears in contexts where the action of swallowing is violent. It is either an animal, a dragon or the earth that swallows up someone. However, it need not necessarily imply a violent act. In example (241) the earth swallowed up the cruel devil, but the violent effect is enhanced by the adverb *grimlice* 'fiercely, in a terrible fashion'.

(241) *And hrædlice seo eorþe forswalg þone wælhreowan deofol grimlice.*
and immediately the earth *for*-**swallowed** the cruel devil terribly
'And immediately in a terrible manner the earth **swallowed up** the cruel devil.'

*c*1050. comargaT,LS_16_[MargaretCot.Tib._A.iii]:16.8.212

Again, it is ambiguous whether this adverb serves to increase the violent effect or is redundant. The act of the earth swallowing a cruel devil in itself is an image violent enough. The question is whether there is any additional, lexical meaning contained within the prefix *for-* that it adds to the meaning of the sentence – or merely perfectivity.

That *forswelgan* need not mean swallowing in a violent context is exemplified in sentence (242):

(242) *And he sceal husligan unhale and seoce, þa hwile þe se seoca mage*
and he shall housel infirm and sick then while the sick may
þæt husl forswelgan;
the housel *for*-**swallow**

---

[43] *Manna* is the name of sweet-tasting food that God gave the Israelites when they travelled across the desert.

'And he shall housel the infirm and sick, while the sick can **swallow** the housel'

c1075. colwsigeXa,ÆLet_1_[Wulfsige_Xa]:84.100

The housel[44] is not something that can be swallowed in a violent manner. The choice of a perfective form of the verb is also logical, as the housel is something that is swallowed in one gulp, so the action is performed in its entirety in one single occasion.

Example (243) shows the Old English imperfective pair of the verb in a context that would more likely be translated into Croatian with a perfective than an imperfective form:

(243)*þy læs cild sy hreosende, þæt is fylleseoc, oþþe scinlac mete,*
the less child be falling that is falling-sickness or phantom dream
*fyregate brægen teoh þurh gyldenne hring, syle þam cilde **swelgan***
mountain-goat brain draw through golden ring give that child **swallow**
ærþam hyt meolc onbyrge.
before it milk tastes
'Lest a child would fall, that is sick of epilepsy, or dream of an apparition, draw a mountain goat's brain through a golden ring, give it to the child to **swallow** before it tastes milk.'

c1025. coquadru,Med_1.1_[de_Vriend]:6.12.248-9

The aspectual meaning of the verb *swelgan* is ambiguous. Why is the verb used without a prefix here? We could say that that the child should swallow all of the mountain goat's brain, in which case we have an imperfective form used with a perfective meaning. The perfective meaning is deduced from the context because the clause that follows signifies a sequence of events introduced by the conjunction *ærþam* 'before'. Moreover, that clause contains the perfective verb *onbyrgan* 'taste'. The imperfective form could also be accounted for by the focus of action. If the stress is on the actual performance of the action or if the action is to be repeated, the imperfective is used. The imperfective form is possible in Croatian translation *dajte djetetu da guta/jede* 'let the child swallow/eat', but it is stylistically different. We might also argue that *swelgan* 'swallow' is metonymically used instead of *etan* 'eat', where eating consists of a series of swallows – hence the repetition of the action.

The verb *swelgan* is used with the prefix *for-* well into the Middle English period, as eamples (244) and (245) show.

(244)*Þat deuel **forswuelgeð** þe man...and gif ure ani is þus **forswolgen**,..*
that devil *for*-swallows the man and if our any is thus *for*-swallowed
clupe we to ure louerd.
call we to our lord
That devil **swallows** a man... and if any of us is thus **swallowed up**, let us call upon our Lord.

c1225. Trin.Hom.(Trin-C B.14.52) 43:

The last attested use is dated in 1340:

---

[44] Housel is a medieval word for the Eucharist, a consecrated piece of bread or wafer.

(245) *Vor þise zenne, onleak þe erþe and **uorzual3** datan and abyron.*
      for this sin unlock the earth and *for*-swallow Datan and Abyron
'For this sin, unlock the earth and **swallow** Datan and Abyron.'
Ayenb. (Arun 57) 67

It is worth noting here that the Modern English simplex verb *swallow* is aspectually ambivalent when taken out of context. It can be both perfective and imperfective. An object or adverbial determine its aspectual meaning on the sentence level. The postverbal particle *up* has a perfectivizing force when added to the simplex *swallow*. However, the particle verb *swallow up* can also be imperfective if the verb is in the progressive form. The Old English verb *forswelgan* (counterpart to *swallow up*) appears to be perfective in all contexts, as there were no progressive tenses that could overrule its perfective value. The simplex *swelgan*, on the other hand, need not be imperfective exclusively, but being semantically unmarked (as discussed in section 2.8.2) can also take a perfective reading.

Another example of *for*- acting as a perfectivizer with the overall meaning of something negative is *forrotan* 'rot away', as we see in (246).

(246) *& hat wyrcean twegen stengas of ðæm treowe, ðe is haten sethim,*
      and order made two poles of the tree that is called sethim
*ðæt ne wyrð næfre **forrotad**;*
      that not becomes never *for*-rotten
'and order two poles to be made of the tree which is called sethim, and will never be **rotten**'
c894. cocura,CP:22.169.22.1155

A few lines later in the same text, the verb *forrotan* appears in its simplex form *rotan* in a rather similar context, co-occurring with the adverb *næfre* 'never' and referring to the sethim tree:

(247) *Ða saglas ðonne ðe mon ða earce big beran sceal, sticiað eallne weg inn*
      the poles that the man the ark be borne shall remains all way in
on ðam hringum ða earce mid to beranne, ða beoð geworht of ðæm
      in the rings that ark with to bear that is made of the
*treowe sethim, ðæt næfre ne **rotað**.*
      tree sethim that never not **rots**
'The poles with which the ark was to be carried, remained always inside the rings, to carry the ark with, and were made of the tree sethim, which never **rots**.'
c894. cocura,CP:22.171.5.1161-2

The pragmatic meaning of both clauses (*ðæt ne wyrð næfre forrotad*) and (*ðæt næfre ne rotað*) is the identical, although different structures are used. In example (246), the verb is in the past participle form which typically takes a perfectivizing prefix, so in this case *for*- acts like one rather than the prefixes *ge*- or *a*-. In other words, *for*- can also function as a past participle marker. Furthermore, when contrasted with Croatian, those two clauses can be translated both with the perfective and the imperfective form of the verb without a pragmatic difference in meaning:

(248)*To drvo nikad ne trune.* 'That tree never rots'
To drvo nikad ne istrune. 'That tree never rots away'

Destructive meanings of the prefix *for-* are best exemplified with verbs like *forspillan* 'destroy' or *forslean* 'break' as in numbers (249) and (250).

(249)*Se gerefa wæs þa swiþe yrre and het   þa halgan Margaretan on*
the prefect was the very angry and ordered the   holy   Margaret   in
karcerne betynan oþþæt he geþohte   hu he hire mægþhad   forspilde.
prison   confined   while   he ge-thought how he her   maidenhood   **for-destroy**
'The prefect was very angry then and he ordered the holy Margaret to be imprisoned while he considered how he might **deflower** her virginity.'
*c*1050. comargaT,LS_16_[MargaretCot.Tib._A.iii]:6.13.66-7

(250)*Gif mon oþrum   rib forslea binnan gehaldre hyde, geselle X scillinga*
   if   man another.DAT rib *for*-**strike** inside   held   skin   give   10 shillings
to bote.
to compensation
'If one man **breaks** another's rib without breaking the skin, 10 shillings shall be given as compensation.'
*c*900. colawaf,LawAf_1:70.201

While the prefix adds to the intensity of destructiveness, it also acts as a perfectivizer. However, perfectivization in this case should be regarded only as its secondary effect.

The prefixless form of this verb, *slean* 'strike' as appears in number (251), can be interpreted in different ways in terms of aspect:

(251)*gif he þonne ful beo,   slea man hine, þæt him forberste se sweora.*
   if   he then   foul be   strike man   him   that him *for*-**burst** the neck
'If he is then guilty, **strike** him, so that his neck breaks.'
Law IIIAtr 4.1

On the one hand, it could be imperfective, which in this particular case would imply an iterative action – one should strike him several times until the guilty person's neck breaks. Furthermore, the form *beo* of the verb "to be" is known to express habitualness, which would make the verb form *slea* 'strike' habitual as well, which can in turn account for the imperfective form. On the other hand, the simplex form, being semantically unmarked, could also have a perfective meaning if we conceptualize the situation as a single, instantaneous (semelfactive) action.

Incidentally, example (251) also contains a *for-* verb (*forberstan* 'break, fracture'), whose meaning is definitely perfective (the action of breaking a neck is performed until its end), but again, it is a destructive verb. It is arguable that even intensive meaning can be felt in the prefix, as the simplex verb *berstan* has a natural end-point, so its imperfective reading can only imply iterativity. An example of the simplex *berstan* is often used in laws where it means 'to be broken, to fail', often referring to oaths, ordeals or formal exculpations, as we can see in number (252):

(252)*gif landagende man ætsace, þonne nemne man him his gelican ealswa*
   if   land-owner   man denies   then   named man him   his alike   also

micel wente swa cyninges þegne; gif him þæt **berste***, gilde lahsliht:*

great went so king's thegn if him that burst pay lahslit

VI healfmarc.

6 half-marks

'If a land owner denies it, then as many compurgators, his equals, are to be nominated for him as for a king's thegn; if that **fails**, he is to pay lahslit: six half-marks.'

c1010. LawNorthu 52

In example (252), as well as in other examples of *berstan* appearing in laws, the meaning can only be perfective.

The following example features the verb *forstelan* 'steal' twice. The verb has a negative connotation even without the prefix and it is not really a destructive verb like the previous two examples, though we could argue that stealing has destructive consequences. However, in these two cases, it is the perfectivizing property of *for-* that is in focus rather than contributing to a destructive effect:

(253) *Gif ceorl ceap* **forstilð** *& bireð into his ærne, & befehð þærinne mon,*

if husband livestock **for-steals** and bears into his building and seized therein man

þonne bið se his dæl synnig butan þam wife anum, forðon hio sceal hire

then be the his share guilty except the wife only since she shall her

ealdore hieran: gif hio dear mid aðe gecyðan, þæt hio þæs **forstolenan**

elder hear if she dare with oath show that she the.GEN **for-stolen**

ne onbite, nime hire ðriddan sceat.

not taste take her third property

'If a husband **steals** livestock and brings it into his house, and it is seized there, he shall forfeit his share, his wife only being exempt, since she must obey her lord: If she dares to confirm with an oath that she has not tasted the **stolen** [meat], she shall retain her third of property.'

c1100. colawine,LawIne:57.153-4

The third most frequent *for-*prefixed verb is *forleosan*, where *for-* has a perfectivizing meaning, much like the Croatian prefix *iz-* 'from' in *izgubiti* 'lose'. In other words, OE *leosan* would make the imperfective pair on a par with Croatian *gubiti*. The following example shows a clearly perfective reading of *forleosan*:

(254) *alesan we ure saule þa hwile þe we þæt lif & þæt weorþ on urum*

rescue we our souls while we that life and that worth on our

gewealde habban, þe læs se deaþ ær cume, & we þonne ætsomne

control have the less the death before come and we then at once

forleosan *þæt lif & þæt weorþ, & þonne syn gelædde mid urum feondum*

for-lose the life and the worth and then be led with our fiends

on ece forwyrde.

in eternal destruction

'Let us save our souls while we have life and worth at our command, for fear that death should come and we will at once **lose** life and worth, and be led by our enemy into eternal punishment.'

c971. coblick,HomU_19_[BlHom_8]:101.70.1296

The verb *forlætan* 'let, permit, allow; leave', also featured later in (262), is by far the most frequent type in the present corpus. Every fourth token of the *for*-prefixed verbs is the verb *forlætan*. It is highly polysemous and its prefix can sometimes show grammaticalizing and other times lexicalizing properties. Its function in both (262) and (255) is perfectivizing. This meaning of *forlætan* as featured in the next example also appears later in number (261) where it has been underlined.

(255) *Hig þa **forlættan** þone wall & heora burh,*
    they then **for-let** the wall and their fort
'Then they **left** the wall and their fort,'
c897. cobede,Bede_1:9.46.20.406

It is interesting that the Croatian equivalents to *forlætan* are the verb *pustiti* 'let' and its prefixed derivations such as *napustiti* 'leave' or *dopustiti* 'permit, allow', all of which (including the simplex) are perfective and would be used in translating the sentences in (262) and (255).

The verb *forlættan* appears in two different meanings, 'abandon' and 'neglect' in example (256). Both have a perfective reading, which is expected from a past participle form.

(256) *ac ic wille nu þurh Godes wissunge þa **forlætenan** mynstru on minum*
    but I wish now through God's guidance that ***for*-let**.PTCP.PL monasteries in my
anwealde gehwær mid munecum gesettan & eac mid mynecenum &
    dominion everywhere with monks   ge-set and also with   nuns   and
*Godes lof geedniwian ðe ær wæs **forlæten**.*
    God's praise restore   that before was ***for*-let**.PTCP
'But I wish now through the guidance of God to fill the **abandoned** monasteries everywhere in my dominion with monks and also with nuns and to restore the worship of God which has been **neglected**.'
Ch 779 8

The meaning of the simplex *lætan* is imperfective, as in the following example:

(257) *He **læteð** his sunne scinen ofer þa goden, & ofer þa yfelen,*
    he **lets** his sun   shine over the good and over the evil
'He **lets** his sun shine over the good and over the wicked'
c1150. coalcuin,Alc_[Warn_35]:150.113

In a different context, the simplex *lætan* could also have a perfective meaning:

(258) *þa bæd Eustachius þæt hi him fyrst **leton** þæt hi him to Gode gebædon,*
    then asked Eustachius that they them first let   that they them to God recommend
'Then Eustachius asked them to **permit** them to recommend themselves to God first,'
c1010. coeust,LS_8_[Eust]:424.449

Yet another meaning of *forlættan* can be observed in the following sentence, whose reading is more likely to be imperfective.

(259) ***Forlæt** þæt þu næbbe to oþres monnes gode andan, forðam þu*
    ***for*-let** that you not-have to other.GEN man.GEN fortune envy because you

swencst ðe sylfne swiðor þonne hine.
swank the self greater   than   him
Avoid being envious of another man's good fortune, because you'll distress yourself more than him.
c1100. codicts,Prov_1_[Cox]:1.31.56

The prefixed verb in example (259) involves a spatial metaphor.

7.4 Lexicalizing *for-*

In a significant number of examples the prefix *for-* is lexicalized, such as *forseon* 'despise', whose simplex verb *seon* means 'to see', as in (260). The prefix *for-* contributes negative meaning to the whole (to see in a negative way = to despise), so the resulting metaphor arising from the combination of the prefix and the verb is rather transparent, though not entirely predictable. In fact, the two Modern English verbs that have replaced *forseon* are also based on the same metaphor: the Latinate verb *despise* from *de-* 'down, off, away' and *spicere* 'look' and the phrasal verb *look down on*. The Old English verb *forseon* is very frequent with about 600 occurrences in the DOE and 58 in the present corpus.

(260) *ac geðence he ðone inncundan ege Godes, & **forsio** ælce olicunge*
but consider he the   inner   fear God.GEN and ***for*-see** each   flattery
ðisses middangeardes, & eac his ege for ðære wynsuman suetnesse Godes.
this.GEN   earth   and also his fear for the winsome   sweetness God.GEN
'But consider the inner fear of God, and **despise** all worldly flattery and fears for the pleasant sweetness of God.'
c894. cocura,CP:14.83.3.538-9

This verb also has two synonymous verbs, *forhogian* and *forhycgan* 'scorn, despise, disdain', whose simplexes *hogian* and *hycgan* mean 'think, consider'.

(261) *He **forhogde** ðæt he hit gehierde, &   nolde hine forlætan.*
he ***for*-thought** that he it *ge*-heard and not-wanted him *for*-let
'He **scorned** to listen and would not leave him.'
c894. cocura,CP:40.295.16.1948-1949

There are two different *for-*prefixed verbs in the next example whose meanings are lexicalized rather than grammaticalized:

(262) *Ne wurðe þe næfre to þys wa, þæt ðu þe ne wene betran, forþon þe*
not become the never to this woe that you that not hope better   for th
*se wena þe ne **forlæt** næfre **forweorðan**.*
the hope that not ***for*-let** never ***for*-become**
'Be never sorrowful as not to hope for better retribution, for that hope will **let** you never **perish**'.
c1100. codicts,Prov_1_[Cox]:1.39.70

The simplex counterpart to the verb *forweorðan* 'perish, die' is *weorðan* 'come to be, be made, arise, come, be'. They are not aspectual partners. The sum of the parts *for-* + *weorðan* points to an idiomatic nature of the resultant combination, although the negative, destructive component carried by the prefix can be readily observed in this *for*-prefixed verb. In other words, in this case we see lexicalization rather than grammaticalization of the prefix *for*-.

A similar meaning of the prefix *for*- can be observed in the verb *forfaran* whose meaning is synonymous to *forweorðan*. The simplex counterpart is the verb *fare* 'go, travel, proceed, fare'. When the prefix *for*- is added to this verb, the original spatial meaning 'away' gives rise to the newly derived metaphorical meaning 'perish, destroy', as exemplified in the following sentence:

(263) *ac beorge man georne, þæt man þa sawla ne* **forfare**, *þe Crist*
but protect man eagerly that man the souls not ***for*-fare**.3SG.SUBJ the Christ
mid his agenum life gebohte.
with his own life *ge*-bought
'but one should take good care that the souls which Christ bought with his own life should not be **destroyed**.'
*c*1050. colaw5atr,LawVAtr:2.7

An interesting example of a lexicalized *for*- is the verb *forlicgan* 'fornicate', whose simplex is *licgan* 'lie, be at bed, be in rest', as illustrated by the following example:

(264) *Gif hwa wið nunnan* **forlicge**, *sy ægðer his weres scildig, ge he ge heo.*
if who with nun ***for*-lies**, be either his wergild both he both she
'If anyone **fornicates** with a vowess, both are to be liable to pay their wergild, both he and she.'
*c*1010. colawnorthu,LawNorthu:63.91

Example (264) demonstrates how the prefix *for*- can contribute to the negative meaning of the newly derived verb.

Other examples of lexicalized *for*- include verbs which have survived *with* the prefix into Modern English, such as *forbid* or *forgive*. However, the meaning of the prefix is not transparent to present-day speakers of English. They are not likely to be able to explain how the prefix affects the meaning of the base verb. Example (265) contains both of these verbs.

(265) *And we* **forbeodað** *on Godes forbode, þæt nan man na ma wifa næbbe*
and we **forbid** in God's forbidding that no man no more wife not-have
buton I; & seo beo mid rihte beweddod & **forgifen**.
but 1 and she be with right wedded and ***for*-given**
'And we **forbid** by virtue of God that any man should have more wives than one; and she is to be legally betrothed and **wedded**.'
*c*1010. colawnorthu,LawNorthu:61.88

The evidence that the verb *forbeodan* 'forbid, prohibit' shows a lexicalization of *for*- is seen in the fact that the simplex verb *beodan* 'command, bid' does not act as its aspectual pair, but has a completely different meaning.

The verb *forgyfan* 'give, grant, allow' also had a meaning of 'give in marriage', as example (265) illustrates. The modern sense of 'forgive' as in 'to excuse for a fault or an offense' is said to be a Germanic calque based on Latin *perdonare* (cf. Gothic *fragiban*, German *vergeben*, Dutch *vergeven*). According to the DOE, the modern meaning is listed as the last of four meanings. The basic Old English meaning is exemplified in number (266):

(266) *Salomon eac **forgeaf** þære cwene swa hwæs swa heo gyrnde æt him.*
   Solomon also ***for*-gave** the queen so what so she desired at him
   'Solomon also **gave** the queen whatever she desired from him'.
   *c*995. ÆCHom II, 45 340.169

One could argue that in this case, example (266), *forgyfan* could act as a perfective pair of *gyfan*. In other words, this is a case of one and the same combination of prefix and verb (*for* + *gyfan*) which in certain contexts shows lexicalizing properties, as in number (265) and grammaticalizing in others, as in number (266).

Finally, the verb *forgytan* 'forget' is another example of early lexicalization which survived into Modern English. Its simplex counterpart is the verb *gytan* 'get, obtain'. The prefix in this case contributes to the meaning of the whole verb with its meaning 'away, amiss opposite', so that the newly derived verb comes to mean something like 'to unget', metaphorically standing for "to lose from the mind"[45]. The following corpus example shows that the verb was used in Old English in the same meaning as today.

(267) *Ne **forgit** þu hine þeah ealne weg, þy læs þu þolige þæs ecan lifes.*
   not **forget**.IMP you it though all way the.INS less you suffer the.GEN eternal life
   'Don't **forget** it completely, lest you lose the life eternal.'
   *c*1100. codicts,Prov_1_[Cox]:1.15.27

7.5 *For-* in Middle English

Many Old English *for*-prefixed verbs can still be encountered in Middle English, but as with the prefix *a-*, the ratio of tokens and types points to a drop in productivity. Table 33 shows the most frequent types in Middle English.

	Type	Token frequency	Meaning
1	*forsaken*	214	to forsake, abandon, betray
2	*foryeven*	210	to forgive, give
3	*forleten*	190	to desert, disregard, forsake
4	*foryeten*	126	to forget
5	*forlesen*	119	to lose
6	*forbeden*	79	to forbid, prohibit
7	*forwerpan*	67	to cast off/out, reject
8	*fordon*	46	to destroy, ruin, kill
9	*forgilten*	38	to become guilty, to sin
10	*forberen*	21	to bear, endure

Table 33
The most frequent *for-* types in Middle English

---

[45] In Croatian the verb that denotes this abstract mental action is also an idiomatic prefixed verb: *zaboraviti* consists of *za-* 'for' and *boraviti* 'dwell'.

A closer look at the table above reveals that the most frequent types are actually lexicalized cases of *for-*. Also, the semantic structures of many of these verbs changed. For example, the polysemic structure of the verb *forgyfan* from the last section has changed in the transition to Middle English, where the modern sense 'forgive' prevailed. This is confirmed by all the occurrences found in the present corpus. However, the MED does list the original old meaning still appearing as late as the 15th century.

(268) *Richard Harecourte..and Thomas Lewys hath **foryoven** and relesed..to Iohn Botiller..that dwellyng place..called Cokerelles.*
'Richard Harecourte and Thomas Lewys have **given** and granted to John Botiller that dwelling place called Cokerelles.'
a1475 Godstow Reg. (Rwl B.408) 348/15.

The most frequent type, *forsaken* is purely lexicalized. It does not even appear in its prefixless form *saken* (though there is a noun *sake* which today survives in phrases like *for the sake of*). Although in many cases the verb will give perfective readings, its meaning cannot be considered grammatical. The following example illustrates the verb in context.

(269) *Also whan sche hadde childe sche **forsook** flescheliche likinge and manis companye ,*
'Also when she had a child she **gave up** fleshly liking and the company of men.'
c1387 CMPOLYCH,VI,473.3491

However, in Early Middle English before the preverb aspectual system died out, some examples of *for-* as a perfectivizer can still be encountered. The following sentence shows the prefix *for-* used as a marker of perfectivity in three past participle forms in a row. Undoubtedly, the prefix's phonological structure also helps to achieve alliteration:

(270) *Þe biscopes & lered men heom <u>cursede</u> æure, oc was heom naht þarof,*
    the bishops and learned men them <u>cursed</u> ever but was them nothing thereof
*for hi uueron al **forcursæd** & **forsuoren** & **forloren**.*
    for they were all ***for*-cursed** and ***for*-despised** and ***for*-lost**
'The bishops and educated men always cursed them, but that was nothing to them, because they were entirely condemned and despised and lost.'
c1137 CMPETERB,56.471-473

In example (270) we also see the verb *cursen* 'to curse' (underlined) first used as a simplex with an imperfective reading and then with the prefix in the perfective form (*forcursæd*).

7.6 Conclusion

The prefix *for-* can act a perfectivizer which is often attached to verbs denoting destructive or negative actions. However, this destructive or negative property is typically present in the semantics of the simplex verb, not in the prefix. The prefix has the capacity to intensify or underscore the negative effect of the action that the verb denotes.

In a controlled randomized sample, the prefix acted as a pure perfectivizer without changing the lexical meaning of the verb in 35% of the cases, while in the remaining 65% of the cases the meanings were more lexicalized, ranging from expressing prohibition and neglecting to destructive senses.

Roughly one third of examples point to grammaticalization of this prefix as a marker of perfectivity, but a handful of examples show typical characteristics of lexicalization, such as *forseon* 'despise', *forweorðan* 'perish' or *forbeodan* 'forbid' whose meanings are not entirely predictable from the sum of their parts. However, it is possible that, like in Slavic, the prefix assigns both aspectual and lexical meaning to the newly derived combination, as the majority of *for-* prefixed examples did have a perfective reading.

It is very interesting that *for-* was only the third most frequent prefix in Old English, but has been preserved as a petrified morpheme in a larger number of verbs in Modern English than the prefixes *ge-* and *a-*. Besides *forgive* and *forbid,* other well-known examples include *forget, forbear, forsake, forswear* or deverbal adjectives such as *forlorn.* The prefixed verb as it appears in these Modern English verbs was lexicalized already in Old English.

Chapter 8
Conclusion

The aim of this study was to examine if and how aspect is expressed in English by means of preverbs and post-verbal particles, thus contributing to the longstanding debate about aspect in English, as well as understanding aspect in diachrony.

The theoretical approach taken in this discussion has, of necessity, been wide ranging. The immense scholarship on aspect over the past few centuries has produced a number of ideas that have been discussed at length, but certainly not exhaustively. These ideas have been backed up by some recent theories such as grammaticalization theory and diachronic construction grammar.

In the discussion of the category of aspect – the development of the concept and the term – it must be noted that the term underwent a loan translation (or calquing) process twice: first from Greek *eidos* 'form, kind' to Russian *vid* 'viewpoint', and then to French *aspect*. Such stretching of the term's meaning is also reflected in the understanding of what this category actually constitutes.

Expressing aspect by means of particles and preverbs is more common in languages around the world than by inflectional means. The latter is manifested only in Slavic languages and only a few others. However, Slavic languages also make use of prefixes to express aspect, where these prefixes can act like inflections.

The contrastive analysis with Slavic performed in this research did not involve stretching English on the Procrustean bed of Slavic, to use Hirt's phrase. Sometimes it is useful to compare two languages to see how their forms are different. The presence or absence of a grammatical feature in one language can better be noticed when compared or contrasted with another language. However, with a grammatical chapter as complex as aspect, it was necessary to describe all the characteristics (as in the subchapter on Slavic, 2.8) because it seems that all those linguists who regard Slavic aspect as absolute standard or idiosyncratic exemplar actually did not have an accurate idea of its implications.

In the European linguistic thought, it took more than two millennia to make a differentiation between tense and aspect and then less than a century to make a differentiation between aspect and aktionsarten. Did cognitive linguistics perhaps revert us or downgrade us by highlighting the fuzziness of the borders between the previously established categories? Not really, it can only push us forward into reconsidering the validity of categorizations in language. Aspect is indeed a semantic category that spreads over the entire morpho-syntactic system in bedazzling ways. In the system of preverbs and post-verbal particles, aspect shares its form with a number of other systems, making it difficult for us to identify it and isolate it from the functions of other systems.

Preverbs and post-verbal particles are a prominent example that blurs the boundaries between grammar and lexicon. As a result they also blur the boundaries between grammaticalization and lexicalization, as well as the boundaries between inflection and derivation. They show that there is a gradual rather than a discrete distinction between them.

The preverbs *a-*, *ge-* and *for-* are three of the seven prefixes that played an important role in the synthetic system of aspectual marking, which was gradually replaced by two analytical systems, one of post-verbal particles and the other of progressive tenses.

This research started from the hypothesis similar to Streitberg's – that Old English prefixed verbs express perfectivity and that their simplex counterparts denote imperfective actions, as is often assumed to be the situation in Slavic. The analysis of aspect in Slavic proved that this rule does not always apply, whereas the analysis of Old English showed that the function of the aspectual prefixes was mainly to mark perfectivity. However, their simplex counterparts did not always turn out to give imperfective readings. Nevertheless, Jakobson's concept of semantic markedness can well account for such cases: perfective is semantically marked, while imperfective is the semantically unmarked opposition of the correlate. Prefixed verbs are predominantly perfective, whereas their simplex counterparts are imperfective by default, which means that they can also give a perfective reading.

The preverbs *a-*, *ge-* and *for-* are traditionally thought to be derivational prefixes. However, ample evidence presented and discussed here shows many of their inflectional properties. Their decline and loss coincides with the decline and loss of all other inflectional suffixes that were used to mark case, gender, verb person and other grammatical functions.

From the analysis of the corpus data, one can see that a change was already under way in Old English. As the preverbs started losing their meaning or their diminishing transparency, speakers re-interpreted them and they eventually fell out of use.

Languages change because their speakers re-interpret data in inter-generational transmission of language. The reason why aspectual prefixes died out could be the fact speakers interpreted them as redundant since simplex versions of prefixed verbs had the capacity to convey both imperfective and perfective meanings.

The prefixes *a-*, *ge-* and *for-* show some typical features of grammaticalization. The investigation of their etymologies showed that once they were both content items which changed into grammatical words and then reduced to an inflectional affix. It is in this stage that we find them in the Old English period. The fact that in many cases their meanings are not readily identifiable points to the fact that their semantic properties were undergoing the process of bleaching.

By the end of the Middle English period they reach the final stage of grammaticalization where all semantic and phonological content is lost and the morpheme is reduced to zero or nothing.

Their meanings had already been bleached to a certain extent by the time of Old English as recorded in the corpus, unlike some other prefixes like *be-* which survived into present-day.

The prefix *a-* had a stronger capacity to express aspectuality than the prefix *ge-*. However, frequency charts may be distorting the overall picture. The prefix *ge-* is four times more frequent than the prefix *a-*, but in almost half the cases its meaning is not aspectual. The third most frequent prefix *for-* was also grammaticalized as a marker of perfectivity. Interestingly enough, the prefix *for-*

survived in the highest number of cases, all of which are now lexicalized, or more precisely, fossilized.

This discussion was a journey across time on many levels. First of all, it described a highly abstract system of temporal reference encoded in the morphology and syntax of verbs known as aspect. Then it described how the perception of this system evolved in human (i.e. linguistic) thought during the course of the past 2,500 years. It also explained how this very temporal reference codification evolved in language itself (the chronogenesis theory) taking us back into the past of 5,000 years ago.

Then from the present moment's perspective and understanding of this temporal reference category in language, the theory of aspect was applied to different stages of the English language, taking us again back into the past of 1,600 years ago for the fourth time on a diachronic enterprise.

Even though this book extensively deals with one segment of verbal aspect in English in diachrony, it has merely scratched the surface. There is much further research that should be undertaken, whose questions have been addressed here but not answered. However, it laid foundations and raised some new questions, which is in science often more appreciated than giving answers.

References

Agrell, Sigurd
    1908   "Aspektänderung und Aktionsartbildung beim polnischen Zeitworte: ein Beitrag zum Studium der indogermanischen Praeverbia und ihrer Bedeutungsfunktionen", *Lunds Universitets Årsskrift*, n.s. I, IV.2. Lund: H. Ohlsson.

Allen, Cynthia
    1990   "Review of Laurel J. Brinton, *The development of English aspectual systems.* (Cambridge Studies in Linguistics 49). Cambridge: Cambridge University Press, 1988. Pp. xii + 307.", *Journal of Linguistics* 26: 245-250

Auwera, Johan van der
    1999   "Dutch verbal prefixes. Meaning and form, grammaticalization and lexicalization", in: *Boundaries of morphology and syntax.* L. Mereu. (ed.) Amsterdam: Benjamins, 121-135.

Babić, Stjepan et al.
    1991   *Povijesni pregled, glasovi i oblici hrvatskoga književnog jezika.* Zagreb: HAZU – Nakladni zavod Globus.

Bach, Emmon
    1986   "The algebra of events". *Linguistics and Philosophy* 9: 5–16.

Bache, Carl
    1982.   "Aspect and Aktionsart: towards a semantic distinction", *Journal of Linguistics* 18: 57-72

Bache, Carl
    1985   *Verbal Aspect: A General Theory and its Application to Present-day English.* Odense: Odense University Press.

Bache, Carl
    1995a   *The Study of Aspect, Tense and Action. Towards a Theory of the Semantics of Grammatical Categories.* Frankfurt am Main: Peter Lang

Bache, Carl
    1995b   "Another look at the distinction between aspect and action". *Temporal Reference, Aspect and Actionality,* in: Bertinetto – Bianchi – Dahl – Squartini (eds.), vol. 2, 65–78.

Bechler, Karl
    1909   *Das Präfix* to *im Verlaufe der englischen Sprachgeschichte.* Königsberg: Hartungsche.

Baugh, Albert C. – Thomas Cable
    2002   *A History of the English Language.* Fifth ed. London: Routledge

Beer, Antonín
    1915   *Tři studie o videch slovesného děje v gotštině.* Část prvni: dějiny otázky. Prag

Benson, Thomas
    1701   *Vocabularium Anglo-Saxonicum.* S. Smith & B. Walford

Bertinetto, Pier Marco
    1997   *Il dominio tempo-aspettuale: Demarcazioni, intersezioni, contrasti.* Torino: Rosenberg & Sellier.

Binnick, Robert I.
  1991   *Time and the Verb. A Guide to Tense & Aspect.* New York and Oxford: Oxford University Press
Blažek, Václav
  2001   "Indo-European Prepositions and Related Words" in *SPFFBU* A 49: 15-32
Blom, Corrien
  2005   *Complex predicates in Dutch, synchrony and diachrony.* Utrecht: LOT.
Bloomfield, L.
  1929   "Notes on the Preverb *ge-* in Alfredian English", in: *Studies in English Philology, A Miscellany in Honor of Frederick Klaeber.* Minneapolis, 79-102
Bolinger, Dwight
  1971   *The Phrasal Verb in English.* Cambridge, Mass: Harvard University Press
Bondarko, A. V.
  1967   "K problematike funkcional'no-semantičeskih kategorij (Glagol'nyj vid i "aspektualnost" v russkom jazyke)", in: *Vosprosy jazykoznanija,* 2, Moskva, 18-31
Boogaart, Ronny
  1999   *Aspect and temporal ordering: A contrastive analysis of Dutch and English.* The Hague: Holland Academic Graphics.
Booij, G. E. – van Kemenade
  2003   "Preverbs: an Introduction", in: *Yearbook of Morphology,* G. E. Booij – J. van Marle (Eds.), 2003, Dordrecht: Kluwer, 33-60.
Booij, Geert
  2008   "Constructional idioms as products of linguistic change: the aan het + INFINITIVE construction in Dutch", in: Bergs A. – Diewald G. (Eds.), *Constructions and language change,* Berlin / New York: Mouton de Gruyter, 133-170
Bosworth, Joseph
  1865   *The Gothic and Anglo-Saxon Gospels in parallel columns with the versions of Wycliffe and Tyndale.* London: John Russell Smith
Braune, Wilhelm
  1883   *Gothic Grammar* with Selections for Reading and a Glossary. Translated from the second German edition by GH Balg. London.
Breu, Walter
  1994   'Interactions between lexical, temporal and aspectual meanings', *Studies in Language* 18: 23-44
Brinton, Laurel J.
  1985   "Iconicity and Semantic Change: Old English Verbal Prefixes", in: *Amsterdamer Beiträge zur älteren Germanistik* 23: 55-70
Brinton, Laurel J.
  1985   "Verb particles in English: Aspect or aktionsart?", *Studia Linguistica* 39: 157-168.
Brinton, Laurel J. – Akimoto, Minoji (eds.)
  1999   *Collocational and Idiomatic Aspects of Composite Predicates in the History of English.* Amsterdam/Philadelphia: John Benjamins Publishing Company
Brinton, Laurel J.
  1988   *The Development of English Aspectual Systems. Aspectualizers and post-verbal particles* (Cambridge Studies in Linguistics, 49). Cambridge: Cambridge University Press

Brinton, Laurel J. – Elizabeth Closs Traugott
  2005 *Lexicalization and Language Change.* Cambridge: Cambridge University Press.
Brlobaš, Željka
  2007 *Glagolski vid u hrvatskim gramatikama do 20. stoljeća.* Zagreb: Institut za hrvatski jezik i jezikoslovlje.
Brugmann, Karl
  1904a *Kurze vergleichende Grammatik der indogermanischen Sprachen.* Trübner, Strassburg.
Brugmann, Karl
  1904b *Die Demonstrativpronomina der indogermanischen Sprachen.* Leipzig: Teubner
Bugge, Sophus
  1889 "Etymologische studien über germanische lautverschiebung" In *Beiträge zur Geschichte der deutschen Sprache und Literatur (PBB)* XII: 399-431
Bybee, Joan L.
  1985 *Morphology: a study of the relation between meaning and form*, volume 9 of *Typological studies in language.* Amsterdam/Philadelphia: John Benjamins Publishing Company.
Bybee, Joan L. – Revere D. Perkins – William Pagliuca
  1994 *The Evolution of Grammar: Tense, Aspect and Modality in the Languages of the World.* Chicago, London: University of Chicago Press.
Cappelle, Bert
  2005 *Particle Patterns in English. A Comprehensive Coverage.* PhD dissertation. K.U.Leuven
Chomsky, Noam
  1957 *Syntactic Structures.* The Hague: Mouton
Chomsky, Noam
  1965 *Aspects of the Theory of Syntax.* Cambridge, Mass: The MIT Press.
Chung, Sandra – Alan Timberlake
  1985 "Tense, aspect, and mood", in: *Linguistic typology and syntactic description, vol 3: grammatical categories and the lexicon,* Timothy Shopen (ed.), Cambridge: Cambridge University Press
Coleman, Robert
  1996 "Exponents of futurity in Gothic", in: *Transactions of the Philological Society* 94:1–30.
Comrie, Bernard
  1976 *Aspect.* Cambridge: Cambridge University Press
Comrie, Bernard
  1985 *Tense.* Cambridge: Cambridge University Press
Comrie, Bernard – Greville G. Corbett (eds.)
  1993 *The Slavonic Languages.* London and New York: Routledge
Coseriu, Eugenio
  1980 "Aspect Verbal ou Aspects Verbaux?: Quelques questions de théorie et de méthode.", in: *La notion d'aspect: Colloque organisé par le Centre d'Analyse Syntaxique de l'Univ. de Metz, 18-20 mai 1978.* Jean David – Robert Martin – Bernard Pottier (eds.), Paris: Klincksieck, 13-25.
Croft, William – D. Allan Cruse
  2004 *Cognitive Linguisitcs.* Cambridge: Cambridge University Press

Dabrowska, Ewa
  1996 "The spatial structuring of events. A study of Polish perfectivizing prefixes", in: *The Construal of Space in Language and Thought* (Cognitive Linguistics Research, 8), Dirven René – Putz Martin (eds.), Berlin: Mouton de Gruyter, 467-490.
Dahl, Östen
  1981 "On the Definition of the Telic-Atelic (Bounded-Nonbounded) Distinction", in: *Tense and Aspect,* Philip Tedeschi – Anie Zaenen (eds). Academic Press. New York. 79-90.
Dahl, Östen
  1985 *Tense and Aspect System.* Oxford: Basil Blackwell
Dahl Östen
  1990 Book review: Laurel J. Brinton. *The Development of English Aspectual Systems. Aspectualizers and post-verbal particles* (Cambridge Studies in Linguistics, 49). Cambridge: Cambridge University Press 1988. in: *Journal of Semantics.* 7 (1): 115-119
de la Cruz, Juan M
  1972a "The Origins of the Germanic Phrasal Verb" In *Indogermanische Forschungen* 77:73-96
de la Cruz, Juan M
  1972b "A Syntactical Complex of Isoglosses in the North-Western End of Europe (English, North Germanic and Celtic)", in *Indogermanische Forschungen* 77: 171-180
de la Cruz, Juan M.
  1975 "Old English pure prefixes: structure and function", *Linguistics* 145: 47-81
Declerck, Renaat
  1979 "Aspect and the bounded/unbounded (telic/atelic) distinction", *Linguistics,* 17: 761-794
Declerck, Renaat
  1990 Short review of "The Development of English Aspectual Systems" by Laurel J. Brinton. *Linguistics* 28, vol. 3: 587-594.
Declerck, Renaat
  2006 *The Grammar of the English Tense System, The Grammar of the English Verb Phrase,* Vol. I. Berlin and New York: Mouton de Gruyter
Declerck, Renaat
  2007 "Distinguishing between the Aspectual Categories '(a)telic', '(im)perfective' and '(non)bounded'", in: *Kansas Working Papers in Linguistics* 29, 48-64
Dehé, Nicole, et al.
  2002 *Particle Verbs in English. Syntax, informational structure and intonation.* Amsterdam/Philadelphia: John Benjamins Publishing Company
Denison, David
  1985 "The origin of completive *up* in English", *Neuphilologische Mitteilungen* 86: 37-61.
Depraetere, Ilse
  1995 "On the necessity of distinguishing between (un)boundedness and (a)telicity", *Linguistics and Philosophy* 18, 1-19
Dickey, Stephen
  2000 *Parameters of Slavic aspect: a cognitive approach.* Stanford: CSLI Publications

Dickey, Stephen
    2007   "A prototype account of the development of delimitative *po-* in Russian" In *Cognitive Paths into the Slavic Domain,* Divjak, Dagmar – Agata Kochanska (eds.), Berlin and New York: Mouton de Gruyter

Diensberg, Bernhard
    1992   'English phrasal verbs expressing aspect and aktionsart?' (Review of Brinton 1988), *Folia Linguistica Historica* 11: 187-197

Dietrich, Gerhard
    1960   *Adverb oder Präposition? Zu einem klärungsbedürftigen Kapitel der englischen Grammatik.* Halle: VEB Max Niemeyer

Dik, Simon
    1989   *The Theory of Functional Grammar. Vol. 1.: The Structure of the Clause.* Dordrecht: Foris

Dik, Simon
    1994   "Verbal semantics in Functional Grammar". In Bache, Basbøll – Lindberg (eds.) in: *Tense, Aspect and Action.* Berlin/ New York: de Gruyter, 23-42.

Dirven, Rene
    2001   *The Metaphoric in Recent Cognitive Approaches to English Phrasal Verbs.* Metaphoric.de: 39-54

Dixon, R.M.W.
    1991   *A New Approach to English Grammar, on Semantic Principles.* Oxford: Clarendon.

Dollinger, Stefan.
    2001   "The OE and ME prefix *ge-* as a linguistic replicator; A morphological case study in a neo-Darwinian framework", *Viewz* 10/2: 3-29

Dorfeld, Karl
    1885   *Über die Funktion des Präfixes ge- (got. ga-) in der Composition mit Verben,* Gießen

Dostál, Antonín
    1954   *Studie o vidovém systému v staroslovnštine.* Prague: Státní pedagogicke nakladatelství.

Dowty, David R.
    1979   *Word Meaning and Montague Grammar.* Dordrecht: Reidel

Dufresne, M., F. Dupuis and M. Tremblay.
    2003   "Preverbs and particles in Old French", in: *Yearbook of Morphology,* G.E. Booij – J. van Marle (eds.), 2003, Dordrecht: Kluwer, 33-60

Durst-Andersen, Per
    1992   *Mental Grammar: Russian Aspect and Related Issues.* Columbus, Ohio: Slavica

Durst-Andersen, Per
    1994   *Russian aspects as different statement models,* in: Bache, Basbøll – Lindberg (eds.), *Tense, Aspect and Action.* Berlin/ New York: de Gruyter, 81–112

Durst-Andersen, Per
    2000   "The English progressive as picture description", in: *Acta Linguistica Hafniensia* 32: 45–103

Egerod, Søren
    1994   "Aspect in Chinese" in: *Tense, Aspect and Action. Empirical and Theoretical Contributions to Language Typology,* C. Bache – H. Basbøll – C.-E. Lindberg (eds.), Berlin and New York: Mouton de Gruyter.

Elenbaas, Marion
    2007 *The Synchronic and Diachronic Syntax of the English Verb-Particle Combination*. Dissertation, Radboud University Nijmegen (LOT Dissertations 149)

Ferrell, James
    1951 "The Meaning of the Perfective Aspect in Russian", *Word* 7: 104-135

Filip, Hana
    1999 *Aspect, Eventuality Types, and Nominal Reference,* London: Routledge

Fillmore, Charles J.
    1975 *Santa Cruz Lectures on Deixis, 1971.* Bloomington: University of Indiana Linguistics Club

Forsyth, James
    1970 *A Grammar of Aspect: Usage and Meaning in the Russian Verb,* Cambridge: Cambridge University Press

Fortson, Benjamin W.
    2004 *Indo-European Language and Culture,* Oxford: Blackwell Publishing

Fraser, Bruce
    1976 *The Verb-Particle Construction,* New York: Academic Press

Fraser, Thomas K. H.
    1975 'The preverbs *for-* and *fore-* in Old English', in: *Studies in English Grammar,* A. Joly and T. Fraser (eds.), Paris: Editions universitaires, 17-28

Freed, Alice F.
    1979 *The Semantics of English Aspectual Complementation.* London: Reidel

Galton, Herbert
    1976 *The Main Functions of the Slavic Verbal Aspect.* Skopje: Macedonian Academy of Sciences and Arts

Garey, Howard B.
    1957 "Verbal Aspect in French" In *Language* 33(2), 91-110

Geld, Renata – Irena Zovko Dinković
    2007 "Perfectives, imperfectives and the Croatian present tense", in: *Cognitive Paths into the Slavic Domain,* Dagmar Divjak – Agata Kochanska (eds.), Berlin and New York: Mouton de Gruyter

Geld, Renata
    2009 *From topology to verbal aspect: Strategic construal of* in *and* out *in English particle verbs.* Dissertation, University of Zagreb

Gelderen, Elly van
    2007 "Accelerated grammaticalization in the *Peterborough Chronicle*", in: *The Language of the Peterborough Chronicle,* edited by Alexander Bergs –Janne Skaffari (eds.). Frankfurt am Main: Peter Lang

Givón, Talmy
    1971 "Historical syntax and synchronic morphology: An Archeologist's fieldtrip", in: *Papers from the Seventh Regional Meeting, Chicago Linguistic Society,* Chicago: Chicago Linguistic Society, 394-415

Goedsche, Curt Rudolf
    1934 "Verbal Aspect in German", *The Journal of English and Germanic Philology,* Vol. 33, No. 4 (Oct., 1934), 506-519

Goedsche, Curt Rudolf
　1940　"Aspect versus Aktionsart", *The Journal of English and Germanic Philology*, Vol. 39, No. 2 (Apr., 1940), 189-196
Gojmerac, Mirko
　1980　*Glagolski vid u hrvatskom ili srpskom i njemačkom jeziku*, doktorska disertacija. Zagreb: Filozofski fakultet, Sveučilište u Zagrebu.
Goldberg, Adele Eva
　1995　*Constructions: A Construction Grammar approach to argument structure*, Chicago: Chicago University. Press
Goldberg, Adele Eva
　2006　*Constructions at work. The nature of generalization in language*, Oxford: Oxford University Press.
Gonda, Jan
　1962　*The aspectual function of the Rgvedic present and aorist*. (Disputationes Rheno-Trajectinae, 7), 'S-Gravenhage: Mouton
Gorlach, Marina
　2000　"Resultativeness: Constructions with phrasal verbs in focus", in: *Between Grammar and Lexicon*, Contini-Morava, Ellen – Yishai Tobin (eds.), 255-287
Gray, Louis Herbert
　1939　*Foundations of Language*, New York: The Macmillan Company
Grubišić, Vinko
　1995　*Croatian Grammar*, Zagreb: Hrvatska sveučilišna naklada
Guillaume, Gustave
　1929　*Temps et verbe*, Paris: Champion.
Guillaume, Gustave
　1945　*Architectonique du temps dans les langues classiques*, Copenhagen: Munksgard. (Repr., Paris: Champion, 1965)
Hale, Ken – Samuel Jay Keyser
　1993　'On argument structure and the lexical expression of syntactic relations', in: *The View from Building 20: Essays in Linguistics in Honor of Sylvain Bromberger*, K. Hale – S. J. Keyser (eds.), Cambridge, Mass.: MIT Press, 53–108
Hampe, Beate
　2002　*Superlative Verbs. A corpus-based study of semantic redundancy in English verb-particle constructions*, Tübingen: Gunter Narr Verlag
Harbert, Wayne
　2007　*The Germanic Languages*, Cambridge: Cambridge University Press
Heine, Bernd – Ulrike Claudi – Friederike Hünnemeyer
　1991　*Grammaticalization. A Conceptual Framework*. Chicago: University of Chicago press.
Heine, Bernd
　2003　"On degrammaticalization", in: *Historical Linguistics 2001. Selected Papers from the 15th International Conference on Historical Linguistics, Melbourne, 13-17 August 2001*, (Current Issues in Linguistic Theory, 237.) Amsterdam and Philadelphia: John Benjamins, 165-179
Hesse, Hugo
　1906　*Perfektive und imperfektive Aktionsart im Altenglischen*, Diss. Münster.

Hewson, John – Vit Bubenik
    1997   *Tense and Aspect in Indo-European Languages. Theory, Typology, Diachrony*, Amsterdam: John Benjamins

Hiltunen, Risto
    1983   "Phrasal Verbs in English grammar books before 1800", *Neuphilologische Mitteilungen* 84: 376-386

Hiltunen, Risto
    1983   *The Decline of the Prefixes and the Beginning of the English Phrasal Verb.* (Annales Universitas Turkuensis, Series B., Vol.160.) Turku

Hiltunen, Risto
    1994   "On phrasal verbs in Early Modern English: notes on lexis and style", in: *Studies in Early Modern English*, Dieter Kastovsky (ed.), Berlin/New York: Mouton de Gruyter, 129-140

Hirt, Hermann
    1934   *Handbuch des Urgermanischen. Teil III: Abriss der Syntax*, Heidelberg: Carl Winters Universitätsbuchhandlung

Hogg, Richard
    2002   *An Introduction to Old English*, Edinburgh University Press, Edinburgh

Holt, Jens
    1943   "Études d'aspect", *Acta Jutlandica* 15.2

Hopper, Paul J. – Elizabeth Closs Traugott
    2003 [1993]   *Grammaticalization*, Cambridge: Cambridge University Press

Horgan, D.M. 1980. "Patterns of variation and interchangeability in some Old English prefixes". In *Neuphilologische Mitteilungen* 81. 127-130.

Huntley, David
    1993   "Old Church Slavonic", in: *The Slavonic Languages*, Comrie, Bernard – Greville G. Cordette (eds.), London and New York: Routledge

Isačenko, Alexander Vasilyevich
    1960   *Grammatičeskij stroj russkogo jazyka v sopostavlenii s slovackim – Čast' vtoraja: morfologija*, Bratislava: Izdatel'stvo akademii nauk

Jackendoff, Ray
    2002   "English Particle Constructions", in: *Verb Particle Explorations*, Dehé, Nicole – Ray Jackendoff, Andrew McIntyre (eds.), Berlin/New York: Mouton de Gruyter

Jacobsohn, Hermann
    1920   "Zwei Probleme der gotischen Lautgeschichte, II: Zum gotischen Satzsandhi", *KZ* 49: 129-218

Jakobson, Roman
    1932   "Zur Struktur des russischen Verbums", [first published in *Charisteria Gvilelmo Mathesio qvinqvagenario a discipulis et Circuli Lingvistici Pragensis sodalibus oblata*], translated into English as "Structure of the Russian verb", in: Waugh, Linda R. – Morris Halle (eds.), 1-14.

Jakobson, Roman
    1957[1971]. "Shifters, verbal categories, and the Russian verb", in: *Selected writings*, vol. 2, 130-147

Janda, Laura Alexis
    2004   "A metaphor in search of a source domain: the categories of Slavic aspect", *Cognitive Linguistics* 15, 471-527

Janda, Laura Alexis
    2007   "What makes Rusian bi-aspectual verbs special?", in: *Cognitive Paths into the Slavic Domain,* Dagmar Divjak – Agata Kochanska (eds.), Berlin and New York: Mouton de Gruyter

Jespersen, Otto
    1924   *The Philosophy of Grammar.* New York: Norton

Jespersen, Otto
    1928   *A Modern English Grammar. On Historical Principles.* 7 volumes. Copenhangen/London: Ejnar Munksgaard/Allen&Unwin/Heidelberg: Carl Winter

Johanson, Lars
    1996   "Terminality operators and their hierarchical status", in: *Complex Structures: A Functionalist Perspective.* Betty Devriendt – Louis Goossens – Johan van der Auwera (eds.), Berlin: Mouton de Gruyter, 229–258

Johnson, Mark
    1987   *The Body in the Mind,* Chicago: University Press of Chicago.

Kabakčiev, Krasimir
    2000   *Aspect in English; A 'Common - Sense' View of the Interplay between Verbal and Nominal Referents,* Studies in Linguistics and Philosophy 75. Dordrecht: Kluwer Academic Publishers

Karčevski, Serge
    1927   *Système du verbe russe: essai de linguistique synchronique,* volume I. Prague: Plamja.

Kastovsky, Dieter
    1992   "Semantics and Vocabulary" in *Cambridge History of the English Language,* Volume 1. Cambridge: Cambridge University Press

Kastovsky, Dieter
    2006   "Vocabulary," in: *A history of the English language,* Hogg, Richard – David Denison (eds.), Cambridge: Cambridge University Press, 199-270

Kemenade, A. van – B. Los
    2003   "Particles and prefixes in Dutch and English", in: *Yearbook of Morphology,* G.E. Booij – J. van Marle (Eds.), Dordrecht: Kluwer, 79-117

Kennedy, A.G.
    1920   *The Modern English Verb-Adverb Combination,* Reprint: New York 1967

Kiefer, Ferenc
    1994   "Some peculiarities of the aspectual system in Hungarian", in: *Tense, Aspect and Action. Empirical and Theoretical Contributions to Language Typology,* C. Bache, H. Basbøll – C.-E. Lindberg (eds.). Berlin and New York: Mouton de Gruyter.

Klein, Wolfgang
    1995   "A time-relational analysis of Russian aspect", *Language* 71: 669–695

Krause, Wolfgang
    1953   *Handbuch des Gotischen.* München: Beck

Krause, Maxi
    1987   *Sémantique et syntaxe des préverbes en Gotique,* 4 vol. Thèse Paris.

Kravar, Miroslav
    1976   "Glagolski vid kao tipološko-komparativni problem", in: *Radovi Filozofskoga fakulteta u Zadru,* 14-15, Zadar, 289-312

Kruisinga, Etsko
    1931   *A handbook of present-day English,* part II. English accidence and syntax, vol. 1, 5th edition, Groningen: P. Noordhoff

Kuryłowicz, Jerzy
    1964   *The Inflectional Categories of Indo-European,* Heidelberg: Carl Winter

Kuryłowicz, Jerzy
    1965   "The evolution of grammatical categories", *Diogenes* 51:55-71.

Labeau, Emmanuelle
    2005   *Beyond the aspect hypothesis: tense-aspect development in advanced L2 French,* Bern: Peter Lang AG

Lakoff, George – Mark Johnson
    1980   *Metaphors We Live By.* Chicago: University of Chicago Press.

Lehmann, Christian
    2002 [1982, 1995]. *Thoughts on Grammaticalization: A programmatic sketch, Vol. 1,* Arbeiten des Kölner Universalien-Projekts, 48, Köln: Institut für Sprachwissenschaft. Revised edition published by LINCOM Europa, München, 1995. Second revised edition reprinted as Arbeitspapiere des Seminars für Sprachwissenschaft der Universität Erfurt, 9. Erfurt: Seminar für Sprachwissenschaft der Universität.

Lehmann, Volkmar
    1988   "Der russische Aspekt und die lexicaische Bedeutung des Verbs", in: *Zeitschrift für slavische Philologie* 48: 170-181

Lehmann, Winfred P.
    1986   *A Gothic Etymological Dictionary,* Leiden: E.J. Brill

Lehmann, Winfred P.
    1994   "Gothic and the Reconstruction of Proto-Germanic", in: *The Germanic Languages,* König, Ekkehard – Johan van der Auwera (eds.), London and New York: Routledge

Leiss, Elisabeth
    2000   *Artikel und Aspekt. Die grammatischen Muster von Definitheit,* Berlin & New York: Walter de Gruyter

Lenze, Josef
    1909   *Das Präfix bi- in der altenglischen Nominal- und Verbalkomposition mit gelegentlicher Berücksichtigung der anderen germanischen Dialekte.* Kiel: Fiencke.

Leopold, Max
    1977[1907]   *Die Vorsilbe ver- und ihre Geschichte.* In Germanistische Abhandlungen. Reprint Hildesheim: Olms

Leskien, August
    1909   *Grammatik der altburgarischen (altkirchenslavischen) Sprache,* Heidelberg: Winter

Langacker, Ronald W.
    1987   *Foundations of Cognitive Grammar. Volume 1. Theoretical Prerequisites,* Stanford: Stanford University Press

Limar, L. S.
    1963   "K voprosu o roli glagol'nix pristavok v svjazi s vidovym značeniem glagolov (na materiale drevneanglijskogo)", in: *Učenye Zapiski,* xxviii, č. 2-ja, Moscow

Lindemann, J. W. R.
    1965 "Old English Preverbal ge-: a Re-Examination of some Current Doctrines", *Journal of English and Germanic Philology* 64, 65-83

Lindemann, J. W. R.
    1970 *Old English preverbal ge-: Its meaning,* Charlottesville: The University Press of Virginia

Lindner, S. J.
    1983 *A lexico-semantic analysis of English verb particle constructions with* out *and* up, Bloomington, Ind.: Indiana University Linguistics Club

Lindström, Therese
    2004 *The history of the concept of grammaticalization*, PhD Thesis, University of Sheffield.

Lipka, Leonhard
    1972 *Semantic Structure and Word Formation, Verb-Particle Construction in Contemporary English.* München

Live, Anna H.
    1965 "The discontinuous verb in English", *Word* 21, 428-451

Lloyd, Albert Larry
    1979 *Anatomy of the Verb: The Gothic Verb as a Model for a Unified Theory of Aspect, Actional Types, and Verbal Velocity,* Amsterdam: John Benjamins

Lloyd, Albert Larry
    1990 "A Reply to Oswald Szemerényi: 'The Origin of Aspect in the Indo-European Languages'", Replies to Szemerényi (1987), *Glotta* 68, 129-131

Lyons, John
    1977 *Semantics, Volume 2.* Cambridge: Cambridge University Press.

Lunt, Horace Gray
    2001 *Old Church Slavonic Grammar.* 7. rev. ed. Berlin and New York: Mouton de Gruyter

Lutz, Angelika
    1997 "Sound change, word formation and the lexicon: The history of the English prefix verbs", *English Studies* 78 (3), 258-290

Macaulay, R. K. S.
    1978 "Review, Comrie (1976) and Friedrich (1974)", *Language* 54, 416-420

Marsden, Richard
    2004 *The Cambridge Old English Reader*, Cambridge: Cambridge University Press

Martín Arista, Javier
    2006 "Alternations, Relatedness and Motivation: Old English *A-*", in: *Where Grammar Meets Discourse: Functional and Cognitive Perspectives,* Guerrero Medina, Pilar – Estela Martínez Jurado (eds.), Córdoba: Servicio de Publicaciones de la Universidad de Córdoba, 113-132

Martín Arista, Javier
    2008 "The *ge*-alternation and the descriptive power of *Nerthus*", *Journal of English Studies* 5-6: 209-231

Maslov, Jurij S.
    1959 "Glagol'nyj vid v sovremennom bolgarskom literaturnom jazyke", in: *Voprosy grammatiki bolgarskogo literaturnogo jazyka,* 157–312

Matasović, Ranko
    2008 *Poredbeno povijesna gramatika hrvatskoga jezika,* Zagreb: Matica hrvatska

Maylor, Roger B.
    2002   *Lexical template morphology: change of state and the verbal prefixes in German*, Amsterdam/Philadelphia: John Benjamins

McEnery, Tony – Andrew Wilson
    2001   *Corpus linguistics. An introduction*. 2nd edition, Edinburgh University Press: Edinburgh.

McIntyre, Andrew
    2001   *Introduction to the Verb-Particle Experience*, Ms., University of Leipzig

McIntyre, Andrew
    2003   "Preverbs, argument linking and verb semantics: German prefixes and particles", in: *Yearbook of Morphology*, Booij, Geert E. – Jaap van Marle (eds.), Dordrecht: Kluwer, 119-144

Michaelis, Laura A.
    1998   *Aspectual Grammar and Past-Time Reference*, London: Routledge

Migdalski, Krzysztof
    2006   *The Syntax of Compound Tenses in Slavic*, LOT 130

Millward, C. M.
    1996   *A Biography of the English Language*, Holt, Rinehart and Winston, Inc. Boston

Mirowicz, Anatol
    1935   *Die Aspektfrage im Gotischen*, Wilno: Nakladem Towarzystrwa Prsyjaci-L Nauk

Mitchell, Bruce
    1985   *Old English Syntax*, 2 vols, Oxford: Clarendon Press

Mitchell, Bruce – Fred C. Robinson
    2007   *A Guide to Old English*, 7th edition, Oxford: Blackwell

Mlynarczyk, Anna Katarzyna
    2004   *Aspectual Pairing in Polish*, PhD thesis, Proefschrift Universiteit Utrecht

Moens, Marc
    1987   *Tense, aspect and temporal reference*, PhD Dissertation, University of Edinburgh

Morgan, Pamela S.
    1997   "Figuring out *figure out:* Metaphor and the semantics of the English verb-particle construction", *Cognitive Linguistics* 8 (4), 327-357

Mossé, Fernand
    1938   *Histoire de la forme périphrastique être + participe present en germanique*, deuxième partie: moyen-anglais et anglais moderne, Paris: C. Klincksieck

Mourelatos, Alexander P. D.
    1978   "Events, processes, and states", *Linguistics and Philosophy* 2, 415-434, (Reprinted in Tedeschi and Zaenen 1981: 191-212)

Mustanoja, Tauno F.
    1960   *A Middle English Syntax, Part 1. Parts of Speech*, Helsinki: Société Néophilologique.

Newman, Lawrence W.
    1976   "The Notion of Verbal Aspect in Eighteenth Century Russia", in: *Russian Linguistics*, Vol. 3, No. 1, 35-53

Nevalainen, Terttu
    1999   *Lexis and Semantics*, in: *The Cambridge History of the English Language. Volume III (1476-1776)*, Lass, Roger (ed.), Cambridge University Press. Cambridge.

Niwa, Yoshinobu
    2008   "Why does *ga-* not appear in the Gothic past participle?", *Studia Anglica Posnaniensia* 44, 13-23

Noël, Dirk
    2007   "Diachronic construction grammar and grammaticalization theory", in: *Functions of Language* 14 (2), 177-202

Norde, Muriel
    2009   *Degrammaticalization*, Oxford: Oxford University Press

O'Dowd, Elizabeth M.
    1998   *Prepositions and Particles in English. A Discourse-Functional Account*, Oxford, Oxford University Press

Ogura, Michigo
    1994   "Grammatical choices in Old and early Middle English: A choice between a simple verb, the prefix/particle-verb or verb-particle combination, and the "auxiliary + infinitive" construction in Old and early Middle English", in: *English Historical Linguistics 1992. Papers from the 7th international conference on English historical linguistics,* Fernández, Francisco – Miguel Fuster – Juan José Calvo (eds.), Amsterdam: Benjamins.

Ogura, Michiko
    1995   "The Interchangeability of Old English Verbal Prefixes", *Anglo-Saxon England* 24, 67-93.

Padučeva, Elena V.
    1995   "Taxonomic categories and semantics of aspectual opposition", in: *Temporal Reference, Aspect, and Actionality, vol. I, Semantic and Syntactic Perspectives,* Bertinetto, Pier Marco – Valentina Bianchi – Östen Dahl – Mario Squartini (eds.), Torino: Rosenberg and Sellier, 71-90

Padučeva, Elena V.
    1996   *Semantičeskie issledovanija* [Essays in semantics], Moskva: Jazyki russkoj kul'tury

Petré, Peter – Hubert Cuyckens
    2008   "Bedusted, yet not beheaded: the role of *be-*'s constructional properties in its conservation", in: *Constructions and language change,* Bergs, Alexander – Gabriele Diewald (eds.), Berlin / New York: Mouton de Gruyter, 133-170

Petré, Peter
    2005   *On the variables determining the life span of English prefix constructions: A case study of the two prefixes* be- *and* to- *(NHG* zer-*),* Unpublished MA thesis, University of Leuven

Pilch, Herbert
    1953   "Das AE. Präverb *ge-*", *Anglia*, LXXI, 129-139

Pilch, Herbert
    1955   "Der Untergang des Präverbs *ge-* im Englischen", *Anglia*, LXXIII, 37-64

Pollak, Wolfgang
    1960   *Studien zum Verbalaspekt. Mit besonderer Berücksichtigung des Französischen,* Bern: Verlag Peter Lang

Porzig, Walter
    1927   "Zur Aktionsart indogermanischer Präasensbildungen", *Indogermanische Forschungen* XLV, 152–167.

Pudić, Ivan
    1956   *Prefiks ga- u gotskom jeziku. Prilog učenju o glagolskom vidu*, Sarajevo: Naučno delo
Pyles, Thomas – John Algeo
    1993   *The Origins and Development of the English Language*, Fourth Edition, London: Harcourt Brace
Quirk, Randolph – C.L. Wrenn
    1957   *An Old English Grammar. Second Edition*, London and New York: Methuen
Renicke, Horst
    1961   "Deutsche Aspektpaare", *Zeitschrift für deutsche Philologie* 80, 86–99
Rice, Allan Lake
    1932   *Gothic Prepositional Compounds in their Relation to their Greek Originals*, Diss. Philadelphia.
Riemer, Nick
    2010   *Introducing Semantics,* Cambridge: Cambridge University Press
Ringe, Donald A.
    2006   *From Proto-Indo-European to Proto-Germanic*, Oxford University Press
Rothstein, Susan
    2004   *Structuring Events: A Study in the Semantics of Lexical Aspect*, Blackwell: Oxford
Rudzka-Ostyn, Brygida
    2003   *Word Power: Phrasal Verbs and Compounds, A Cognitive Approach*, Berlin and New York: Mouton de Gruyter
Sadej, Kinga
    2009   "The grammaticalization of 'down'", *Studia Anglica Posnaniensia* vol. 45, number 1, 103-115
Samuels, M. L.
    1972   *Linguistic Evolution. With Special Reference to English.* Cambridge: Cambridge University Press
Sapir, Edward
    1921   *Language,* New York: Harcourt, Brace and Company
Sasse, Hans Jürgen
    1991   "Aspect and Aktionsart: A Reconciliation", in: *Perspectives on Aspect and Aktionsart. (Belgian Journal of Linguistics 6, 31-45).* Vetters, Carl – Willy Vandeweghe (eds.), Bruxelles: Editions de l'Université de Bruxelles
Sasse, Hans Jürgen
    2002   "Recent activity in the theory of Aspect: accomplishments, achievements, or just non-progressive state?", *Linguistic Typology* 6, 199-271
Scherer, Philip
    1954   "Aspect in Gothic" In *Language* 30, No. 2. pp. 211-223
Scherer, Philip
    1956   "Aspect in the Old High German of Tatian", in: *Language* 32, 423-434
Scherer, Philip
    1958   "Aspect in the Old English of the Corpus Christi MS", in: *Language* 34, 245-251
Schmidt, Johannes
    1889   *Die Pluralbindungen der indogermanischen Neutra,* Weimar: Herman Böhlau
Senn, Alfred
    1949   "Verbal Aspects in Germanic, Slavic and Baltic", *Language* 35, 402-409

Silić, Josip
    1978   "An Approach to the Study of Aspectuality in the Croatian Literary Language", in: *Kontrastivna analiza engleskog i hrvatskog ili srpskog jezika* [Contrastive Analysis of English and Serbo-Croatian]. Volume 2. Rudolf Filipović (ed.), Zagreb: Institute of Linguistics, Faculty of Philosophy, University of Zagreb, 42–70

Silić, Josip – Ivo Pranjković
    2007   *Gramatika hrvatskoga jezika,* Zagreb: Školska knjiga

Singh, Ishtla
    2005   *The History of English: A Student's Guide,* London: Hodder Arnold

Smith, Carlota
    1983   "A Theory of Aspectual Choice", *Language* 59, 479-501

Smith, Carlota
    1991   *The Parameter of Aspect,* Dordrecht: Kluwer.

Somner, William
    1659   *Dictionarium Saxonico-Latino-Anglicum,* Oxford: William Hall

Spencer, Andrew
    1991   *Morphological Theory: An Introduction to Word Structure in Generative Grammar,* Oxford: Blackwell Strauss

Sroka, Kazimiers
    1972   *The Syntax of English Phrasal Verbs,* The Hague/Paris: Mouton

Streitberg, Wilhelm
    1891   "Perfective und imperfective actionsart im Germanischen", in: *Beiträge zur Geschichte der deutschen Sprache und Literatur* 15, 70-177

Szemerényi, Oswald J. L.
    1987   "The Origin of Aspect in the Indo-European Languages", *Glotta* 65, 1-18

Szemerényi, Oswald J. L.
    1996   *Introduction to Indo-European Linguistics,* Oxford: Clarendon Press

Tabakowska, Elżbieta
    2003   "Space and Time in Polish. The preposition za and the verbal prefix za-' ", in: *Motivation in Language. Studies in honor of Günter Radden* (Current Issues in Linguistic Theory, 243), Cuyckens, Hubert – Thomas Berg – René Dirven – Klaus Uwe Panther (eds.), Amsterdam: Benjamins, 153-177

Tandy, Keith Alan
    1976   *Aspect and Ælfric,* Ph.D. Thesis, University of California, Berkeley

Tandy, Keith Alan
    1978   "Verbal aspect as a Narrative Structure in Aelfric's *Lives of Saints*", in: *The Old English homily and its backgrounds,* Szarmach, Paul E. – Bernard Felix Huppé (eds.), Albany: State University of New York Press

Tatevosov, Sergei
    2002   "The Parameter of Actionality", in: *Linguistic Typology* 6: 317-401

Thim, Stefan
    2012   *Phrasal Verbs. The English Verb-Particle Construction and its History,* Berlin/Boston: De Gruyter Mouton

Tichy, Eva
    2000   *Indogermanistisches Grundwissen für Studierende sprachwissenschaftlicher Disziplinen,* Bremen: Hempen

Timberlake, Alan
    2004   *A Reference Grammar of Russian,* Cambridge: Cambridge University Press
Traugott, Elizabeth Closs
    1978   "On the Expression of Spatio-Temporal Relations in Language", in: *Universals of Human Language,* Vol. III., Greenberg, Joseph H. – Charles A. Ferguson – Edith A. Moravcsik (eds.), Stanford: Stanford University Press, 369-400
Traugott, Elizabeth Closs
    1982   "From propositional to textual and expressive meanings: some semantic-pragmatic aspects of grammaticalization", in: *Perspectives on historical linguistics,* Lehmann, Winfred P. – Yakov Malkiel (eds.), Amsterdam and Philadelphia: John Benjamins
Traugott, Elizabeth Closs
    1990   "Review of Laurel J. Brinton (1988) *The development of English aspectual systems.* (Cambridge Studies in Linguistics 49). Cambridge: Cambridge University Press" In *Studies in Language* 14: 221-226
Traugott, Elizabeth Closs
    2008   "Grammaticalization, constructions and the incremental development of language: Suggestions from the development of degree modifiers in English", in: *Variation, Selection, Development: Probing the Evolutionary Model,* Eckardt, Regine – Gerhard Jäger – Tonjes Veenstra (eds.), Berlin and New York: Mouton de Gruyter, 219-250
Trobevšek Drobnak, Frančiška
    1994   "The Old English preverbal *ge-* in the light of the theory of language changes as strengthening or weakening", *Studia Anglica Posnaniensia* 28, 123-142
Trousdale, Graeme
    2008   "Constructions in grammaticalization and lexicalization: Evidence from the history of a composite predicate construction in English", in: *Constructional Approaches to English Grammar* [Topics in English Linguistics 57], Trousdale, Graeme – Nikolas Gisborne (eds.), Berlin: Mouton de Gruyter, 33-67
Uhlenbeck, Christianus C.
    1906   "Aanteekeningen bij Gotischen etymologieën", TNTL 25, 245-306
Vendler, Zeno
    1957   "Verbs and times", in: *The Philosophical Review* 66, 143-160, Reprinted in Z. Vendler. 1967. Linguistics in philosophy. Ithaca: Cornell University Press.
Verkuyl, Henk J.
    1972   *On the compositional nature of the aspects.* (Foundations of Language Supplementary Series, 15), Dordrecht-Holland: D. Reidel
Verkuyl, Henk J.
    1993   *A theory of aspectuality: The interaction between temporal and atemporal structure,* Cambridge: Cambridge University Press
Weick, Friedrich
    1911   *Das Aussterben des Präfixes ge- im Englischen,* Diss. Darmstadt: Wintersche Buchdruckerei
West, Jonathan
    1982   "The Semantics of Preverbs in Gothic", *Indogermanische Forschungen* 87, 138-165
Wijk, Nicolaas van
    1928   "'Aspect' en 'Aktionsart'", in: *De Nieuwe Taalgids,* Jaargang 22, 225-239

Wischer, Ilse – Mechthild Habermann
    2004   "Der Gebrauch von Präfixverben zum Ausdruck von Aspekt/Aktionsart im Altenglischen und Althochdeutschen", *Zeitschrift für Germanistische Linguistik* 32, 262-285.

Zandvoort, Reinard W.
    1962   "Is 'Aspect' an English Verbal Category?", in: *Studies in English (Gothenburg)* 14

Zbierska-Sawala, Anna
    1997   "Word-formation and the text in Early English: The axiological functions of Old English prefixes", in: *Language history and linguistic modelling: A festschrift for Jacek Fisiak on his 60th birthday*. Hickey, Raymond – Stanisław Puppel (eds.), Berlin - New York: Mouton de Gruyter, 593-602.

Ziegeler, Debra
    2006   *Interfaces with English aspect: Diachronic and empirical studies,* Philadelphia and Amsterdam: John Benjamins

Žic Fuchs, Milena
    2009   *Kognitivna lingvistika i jezične structure: engleski* present perfect, Zagreb: Nakladni zavod Globus

Dictionaries:

BT: Joseph Bosworth and T. Northcote Toller. 1898 (main volume) & 1921 (supplement). *An Anglo-Saxon dictionary, based on the manuscript collections of the late Joseph Bosworth.* Oxford: Oxford University Press. (also in the digital edition: http://bosworth.ff.cuni.cz/ (accessed 24 March 2011)

DOE: *Dictionary of Old English: A to G on CD-ROM.* 2008. Angus Cameron, Ashley Crandell Amos, Antonette diPaolo Healey et al. (eds.). Toronto: Pontifical Institute of Mediaeval Studies.

MED: *Middle English Dictionary.* http://quod.lib.umich.edu/m/med/ (accessed 24 March 2011)

OED: *The Oxford English Dictionary.* 2nd edn. 1989. Simpson, J. A. and Weiner, E. S . C. (eds) on CD-ROM. Oxford: Oxford University Press

Appendix I
Old English Corpus

This is the list of Old English texts from the York-Toronto-Helsinki Parsed Corpus of Old English prose (YCOE) that was used in this research. YCOE was compiled by Ann Taylor Anthony Warner, Susan Pintzuk and Frank Beths in 2003. The texts are listed by their YCOE file name along with their full name and a reference to the text edition.
Further details can be found at
http://www-users.york.ac.uk/~lang22/YCOE/info/YcoeTextInfo.htm

File name	Text name and edition
coadrian	*Adrian and Ritheus* Cross, James E. and Thomas D. Hill. 1982. *The "Prose Solomon and Saturn" and "Adrian and Ritheus"*. Pp. 35-40. Toronto, Buffalo, London: University of Toronto Press.
coalcuin	*Alcuin's De Virtutibus et Vitiis* Warner, Rubie D.-N. 1917 (1971). *Early English Homilies from the 12th Century Ms. Vespasian D.XIV*. EETS 152: 91-105. London: Trübner.
coalex	*Alexander's Letter to Aristotle* Orchard, Andrew P.M. 1995. *Pride and Prodigies: Studies in the Monsters of the "Beowulf" Manuscript*. Pp. 224-52. Cambridge: D.S. Brewer.
coaugust	*Augustine* Warner, Rubie D.-N. 1917 (1971). *Early English Homilies from the 12th Century Ms. Vespasian D.XIV*. EETS 152. P.65. London: Trübner. [repr. 1971]
cobede	*Bede's History of the English Church* Miller, Thomas. 1959-1963 (1890-1898). *The Old English Version of "Bede's Ecclesiastical History of the English People"*. EETS 95, 96, 110, 111. London: OUP.
cobenrul	*Benedictine Rule* Schröer, A. (1885–1888). *Die angelsæchsischen Prosabearbeitungen der Benediktinerregel*. Bibliothek der Angelsæchsischen Prosa, II. Kassel. Reprinted with appendix by H. Gneuss (Darmstadt 1964).
coblick	*Blickling Homilies* Morris, Richard. 1967 (1874-1880). *The Blickling Homilies*. EETS 58, 63, 73. London: Trübner.
cocanedd	*Canons of Edgar* Fowler, Roger. 1972. *Wulfstan's Canons of Edgar*. EETS 266. London: OUP.
cocanedx	*Canons of Edgar* Fowler, Roger. 1972. *Wulfstan's Canons of Edgar*. EETS 266. London: OUP.
cochad	*Other Saints' Lives, The Life of Saint Chad* Vleeskruyer, Rudolf. 1953. *The Life of Saint Chad: An Old English Homily*. Amsterdam: North-Holland.
cochdrul	*Chrodegang of Metz* Napier, Arthur S. 1971 (1916). *The Old English Version, with the Latin Original, of the Enlarged Rule of Chrodegang together with the Latin Original*.

186   Appendix I: Old English Corpus

	EETS 150. London: Kegan Paul, Trench, Trübner & Co., Ltd. and OUP.
cochroph	*Saint Christopher*
	Rypins, Stanley. 1971 (1924). *Three Old English Prose Texts in Ms. Cotton Vitellius A.XV*. EETS 161. London: OUP.
cocura1	*Cura Pastoralis*
	Sweet, Henry. 1958 (1871). *King Alfred's West-Saxon Version of Gregory's Pastoral Care*. EETS 45, 50. London: OUP.
cocurac	*Cura Pastoralis*
	Sweet, Henry. 1958 (1871). *King Alfred's West-Saxon Version of Gregory's Pastoral Care*. EETS 45, 50. London: OUP.
codicts	*Distichs of Cato*
	Cox, R.S. 1972. "The Old English Dicts of Cato." *Anglia* 90:1-42. Tübingen: Max Niemeyer.
codocum2	*Charters and Wills*
	(1) Harmer, F.E. 1914. *Select Historical Documents of the Ninth and Tenth Centuries*. Cambridge: CUP.
	(2) Robertson, A.J. 1956 (1939). *Anglo-Saxon Charters*. Cambridge: CUP.
codocum3	*Charters and Wills*
	(1) Robertson, A.J. 1956 (1939). *Anglo-Saxon Charters*. Cambridge: CUP.
	(2) Whitelock, Dorothy. 1930. *Anglo-Saxon Wills*. Cambridge: CUP.
codocum4	*Charters and Wills*
	Robertson, A.J. 1956 (1939). *Anglo-Saxon Charters*. Cambridge: CUP.
coeluc1	*Honorius of Autun, Elucidarium*
	Warner, Rubie D.-N. 1917 (1971). *Early English Homilies from the 12th Century Ms. Vespasian D.XIV*. EETS 152: 140-3. London: Trübner.
coeluc2	*Honorius of Autun, Elucidarium*
	Warner, Rubie D.-N. 1917 (1971). *Early English Homilies from the 12th Century Ms. Vespasian D.XIV*. EETS 152: 144-5. London: Trübner.
coeuphr	*Saint Euphrosyne*
	Skeat, Walter William. 1966 (1881-1900). *Ælfric's Lives of Saints*. EETS 76, 82, 94, 114: 334-54. London: OUP.
coeust	*Saint Eustace and his Companions*
	Skeat, Walter William. 1966 (1881-1900). *Ælfric's Lives of Saints*. EETS 76, 82, 94, 114: 190-218. London: OUP.
coexodup	*Exodus*
	Crawford, Samuel J. 1922. *The Old English Version of the Heptateuch. Ælfric's Treatise on the Old and New Testament and His Preface to Genesis*. EETS 160: 458-60. London: OUP. Reprinted with additions by N.R. Ker 1969.
cogenesc	*Genesis*
	Crawford, Samuel J. 1922. *The Old English Version of the Heptateuch. Ælfric's Treatise on the Old and New Testament and His Preface to Genesis*. EETS 160: 444-56. London: OUP. Reprinted with additions by N.R. Ker 1969.
coherbar	*Herbarium*
	Vriend, H.J. de (1984). *The Old English Herbarium and Medicina de quadrupedibus*. EETS 286: 30–233. London: OUP.
cojames	*James the Greater*
	Warner, Rubie D.-N. 1917 (1971). *Early English Homilies from the 12th Century Ms. Vespasian D.XIV*. EETS 152: 21-5. London: Trübner.

Appendix I: Old English Corpus 187

colacnu   *Lacnunga*
Grattan, John Henry Grafton and Charles Singer, eds. 1952. *Anglo-Saxon Magic and Medicine.* Publications of the Wellcome Historical Medical Museum n.s. 3. London: OUP.

colaece   *Bald's Leechbook*
Cockayne, Oswald. 1864-1866. *Leechdoms, Wortcunning and Starcraft of Early England.* Rolls Series 35, vol. 1. 70-324. London: Her Majesty's Stationery Office. Reprinted Wiesbaden, Germany: Kraus Reprint Ltd. 1965.

colaw1cn   *Laws of Cnut*
Lieberman, F. (1903–16). Die Gesetze der Angelsachsen. Halle. Reprinted Aalen 1960.

colaw2cn   *Laws of Cnut*
Lieberman, F. (1903–16). Die Gesetze der Angelsachsen. Halle. Reprinted Aalen 1960.F. Lieberman, 308-70 *Die Gesetze der Angelsachsen*, Halle 1903–16 [Aalen 1960]

colaw5at   *Laws of Æthelred V*
Lieberman, F. (1903–16). Die Gesetze der Angelsachsen. Halle. Reprinted Aalen 1960.F. Lieberman, 236-46 *Die Gesetze der Angelsachsen*, Halle 1903-16 [Aalen 1960]

colaw6at   *Laws of Æthelred VI*
Lieberman, F. 246–58 *Die Gesetze der Angelsachsen*, Halle 1903-16 [Aalen 1960].

colawaf1   *Laws of Alfred*
Lieberman, F. 1903-16. Die Gesetze der Angelsachsen. Halle. Reprinted Aalen 1960.

colawafi   *Alfred's Introduction to Laws*
Lieberman, F. 1903-16. Die Gesetze der Angelsachsen. Halle. Reprinted Aalen 1960.

colawger   *Gerefa*
Lieberman, F. 1903-16. Die Gesetze der Angelsachsen. Halle. Reprinted Aalen 1960.

colawine   *Laws of Ine*
Lieberman, F. 1903-16. Die Gesetze der Angelsachsen. Halle. Reprinted Aalen 1960

colawnor   *Northumbra Preosta Lagu*
Lieberman, F. 1903-16. Die Gesetze der Angelsachsen. Halle. Reprinted Aalen 1960.

colawwll   *Laws of William*
Lieberman, F. 1903-16. Die Gesetze der Angelsachsen. Halle. Reprinted Aalen 1960.

coleofri   *Vision of Leofric*
Napier, Arthur S. 1907-10. "An Old English Vision of Leofric, Earl of Mercia". *Transactions of the Philological Society*: 180-88

colsigez   Ælfric's Letter to Sigeweard (Z)
Crawford, Samuel J. 1922. *The Old English Version of the Heptateuch. Ælfric's Treatise on the Old and New Testament and His Preface to Genesis.* EETS 160: 14-75. London: OUP. Reprinted with additions by N.R. Ker 1969

colwisgt   *Ælfric's Letter to Wulfsige*

colwsixa	Fehr, B. 1914. *Die Hirtenbriefe Aelfrics in Altenglischer und Lateinischer Fassung*. Bibliothek der Angelsaechsischen Prosa, IX: 1-34. Hamburg: Verlag von Henri Grand. Reprinted with a supplement by P. Clemoes, Darmstadt 1966 Ælfric's Letter to Wulfsige Fehr, B. 1914. *Die Hirtenbriefe Aelfrics in Altenglischer und Lateinischer Fassung*. Bibliothek der Angelsaechsischen Prosa, IX: 1-34. Hamburg: Verlag von Henri Grand. Reprinted with a supplement by P. Clemoes, Darmstadt 1966.
comargac	*Saint Margaret* Clayton, Mary and Hugh Magennis. 1994, "The Old English Lives of St Margaret." *Cambridge Studies in Anglo-Saxon England* 9:152-70. Cambridge: CUP.
comargat	*Saint Margaret* Clayton, Mary and Hugh Magennis. 1994, "The Old English Lives of St Margaret." *Cambridge Studies in Anglo-Saxon English* 9:112-38. Cambridge: CUP.
comart1	*Martyrology* Herzfeld, George. 1973 (1900). *An Old English Martyrology*. EETS 116: 2-10. London: Trübner. Corrected by Kotzor, G. 1981. *Das Alternglische Martyrologium, vol. II*. Bayerische Akademie der Wissenschaften, Philosophisch-Historische Klasse. Abhandlunge, Neue Folge, Heft 88/2. München: Verlag der Bayerischen Akademie der Wissenschaften.
comart2	*Martyrology* Herzfeld, George. 1973 (1900). *An Old English Martyrology*. EETS 116: 40-222. London: Trübner. Corrected by Kotzor, G. 1981. *Das Alternglische Martyrologium, vol. II*. Bayerische Akademie der Wissenschaften, Philosophisch-Historische Klasse. Abhandlunge, Neue Folge, Heft 88/2. München: Verlag der Bayerischen Akademie der Wissenschaften.
comart3	*Martyrology* Kotzor, G. 1981. *Das Alternglische Martyrologium, vol. II*. Bayerische Akademie der Wissenschaften, Philosophisch-Historische Klasse. Abhandlunge, Neue Folge, Heft 88/2. München: Verlag der Bayerischen Akademie der Wissenschaften.
comarvel	*Marvels of the East* Orchard, Andrew P.M. 1995. *Pride and Prodigies: Studies in the Monsters of the "Beowulf" Manuscript.* Pp. 184-202. Cambridge: D.S. Brewer.
comary	*Mary of Egypt* Skeat, Walter William. 1966 (1881-1900). *Ælfric's Lives of Saints*. EETS 76, 82, 94, 114: 2-52. London: OUP.
coneot	*Saint Neot* Warner, Rubie D.-N. 1917 (1971). *Early English Homilies from the 12th Century Ms. Vespasian D.XIV*. EETS 152: 129-34. London: Trübner.
conicoda	*The Gospel of Nichodemus* Cross, J.E. 1996. *Two Old English Apocrypha and Their Manuscript Source: The Gospel of Nichodemus and The Avenging of the Saviour, with contributions by Denis Brearley, Julia Crick, Thomas Hall and Andy Orchard.* Cambridge Studies in Anglo-Saxon England 19: 139-247. Cambridge: CUP
conicodd	*The Gospel of Nichodemus* Hulme, William H. 1903-4. "The Old English Gospel of Nicodemus". *Modern*

	Philology 1: 610-14.
conicode	*The Gospel of Nichodemus*
	Torkar, Roland. ed. from ms. for Dictionary of Old English Project
coprefcu	*Preface to Cura Pastoralis*
	Sweet, Henry. 1958 (1871). *King Alfred's West-Saxon Version of Gregory's Pastoral Care.* EETS 45, 50: 3-9. London: OUP.
coprefso	*Preface to St Augustine's Soliloquies*
	Endter, W. 1922. *König Alfreds des Grossen Bearbeitung der Soliloquien des Augustinus.* Bibliothek der Angelsaechsischen Prosa, 11: 1-2. Darmstadt: Wissenschaftliche Buchgesellschaft. Reprinted Darmstadt 1964. Corrections by Carnicelli, T.A. 1969. *King Alfred's Version of St. Augustine's Soliloquies.* Cambridge, MA: Harvard University Press.
coquadru	*Quadrupedibus*
	de Vriend, Hubert Jan. 1984. *The Old English Herbarium and Medicina de quadrupedibus.* EETS 286: 234-73. London: OUP.
corood	*The History of the Holy Rood-Tree*
	Napier, Arthur S. 1973 (1894). *History of the Holy Rood Tree.* EETS 103. London: Kegan Paul, Trench, Trübner & Co
cosolsa1	*Solomon and Saturn I*
	Cross, James E. and Thomas D. Hill. 1982. *The "Prose Solomon and Saturn" and "Adrian and Ritheus".* Pp. 25-34. Toronto, Buffalo, London: University of Toronto Press.
cosolsa2	*Solomon and Saturn II*
	Menner, Robert J. 1941. *The Poetical Dialogues of Solomon and Saturn.* MLA Monograph Series 13: 168-71. New York: The Modern Language Association of America.
coverhoe	*Vercelli Homilies*
	Scragg, D.G. 1992. *The Vercelli Homilies and Related Texts.* EETS 300. Oxford: OUP.
coverhol	*Vercelli Homilies, Homily IX*
	Scragg, D.G. 1992. *The Vercelli Homilies and Related Texts.* EETS 300. Oxford: OUP.
coverhom	*Vercelli Homilies*
	Scragg, D.G. (1992). *The Vercelli Homilies and Related Texts.* EETS 300. Oxford: OUP.
covinceb	*The Martyrdom of Saint Vincent (2nd half)*
	Irvine, Susan. 1993. *Old English Homilies from Ms Bodley 343.* EETS 302. Oxford: OUP.
covisal	*Vindicta Salvatoris*
	Cross, J.E. 1996. *Two Old English Apocrypha and Their Manuscript Source: The Gospel of Nichodemus and The Avenging of the Saviour, with contributions by Denis Brearley, Julia Crick, Thomas Hall and Andy Orchard.* Cambridge Studies in Anglo-Saxon England 19: 249-93. Cambridge: CUP.

Appendix II
Middle English Corpus

This is the list of Middle English texts from the Penn-Helsinki Parsed Corpus of Middle English, second edition (PPCME2) that was used in this research. The PPCME2 was compiled by Anthony Kroch and Ann Taylor in 2000. The texts are listed by their PPCME2 file name along with their full name and a reference to the text edition. Further details can be found at http://www.ling.upenn.edu/hist-corpora/PPCME2-RELEASE-3/index.html.

File name	Text name and edition
cmaelr3	*Rievaulx's De Institutione Inclusarum*
cmaelr4	Aelred of Rievaulx's De Institutione Inclusarum (Ms. Vernon)
	Ayto, John and Alexandra Barratt. 1984. *Aelred of Rievaulx's De institutione inclusarum: Two English versions.* EETS O.S. 287. London: Oxford University Press.
cmancri1	*Ancrene Riwle*
cmancri2	Ackerman, Robert W. and Roger Dahood. 1984. *Ancrene riwle. Introduction and Part I.* Medieval and Renaissance Texts and Studies 31. Binghamton, NY: Center for Medieval and Early Renaissance Studies, State University of New York at Binghamton.
	Dobson, Eric J. 1972. *The English text of the Ancrene riwle edited from B.M. Cotton ms. Cleopatra C vi.* EETS O.S. 267. London: Oxford University Press.
cmastro	*A Treatise on the Astrolabe*
cmboeth	*Boethius*
cmctmeli	*The Tale of Melibee*
cmctpars	*The Parson's Tale*
	Benson, Larry D. 1987. *The Riverside Chaucer.* Boston: Houghton Mifflin. Third edition.
cmayenbi	*Ayenbite of Inwyt*
	Morris, Richard. 1979. *Dan Michel's Ayenbite of inwyt.* EETS O.S. 278. London: Oxford University Press. Originally published by Trübner (London, 1866) as EETS O.S. 23.
cmbenrul	*The Northern Prose Rule of St. Benet*
	Kock, Ernst A. 1902. *The Northern prose version of the Rule of St. Benet.* In Ernst A. Kock (ed.), *Three Middle-English versions of the Rule of St. Benet and two contemporary rituals for the ordination of nuns.* EETS O.S. 120. London: K. Paul, Trench, Trübner & Co.
cmbrut3	*The Brut or the Chronicles of England*
	Brie, F.W.D. 1906. *The Brut or the Chronicles of England. Part I.* EETS O.S. 131. London: K. Paul, Trench, Trübner & Co.
cmcapchr	*Capgrave's Chronicle*
	Lucas, Peter J. 1983. *John Capgrave's Abbreuiacion of cronicles.* EETS O.S. 285. Oxford: Oxford University Press
cmcapser	*Capgrave's Sermon*
	Munro, John J. 1910. *John Capgrave's Lives of St. Augustine and St. Gilbert*

	of Sempringham, and a sermon. EETS O.S. 140. New York: K. Paul, Trench, Trübner & Co.
cmcloud	*The Cloud of Unknowing* Hodgson, Phyllis. 1944 (for 1943). *The cloud of unknowing and The book of privy counselling.* EETS O.S. 218. London: Oxford University Press.
cmearlps	*The Earliest Complete English Prose Psalter* Bülbring, Karl D. 1891. *The earliest complete English prose psalter.* EETS O.S. 97. London: K. Paul, Trench, Trübner & Co.
cmedmund	*The Life of St. Edmund* Blake, Norman F. 1972. *The life of St. Edmund.* In Norman F. Blake (ed.), *Middle English religious prose.* York Medieval Texts. London: Arnold.
cmedthor	*The Mirror of St. Edmund (Thornton Ms.)* Perry, George G. 1969. *The mirror of St. Edmund.* In George G. Perry (ed.), *Religious pieces in prose and verse.* EETS O.S. 26. London: K. Paul, Trench, Trübner & Co. Third edition (first edition 1867, second edition 1914).
cmedvern	*The Mirror of St. Edmund* (Vernon Ms.) Horstman, C. 1895-1896. *Yorkshire writers: Richard Rolle of Hampole.* London: Swan Sonnenschein & Co.
cmequato	*The Equatorie of the Planets* Price, Derek J. 1955. *The equatorie of the planetis.* Cambridge: Cambridge University Press.
cmfitzja	*Richard Fitzjames' Sermo die Lune* Jenkinson, Francis J.H. 1907. *Sermo die lune in ebdomada Pasche, by Richard Fitz-James. Printed at Westminster by Wynkyn de Worde about the year 1495.* Cambridge: Cambridge University Press. Facsimile edition.
cmgaytry	*Dan Jon Gaytryge's Sermon* Perry, George G. 1969. *Dan Jon Gaytryge's sermon.* In George G. Perry (ed.), *Religious pieces in prose and verse.* EETS O.S. 26. New York: K. Paul, Trench, Trübner & Co. Third edition (first edition 1867, second edition 1914).
cmgregor	*Gregory's Chronicle* Gairdner, James. 1876. *The historical collections of a citizen of London in the fifteenth century.* Camden Society, N.S. XVII. Westminster: Camden Society.
cmhali	*Hali Meidhad*
cmkathe	*St. Katherine*
cmjulia	*St. Juliana*
cmmarga	*St. Margaret*
cmsawles	*Sawles Warde* D'Ardenne, S.R.T.O. 1977. *The Katherine Group edited from ms. Bodley 34.* Bibliothèque de la Faculté de philosophie et lettres de l'Université de Liège fasc. 215. Paris: Société d'Edition Les Belles Lettres.
cmhilton	*Hilton's Eight Chapters on Perfection* Kuriyagawa, Fumio. 1967. *Walter Hilton's Eight chapters on perfection.* Tokyo: Keio Institute of Cultural and Linguistic Studies.
cmhorses	*A Late Mile English Treatise on Horses* Svinhufvud, Anne Charlotte. 1978. *A Late Middle English treatise on horses.* Stockholm Studies in English 47. Stockholm: Almqvist & Wiksell.

cminnoce	*In Die Innocencium* Nichols, J.G. 1875. *Two sermons preached by the boy bishop, at St. Paul's Temp. Henry VII, and at Gloucester Temp. Mary.* Camden Society Miscellany VII. Camden Society N.S. XIV. London: [publisher unknown].
cmjulnor	*Revelations of Divine Love* Beer, Frances. 1978. *Julian of Norwich's revelations of divine love: The shorter version edited from B.L. Add. Ms 37790.* Middle English Texts 8. Heidelberg: Winter.
cmkentse	*Kentish Sermons* Hall, Joseph. 1963. *Selections from Early Middle English 1130-1250. Part I.* Oxford: Clarendon. Second edition (first edition 1920).
cmlamb1 cmlambx1	*The Lambeth Homilies* Morris, Richard. 1969. *Old English homilies and homiletic treatises. Part I.* EETS O.S. 29, 34. New York: Greenwood Press. Originally published by Trübner (London, 1868).
cmmalory	*Malory's Morte Darthur* Vinaver, Eugène. 1954. *The works of Thomas Malory.* London: Oxford University Press.
cmmirk	*Mirk's Festial* Erbe, Theodore. 1905. *Mirk's Festial: A collection of homilies, by Johannes Mirkus (John Mirk). Part I.* EETS E.S. 96. London: K. Paul, Trench, Trübner & Co.
cmntest	*The New Testament* (Wycliffite) Forshall, Josiah and Frederic Madden. 1879. *The New Testament in English according to the version of John Wycliffe about A.D. 1380 and revised by John Purvey about A.D. 1388.* Oxford: Clarendon
cmorm	*The Ormulum* Holt, Robert. 1878. *The Ormulum, with the notes and glossary of Dr. R.M. White. Vols. I-II.* Oxford: Clarendon.
cmotest cmpurvey	*The Old Testament* (Wycliffite) *Purvey's General Prologue to the Bible* Forshall, Josiah and Frederic Madden. 1850. *The Holy Bible, containing the Old and New Testaments, with the apocraphal books, in the earliest English versions made from the Latin Vulgate by John Wycliffe and his followers, Vol. 1.* Oxford: Oxford University Press. Reprinted 1982 (New York: AMS Press).
cmpeterb	*The Peterborough Chronicle* Clark, Cecily. 1970. *The Peterborough Chronicle 1070-1154.* Oxford: Clarendon. Second edition (first edition 1958).
cmpolych	*John Trevisa's Polychronicon* Lumby, Joseph R. 1876, 1882. *Polychronicon Ranulphi Higden, monachi cestrensis, Vols. VI, VIII, English translations of John Trevisa and of an unknown writer of the fifteenth century.* Rolls Series 41. London: [publisher unknown].
cmreynar	*Caxton's History of Reynard the Fox* Blake, Norman F. 1970. *The History of Reynard the fox. Translated from the Dutch original by William Caxton.* EETS O.S. 263. London: Oxford University Press.

Appendix II: Middle English Corpus 193

cmreynes	*The Commonplace Book of Robert Reynes*
	Louis, Cameron. 1980. *The commonplace book of Robert Reynes of Acle: An edition of Tanner Ms. 407.* Garland Medieval Texts 1. New York: Garland.
cmrollep	*The Psalter or Psalms of David*
	Allen, Hope E. 1931. *English writings of Richard Rolle, hermit of Hampole.* Oxford: Clarendon.
cmrolltr	*Rolle, Prose Treatises (Thornton Ms.)*
	Perry, George G. 1921. *English prose treatises of Richard Rolle de Hampole.* EETS O.S. 20. London: Oxford University Press.
cmroyal	*Middle English Sermons*
	Ross, Woodburn O. 1940 (for 1938). *Middle English sermons edited, from British Museum ms. Royal 18 B. xxiii.* EETS O.S. 209. London: Oxford University Press.
cmsiege	*The Siege of Jerusalem*
	Kurvinen, Auvo. 1969. *The siege of Jerusalem in prose.* Mémoires de la Société Néophilologique de Helsinki 34. Helsinki: Société Néophilologique de Helsinki.
cmthorn	*Liber de Diversis Medicinis*
	Ogden, Margaret S. 1969. *The `Liber de diversis medicinis' in the Thornton Manuscript.* EETS O.S. 207. London: Oxford University Press. Originally published in 1938 (for 1936).
cmtrinit	*Trinity Homilies*
	Morris, Richard. 1873. *Old English homilies of the twelfth century. Second series.* EETS O.S. 53. London: Trübner.
cmvices1	*Vices and Virtues*
	Holthausen, Ferdinand. 1888. *Vices and virtues. Part 1.* EETS O.S. 89. London: Trübner.
cmvices4	*The Book of Vices and Virtues*
	Francis, Winthrop N. 1942. *The book of vices and virtues: A fourteenth century English translation of the Somme le roi of Lorens D'Orléans.* EETS O.S. 217. London: Oxford University Press.
cmwycser	*English Wycliffite Sermons*
	Hudson, Anne. 1983. *English Wycliffite sermons.* Oxford: Clarendon.

Studies in English Medieval Language and Literature

Edited by Jacek Fisiak

Vol. 1 Dieter Kastovsky / Arthur Mettinger (eds.): Language Contact in the History of English. 2nd, revised edition. 2003.

Vol. 2 Studies in English Historical Linguistics and Philology. A Festschrift for Akio Oizumi. Edited by Jacek Fisiak. 2002.

Vol. 3 Liliana Sikorska: *In a Manner of Morall Playe*: Social Ideologies in English Moralities and Interludes (1350-1517). 2002.

Vol. 4 Peter J. Lucas / Angela M. Lucas (eds.): Middle English from Tongue to Text. Selected Papers from the Third International Conference on Middle English: Language and Text, held at Dublin, Ireland, 1-4 July 1999. 2002.

Vol. 5 Chaucer and the Challenges of Medievalism. Studies in Honor of H. A. Kelly. Edited by Donka Minkova and Theresa Tinkle. 2003.

Vol. 6 Hanna Rutkowska: Graphemics and Morphosyntax in the *Cely Letters* (1472-88). 2003.

Vol. 7 The *Ancrene Wisse*. A Four-Manuscript Parallel Text. Preface and Parts 1-4. Edited by Tadao Kubouchi and Keiko Ikegami with John Scahill, Shoko Ono, Harumi Tanabe, Yoshiko Ota, Ayako Kobayashi and Koichi Nakamura. 2003.

Vol. 8 Joanna Bugaj: Middle Scots Inflectional System in the South-west of Scotland. 2004.

Vol. 9 Rafal Boryslawski: The Old English Riddles and the Riddlic Elements of Old English Poetry. 2004.

Vol. 10 Nikolaus Ritt / Herbert Schendl (eds.): Rethinking Middle English. Linguistic and Literary Approaches. 2005.

Vol. 11 The *Ancrene Wisse*. A Four-Manuscript Parallel Text. Parts 5–8 with Wordlists. Edited by Tadao Kubouchi and Keiko Ikegami with John Scahill, Shoko Ono, Harumi Tanabe, Yoshiko Ota, Ayako Kobayashi, Koichi Nakamura. 2005.

Vol. 12 Text and Language in Medieval English Prose. A Festschrift for Tadao Kubouchi. Edited by Akio Oizumi, Jacek Fisiak and John Scahill. 2005.

Vol. 13 Michiko Ogura (ed.): Textual and Contextual Studies in Medieval English. Towards the Reunion of Linguistics and Philology. 2006.

Vol. 14 Keiko Hamaguchi: Non-European Women in Chaucer. A Postcolonial Study. 2006.

Vol. 15 Ursula Schaefer (ed.): The Beginnings of Standardization. Language and Culture in Fourteenth-Century England. 2006.

Vol. 16 Nikolaus Ritt / Herbert Schendl / Christiane Dalton-Puffer / Dieter Kastovsky (eds): Medieval English and its Heritage. Structure, Meaning and Mechanisms of Change. 2006.

Vol. 17 Matylda Włodarczyk: Pragmatic Aspects of Reported Speech. The Case of Early Modern English Courtroom Discourse. 2007.

Vol. 18 Hans Sauer / Renate Bauer (eds.): *Beowulf* and Beyond. 2007.

Vol. 19 Gabriella Mazzon (ed.): Studies in Middle English Forms and Meanings. 2007.

Vol. 20 Alexander Bergs / Janne Skaffari (eds.): The Language of the Peterborough Chronicle. 2007.

Vol. 21 Liliana Sikorska (ed.). With the assistance of Joanna Maciulewicz: Medievalisms. The Poetics of Literary Re-Reading. 2008.

Vol.	22	Masachiyo Amano / Michiko Ogura / Masayuki Ohkado (eds.): Historical Englishes in Varieties of Texts and Contexts. The Global COE Program, International Conference 2007. 2008.
Vol.	23	Ewa Ciszek: Word Derivation in Early Middle English. 2008.
Vol.	24	Andrzej M. Łęcki: Grammaticalisation Paths of *Have* in English. 2010.
Vol.	25	Osamu Imahayashi / Yoshiyuki Nakao / Michiko Ogura (eds.): Aspects of the History of English Language and Literature. Selected Papers Read at SHELL 2009, Hiroshima. 2010.
Vol.	26	Magdalena Bator: Obsolete Scandinavian Loanwords in English. 2010.
Vol.	27	Anna Cichosz: The Influence of Text Type on Word Order of Old Germanic Languages. A Corpus-Based Contrastive Study of Old English and Old High German. 2010.
Vol.	28	Jacek Fisiak / Magdalena Bator (eds.): Foreign Influences on Medieval English. 2011.
Vol.	29	Władysław Witalisz: The Trojan Mirror. Middle English Narratives of Troy as Books of Princely Advice. 2011.
Vol.	30	Luis Iglesias-Rábade: Semantic Erosion of Middle English Prepositions. 2011.
Vol.	31	Barbara Kowalik: Betwixt *engelaunde* and *englene londe*. Dialogic Poetics in Early English Religious Lyric. 2010.
Vol.	32	The Katherine Group. A Three-Manuscript Parallel Text. Seinte Katerine, Seinte Marherete, Seinte Iuliene, and Hali Meiðhad, with Wordlists. Edited by Shoko Ono and John Scahill with Keiko Ikegami, Tadao Kubouchi, Harumi Tanabe, Koichi Nakamura, Satoko Shimazaki and Koichi Kano. 2011.
Vol.	33	Jacob Thaisen / Hanna Rutkowska (eds.): Scribes, Printers, and the Accidentals of their Texts. 2011.
Vol.	34	Isabel Moskowich: Language Contact and Vocabulary Enrichment. Scandinavian Elements in Middle English. 2012.
Vol.	35	Joanna Esquibel / Anna Wojtyś (eds.): Explorations in the English Language: Middle Ages and Beyond. Festschrift for Professor Jerzy Wełna on the Occasion of his 70th Birthday. 2012.
Vol.	36	Yoshiyuki Nakao: The Structure of Chaucer´s Ambiguity. 2013.
Vol.	37	Begoña Crespo: Change in Life, Change in Language. A Semantic Approach to the History of English. 2013.
Vol.	38	Richard Dance / Laura Wright (eds.): The Use and Development of Middle English. Proceedings of the Sixth International Conference on Middle English, Cambridge 2008. 2012.
Vol.	39	Michiko Ogura: Words and Expressions of Emotion in Medieval English. 2013.
Vol.	40	Anna Czarnowus: Fantasies of the Other´s Body in Middle English Oriental Romance. 2013.
Vol.	41	Hans Sauer / Gaby Waxenberger (eds.): Recording English, Researching English, Transforming English. With the Assistance of Veronika Traidl. 2013.
Vol.	42	Michio Hosaka / Michiko Ogura / Hironori Suzuki / Akinobu Tani (eds.): Phases of the History of English. Selection of Papers Read at SHELL 2012. 2013.
Vol.	43	Vlatko Broz: Aspectual Prefixes in Early English. 2014.

www.peterlang.com